In the aftermath of a rebellion that set change against tradition, the nation against their king and even the living against the dead...Wakanda must now rebuild.

The forces of rebellion have quieted with the arrest of **Tetu**, one of the rebel leaders, while the other, **Zenzi**, remains at large. The royal family and the people of Wakanda are attempting to move forward together. T'Challa began this process by calling together a council of representatives from each region to write a new constitution and enact a new government. In discussions with his mother **Ramonda** and sister **Shuri**, T'Challa has expressed both trepidation and hope for this new era in Wakandan history.

But just as T'Challa moves forward, he keeps one eye on his past...

AVENGERS OF THE NEW WORLD

PART ONE

Letterer/**VC's Joe Sabino**

Logo Design/**Rian Hughes**

Cover Art/**Brian Stelfreeze**
with **Laura Martin** (#13, #16-18)

Assistant Editors/**Chris Robinson & Charles Beacham**

Associate Editor/**Sarah Brunstad**

Editor/**Wil Moss**

P9-ELR-422

COLLECTION EDITOR/**JENNIFER GRÜNWALD**
ASSISTANT EDITOR/**CAITLIN O'CONNELL**
ASSOCIATE MANAGING EDITOR/**KATERI WOODY**
EDITOR, SPECIAL PROJECTS/**MARK D. BEAZLEY**
VP PRODUCTION & SPECIAL PROJECTS/**JEFF YOUNGQUIST**
SVP PRINT, SALES & MARKETING/**DAVID GABRIEL**
BOOK DESIGNERS/**JAY BOWEN** & **MANNY MEDEROS**

EDITOR IN CHIEF/**AXEL ALONSO**
CHIEF CREATIVE OFFICER/**JOE QUESADA**
PRESIDENT/**DAN BUCKLEY**
EXECUTIVE PRODUCER/**ALAN FINE**

BLACK PANTHER BOOK 4: AVENGERS OF THE NEW WORLD PART 1. First printing 2017. ISBN# 978-1-302-90649-8. Published by MARVEL WORLDWIDE, INC., a subsidiary of MARVEL ENTERTAINMENT, LLC. OFFICE OF PUBLICATION: 135 West 50th Street, New York, NY 10020. Copyright © 2017 MARVEL. No similarity between any of the names, characters, persons, and/or institutions in this magazine with those of any living or dead person or institution is intended, and any such similarity which may exist is purely coincidental. **Printed in the U.S.A.** DAN BUCKLEY, President, Marvel Entertainment; JOE QUESADA, Chief Creative Officer; TOM BREVOORT, SVP of Publishing; DAVID BOGART, SVP of Business Affairs & Operations, Publishing & Partnership; C.B. CEBULSKI, VP of Brand Management & Development, Asia; DAVID GABRIEL, SVP of Sales & Marketing, Publishing; JEFF YOUNGQUIST, VP of Production & Special Projects; DAN CARR, Executive Director of Publishing Technology; ALEX MORALES, Director of Publishing Operations; SUSAN CRESPI, Production Manager; STAN LEE, Chairman Emeritus. For information regarding advertising in Marvel Comics or on Marvel.com, please contact Vit DeBellis, Integrated Sales Manager, at vdebellis@marvel.com. For Marvel subscription inquiries, please call 888-511-5480. **Manufactured between 9/1/2017 and 10/2/2017 by QUAD/GRAPHICS WASECA, WASECA, MN, USA.**

10 9 8 7 6 5 4 3 2 1

Contains material originally published in magazine form as BLACK PANTHER #13-18.

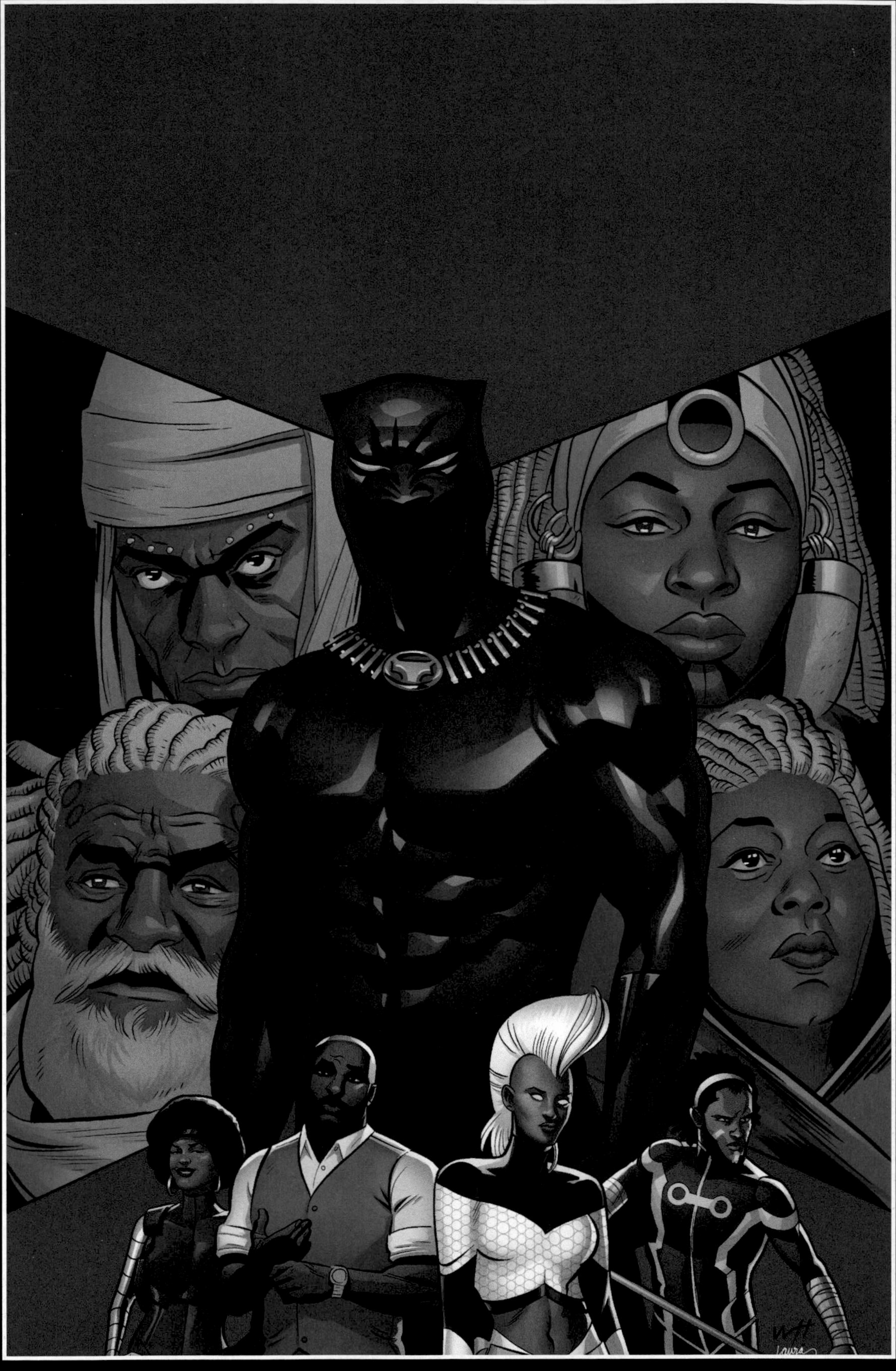

#13 VARIANT BY **WILFREDO TORRES** & **LAURA MARTIN**

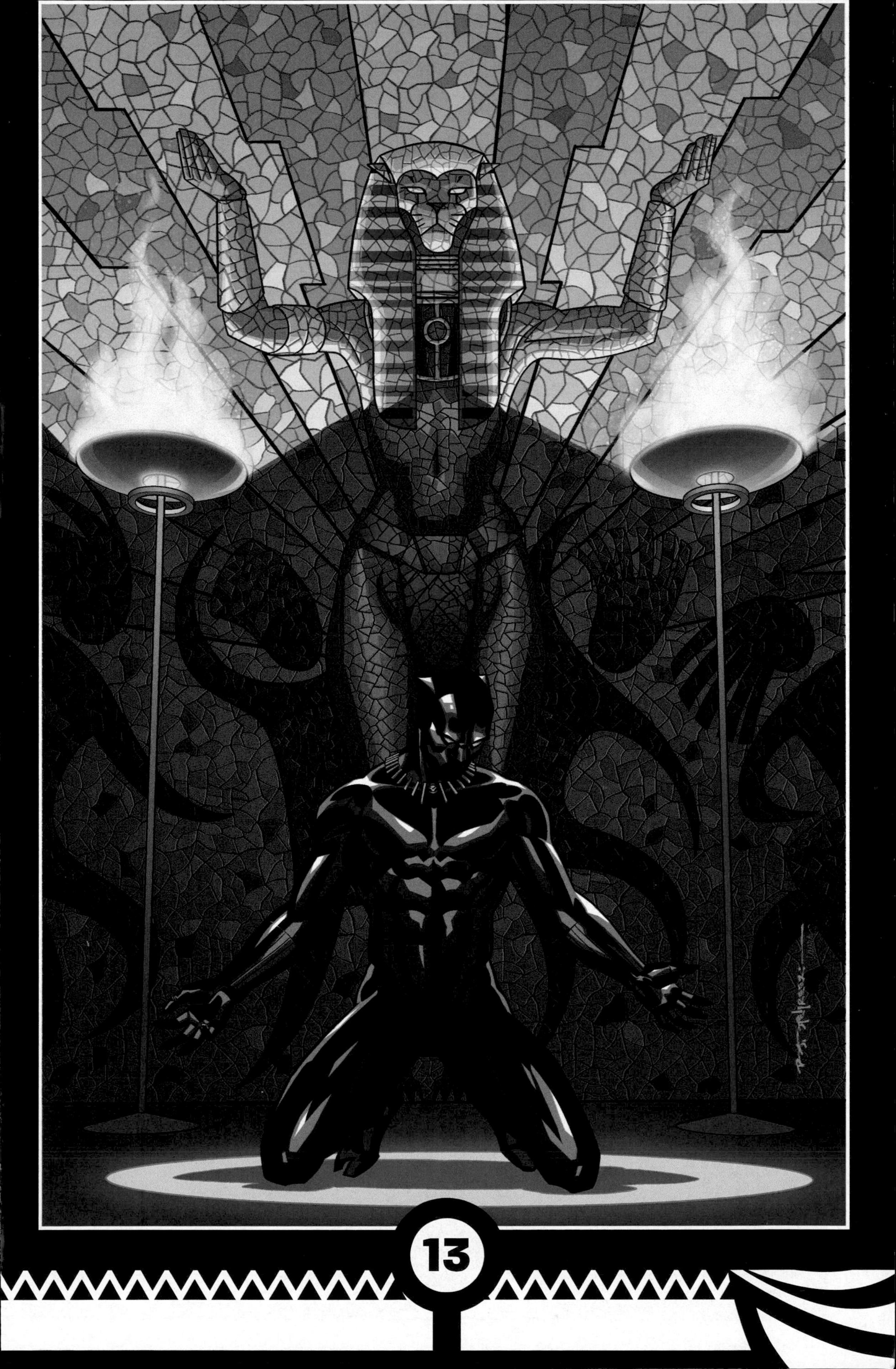
13

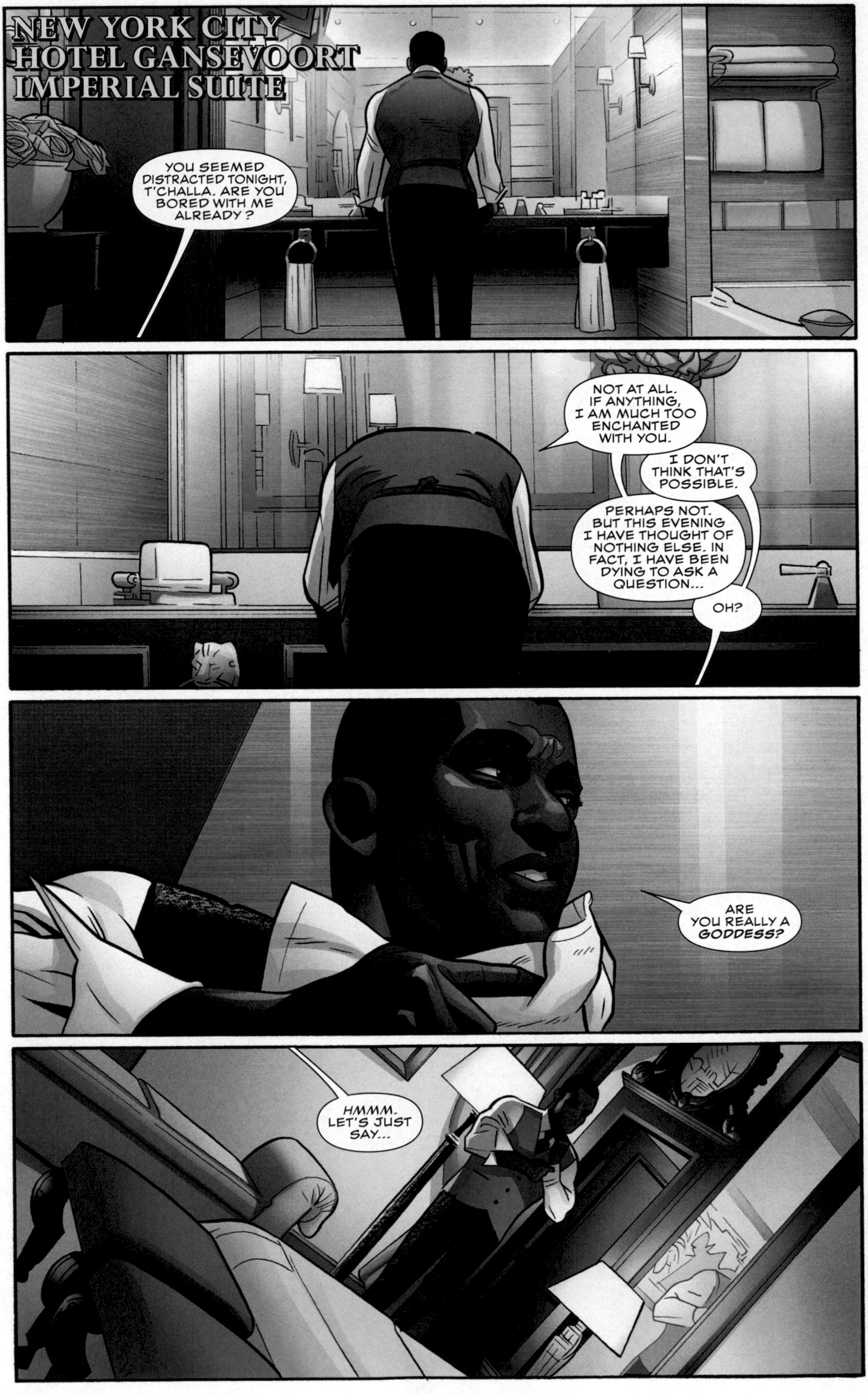
NEW YORK CITY
HOTEL GANSEVOORT
IMPERIAL SUITE
YOU SEEMED DISTRACTED TONIGHT, T'CHALLA. ARE YOU BORED WITH ME ALREADY?
NOT AT ALL. IF ANYTHING, I AM MUCH TOO ENCHANTED WITH YOU.
I DON'T THINK THAT'S POSSIBLE.
PERHAPS NOT. BUT THIS EVENING I HAVE THOUGHT OF NOTHING ELSE. IN FACT, I HAVE BEEN DYING TO ASK A QUESTION...
OH?
ARE YOU REALLY A *GODDESS?*
HMMM. LET'S JUST SAY...

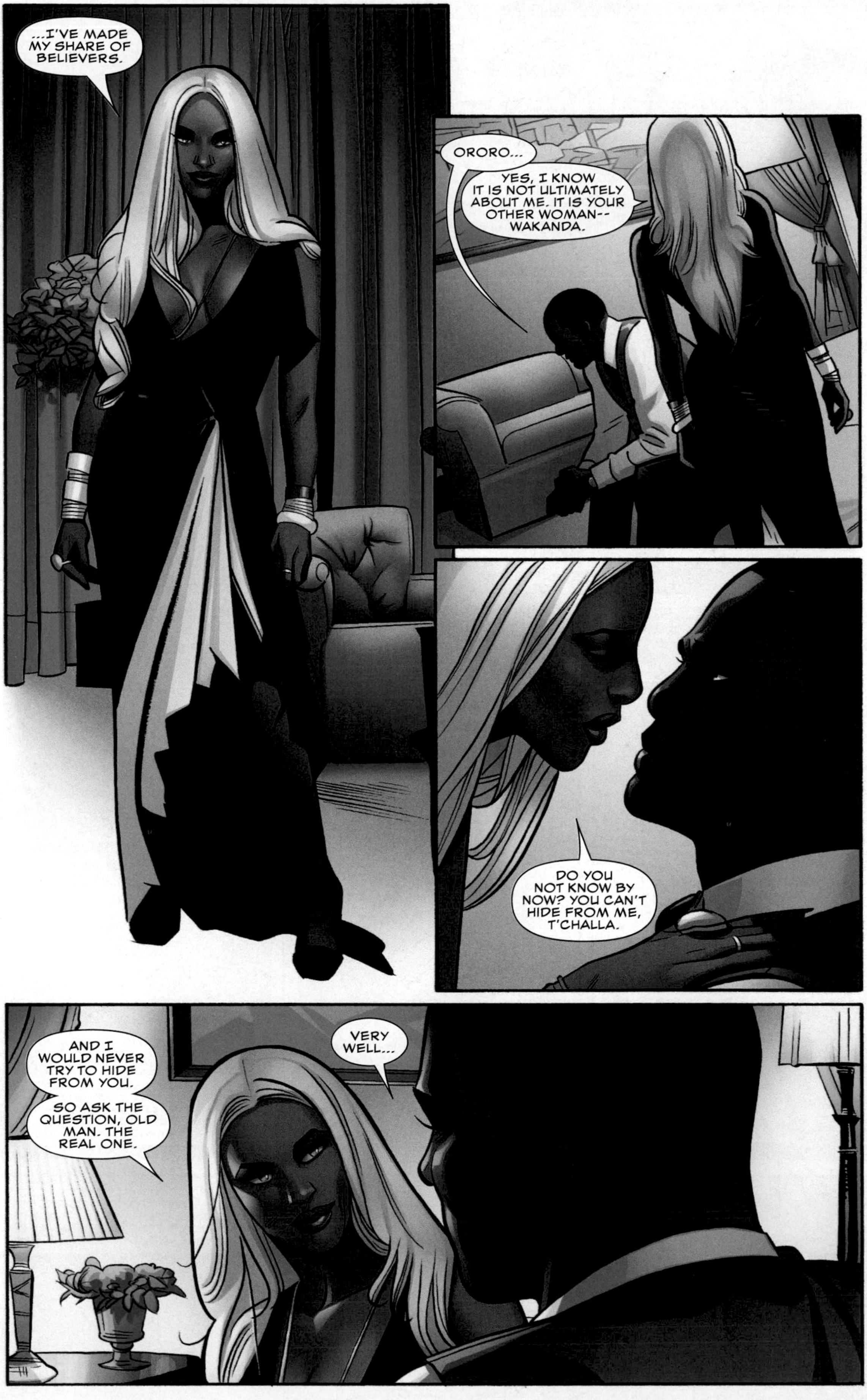
...I'VE MADE MY SHARE OF BELIEVERS.
ORORO...
YES, I KNOW IT IS NOT ULTIMATELY ABOUT ME. IT IS YOUR OTHER WOMAN-- WAKANDA.
DO YOU NOT KNOW BY NOW? YOU CAN'T HIDE FROM ME, T'CHALLA.
VERY WELL...
AND I WOULD NEVER TRY TO HIDE FROM YOU.
SO ASK THE QUESTION, OLD MAN. THE REAL ONE.

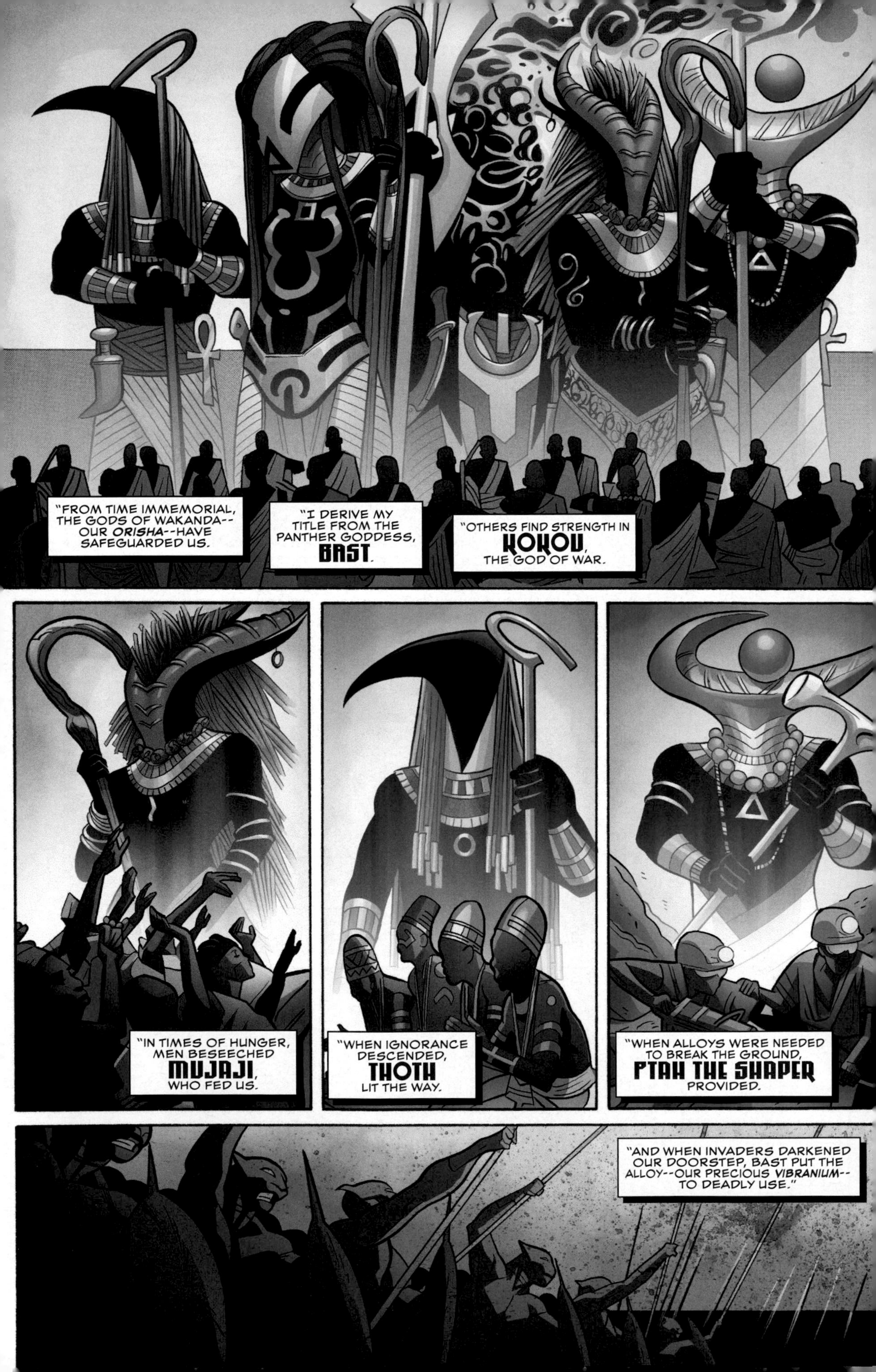
"FROM TIME IMMEMORIAL, THE GODS OF WAKANDA--OUR ORISHA--HAVE SAFEGUARDED US.
"I DERIVE MY TITLE FROM THE PANTHER GODDESS, BAST.
"OTHERS FIND STRENGTH IN KOKOU, THE GOD OF WAR.
"IN TIMES OF HUNGER, MEN BESEECHED MUJAJI, WHO FED US.
"WHEN IGNORANCE DESCENDED, THOTH LIT THE WAY.
"WHEN ALLOYS WERE NEEDED TO BREAK THE GROUND, PTAH THE SHAPER PROVIDED.
"AND WHEN INVADERS DARKENED OUR DOORSTEP, BAST PUT THE ALLOY--OUR PRECIOUS VIBRANIUM--TO DEADLY USE."

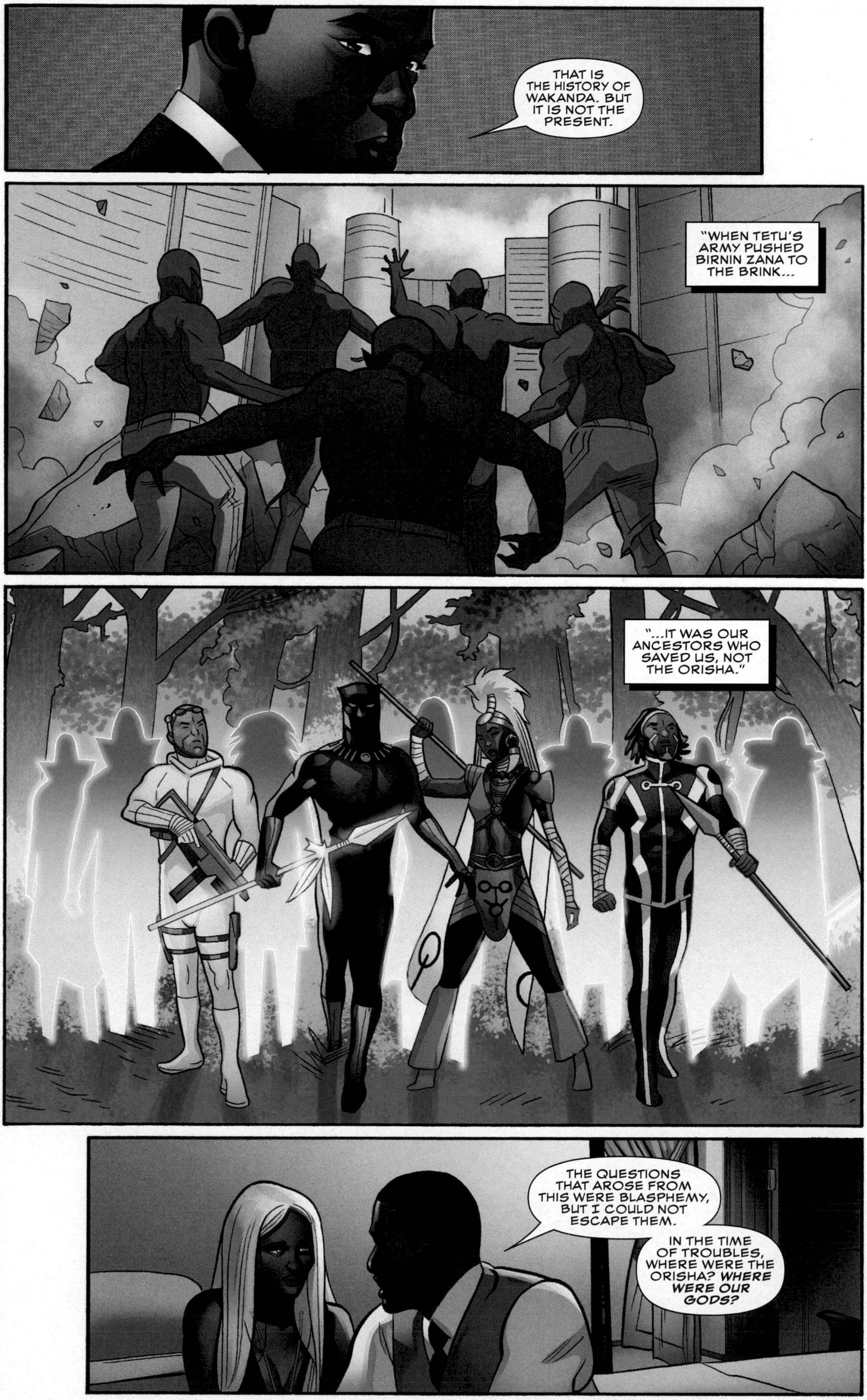
THAT IS THE HISTORY OF WAKANDA. BUT IT IS NOT THE PRESENT.
"WHEN TETU'S ARMY PUSHED BIRNIN ZANA TO THE BRINK...
"...IT WAS OUR ANCESTORS WHO SAVED US, NOT THE ORISHA."
THE QUESTIONS THAT AROSE FROM THIS WERE BLASPHEMY, BUT I COULD NOT ESCAPE THEM.
IN THE TIME OF TROUBLES, WHERE WERE THE ORISHA? *WHERE WERE OUR GODS?*

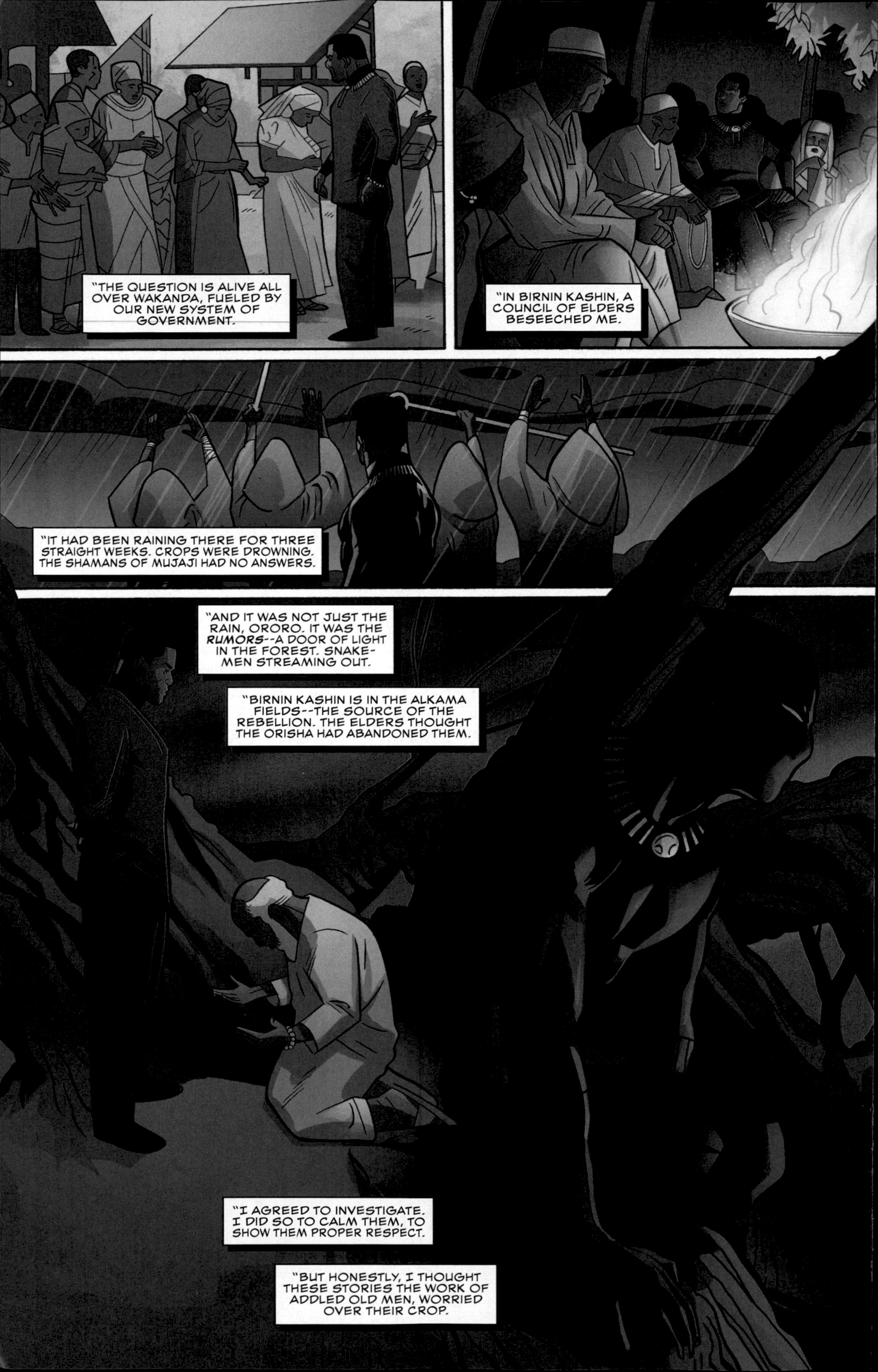
"THE QUESTION IS ALIVE ALL OVER WAKANDA, FUELED BY OUR NEW SYSTEM OF GOVERNMENT.
"IN BIRNIN KASHIN, A COUNCIL OF ELDERS BESEECHED ME.
"IT HAD BEEN RAINING THERE FOR THREE STRAIGHT WEEKS. CROPS WERE DROWNING. THE SHAMANS OF MUJAJI HAD NO ANSWERS.
"AND IT WAS NOT JUST THE RAIN, ORORO. IT WAS THE *RUMORS*--A DOOR OF LIGHT IN THE FOREST. SNAKE-MEN STREAMING OUT.
"BIRNIN KASHIN IS IN THE ALKAMA FIELDS--THE SOURCE OF THE REBELLION. THE ELDERS THOUGHT THE ORISHA HAD ABANDONED THEM.
"I AGREED TO INVESTIGATE. I DID SO TO CALM THEM, TO SHOW THEM PROPER RESPECT.
"BUT HONESTLY, I THOUGHT THESE STORIES THE WORK OF ADDLED OLD MEN, WORRIED OVER THEIR CROP.

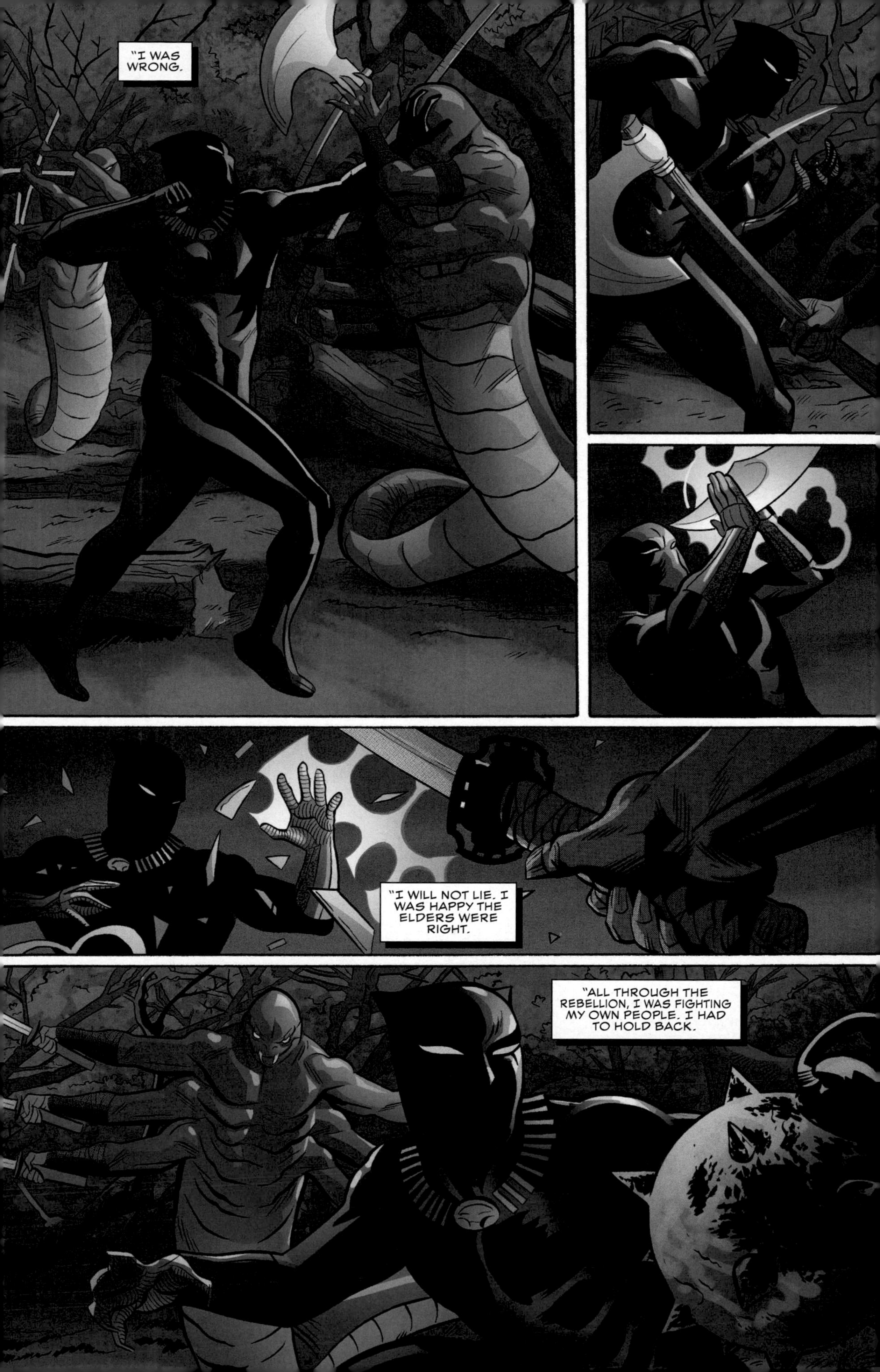
"I WAS WRONG.
"I WILL NOT LIE. I WAS HAPPY THE ELDERS WERE RIGHT.
"ALL THROUGH THE REBELLION, I WAS FIGHTING MY OWN PEOPLE. I HAD TO HOLD BACK.

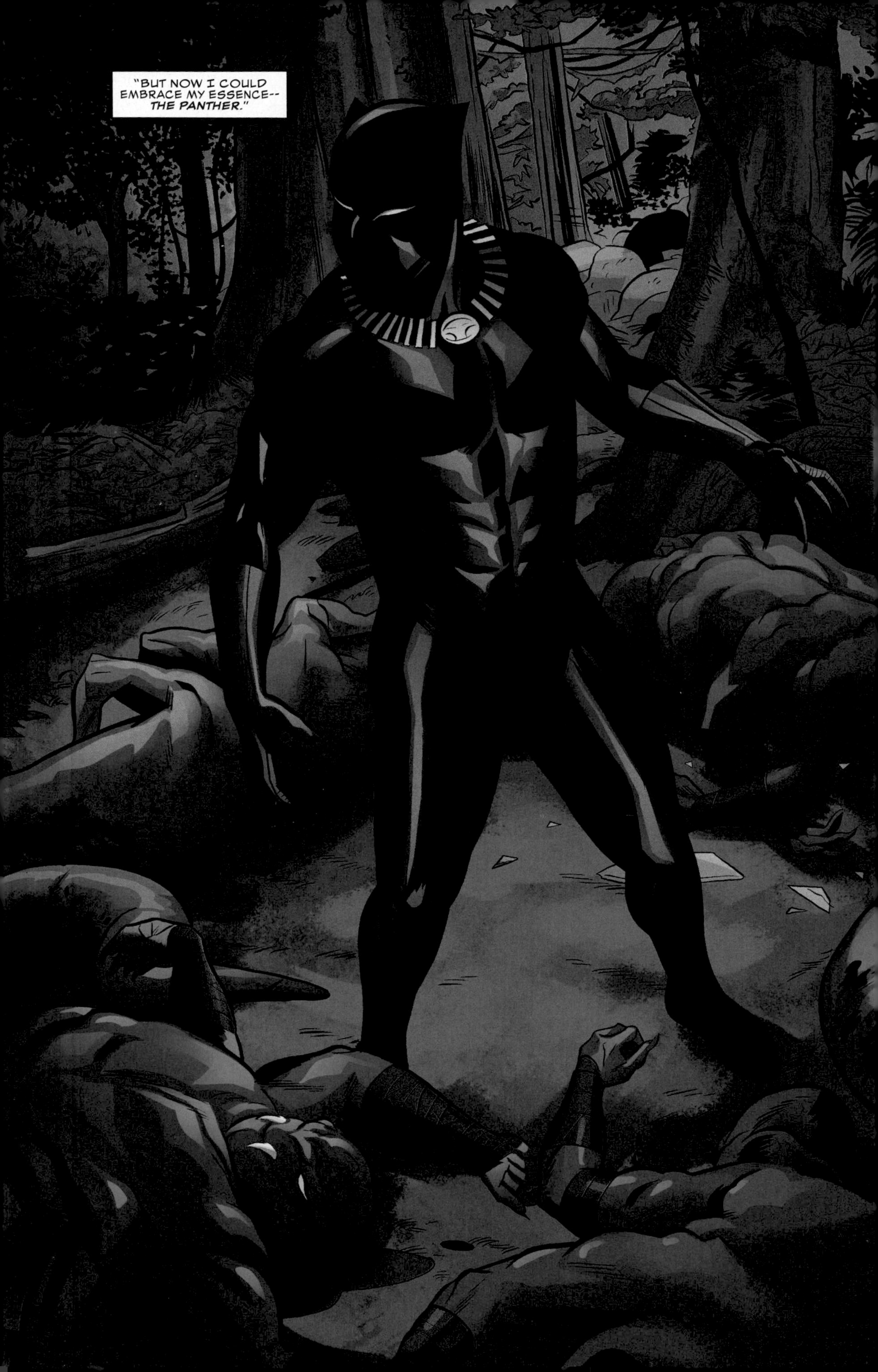
"BUT NOW I COULD EMBRACE MY ESSENCE-- *THE PANTHER.*"

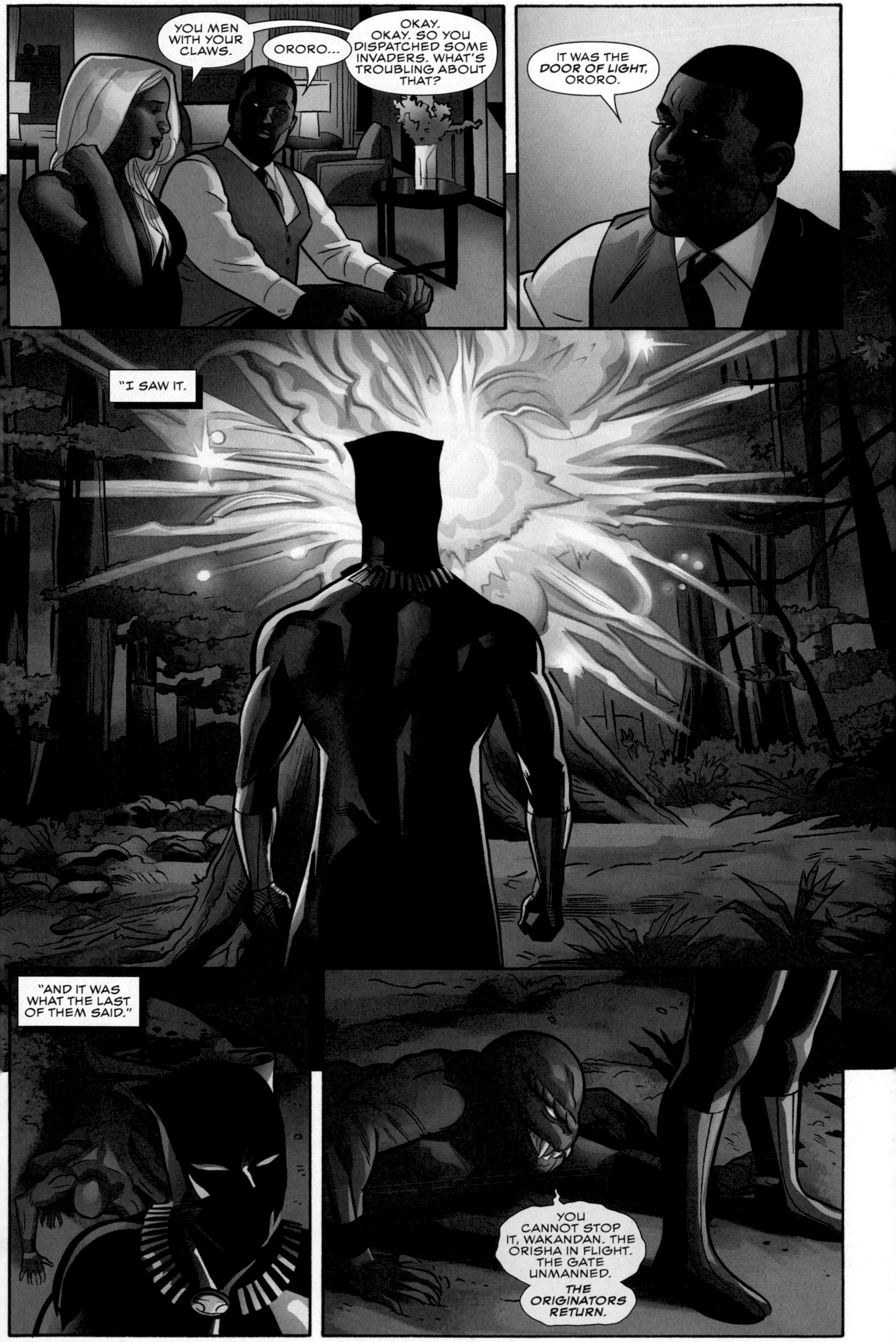

YOU MEN WITH YOUR CLAWS.
ORORO...
OKAY. OKAY. SO YOU DISPATCHED SOME INVADERS. WHAT'S TROUBLING ABOUT THAT?
IT WAS THE *DOOR OF LIGHT,* ORORO.
"I SAW IT.
"AND IT WAS WHAT THE LAST OF THEM SAID."
YOU CANNOT STOP IT, WAKANDAN. THE ORISHA IN FLIGHT. THE GATE UNMANNED. *THE ORIGINATORS RETURN.*

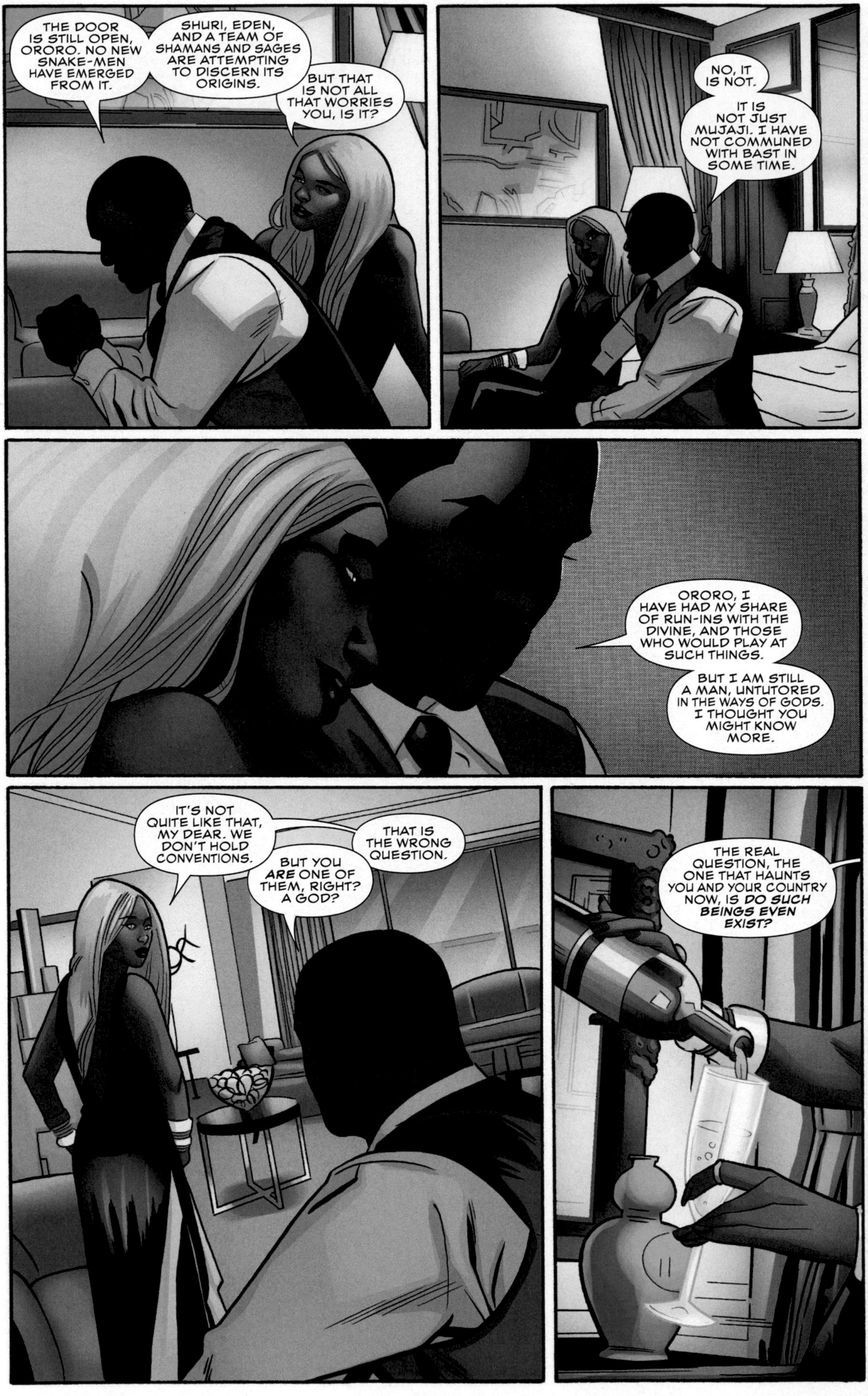
THE DOOR IS STILL OPEN, ORORO. NO NEW SNAKE-MEN HAVE EMERGED FROM IT.
SHURI, EDEN, AND A TEAM OF SHAMANS AND SAGES ARE ATTEMPTING TO DISCERN ITS ORIGINS.
BUT THAT IS NOT ALL THAT WORRIES YOU, IS IT?
NO, IT IS NOT.
IT IS NOT JUST MUJAJI. I HAVE NOT COMMUNED WITH BAST IN SOME TIME.
ORORO, I HAVE HAD MY SHARE OF RUN-INS WITH THE DIVINE, AND THOSE WHO WOULD PLAY AT SUCH THINGS.
BUT I AM STILL A MAN, UNTUTORED IN THE WAYS OF GODS. I THOUGHT YOU MIGHT KNOW MORE.
IT'S NOT QUITE LIKE THAT, MY DEAR. WE DON'T HOLD CONVENTIONS.
BUT YOU *ARE* ONE OF THEM, RIGHT? A GOD?
THAT IS THE WRONG QUESTION.
THE REAL QUESTION, THE ONE THAT HAUNTS YOU AND YOUR COUNTRY NOW, IS *DO SUCH BEINGS EVEN EXIST?*

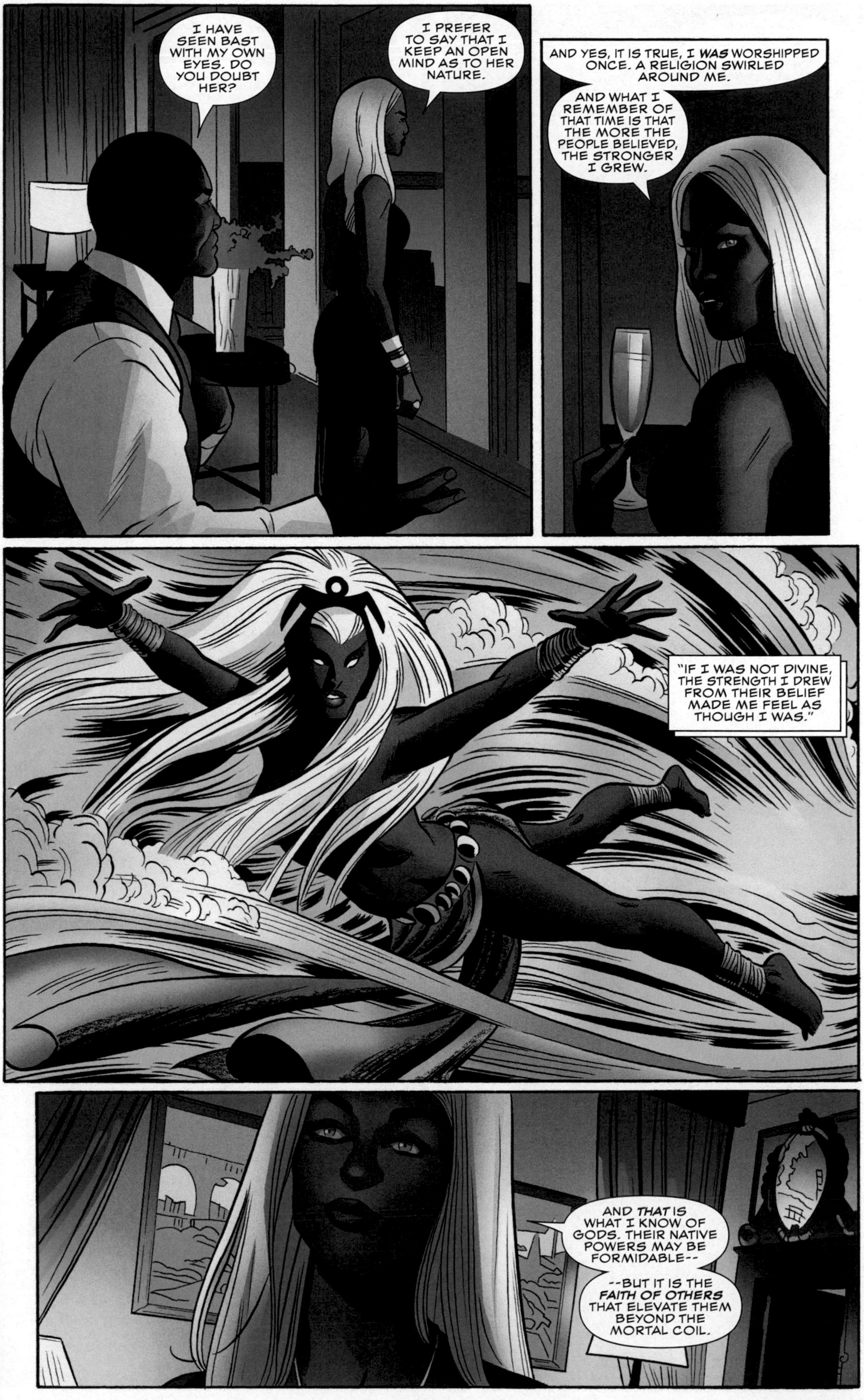

I HAVE SEEN BAST WITH MY OWN EYES. DO YOU DOUBT HER?
I PREFER TO SAY THAT I KEEP AN OPEN MIND AS TO HER NATURE.
AND YES, IT IS TRUE, I *WAS* WORSHIPPED ONCE. A RELIGION SWIRLED AROUND ME.
AND WHAT I REMEMBER OF THAT TIME IS THAT THE MORE THE PEOPLE BELIEVED, THE STRONGER I GREW.
"IF I WAS NOT DIVINE, THE STRENGTH I DREW FROM THEIR BELIEF MADE ME FEEL AS THOUGH I WAS."
AND *THAT* IS WHAT I KNOW OF GODS. THEIR NATIVE POWERS MAY BE FORMIDABLE--
--BUT IT IS THE ***FAITH OF OTHERS*** THAT ELEVATE THEM BEYOND THE MORTAL COIL.

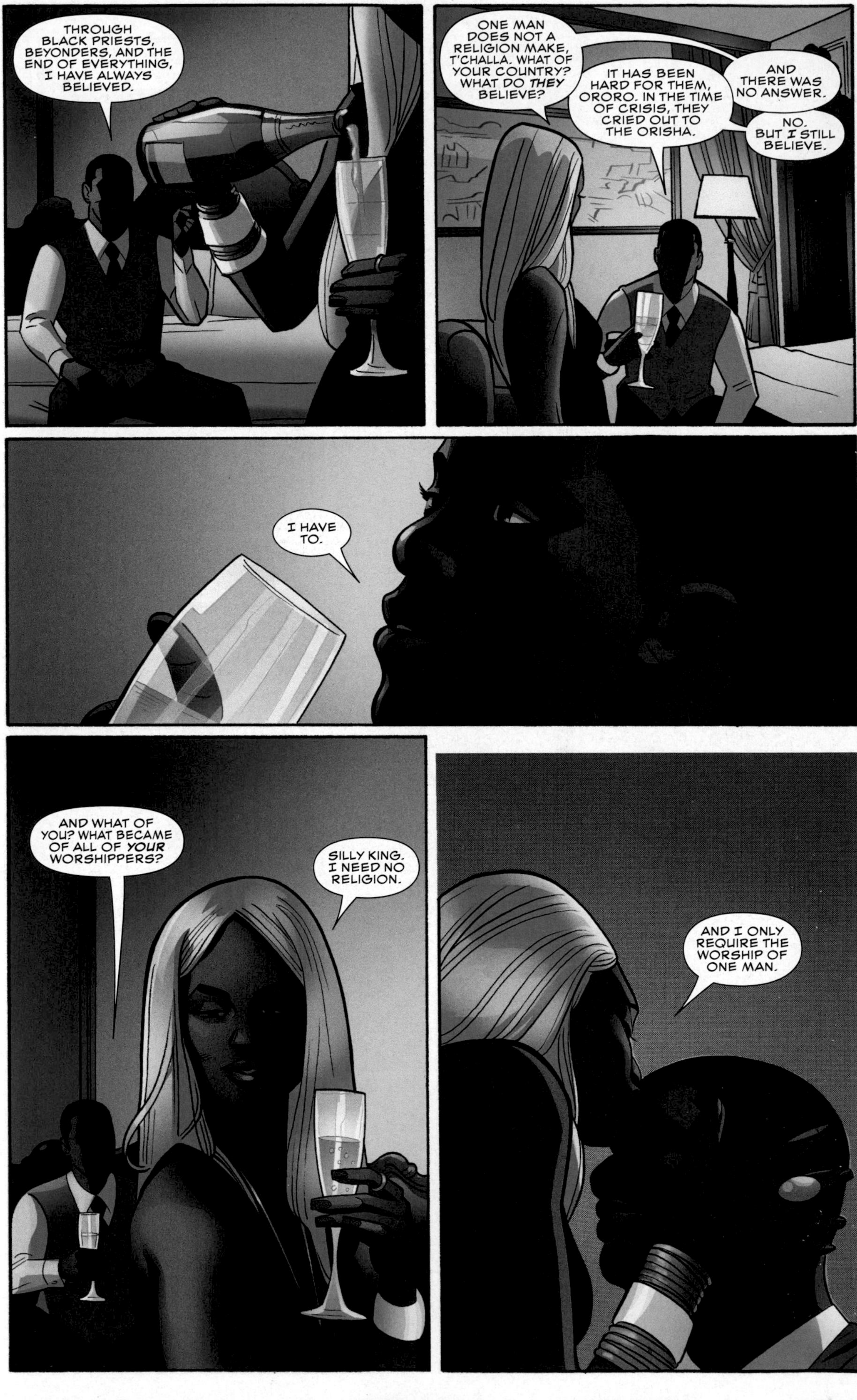
THROUGH BLACK PRIESTS, BEYONDERS, AND THE END OF EVERYTHING, I HAVE ALWAYS BELIEVED.
ONE MAN DOES NOT A RELIGION MAKE, T'CHALLA. WHAT OF YOUR COUNTRY? WHAT DO *THEY* BELIEVE?
IT HAS BEEN HARD FOR THEM, ORORO. IN THE TIME OF CRISIS, THEY CRIED OUT TO THE ORISHA.
AND THERE WAS NO ANSWER.
NO. BUT *I* STILL BELIEVE.
I HAVE TO.
AND WHAT OF YOU? WHAT BECAME OF ALL OF *YOUR* WORSHIPPERS?
SILLY KING. I NEED NO RELIGION.
AND I ONLY REQUIRE THE WORSHIP OF ONE MAN.

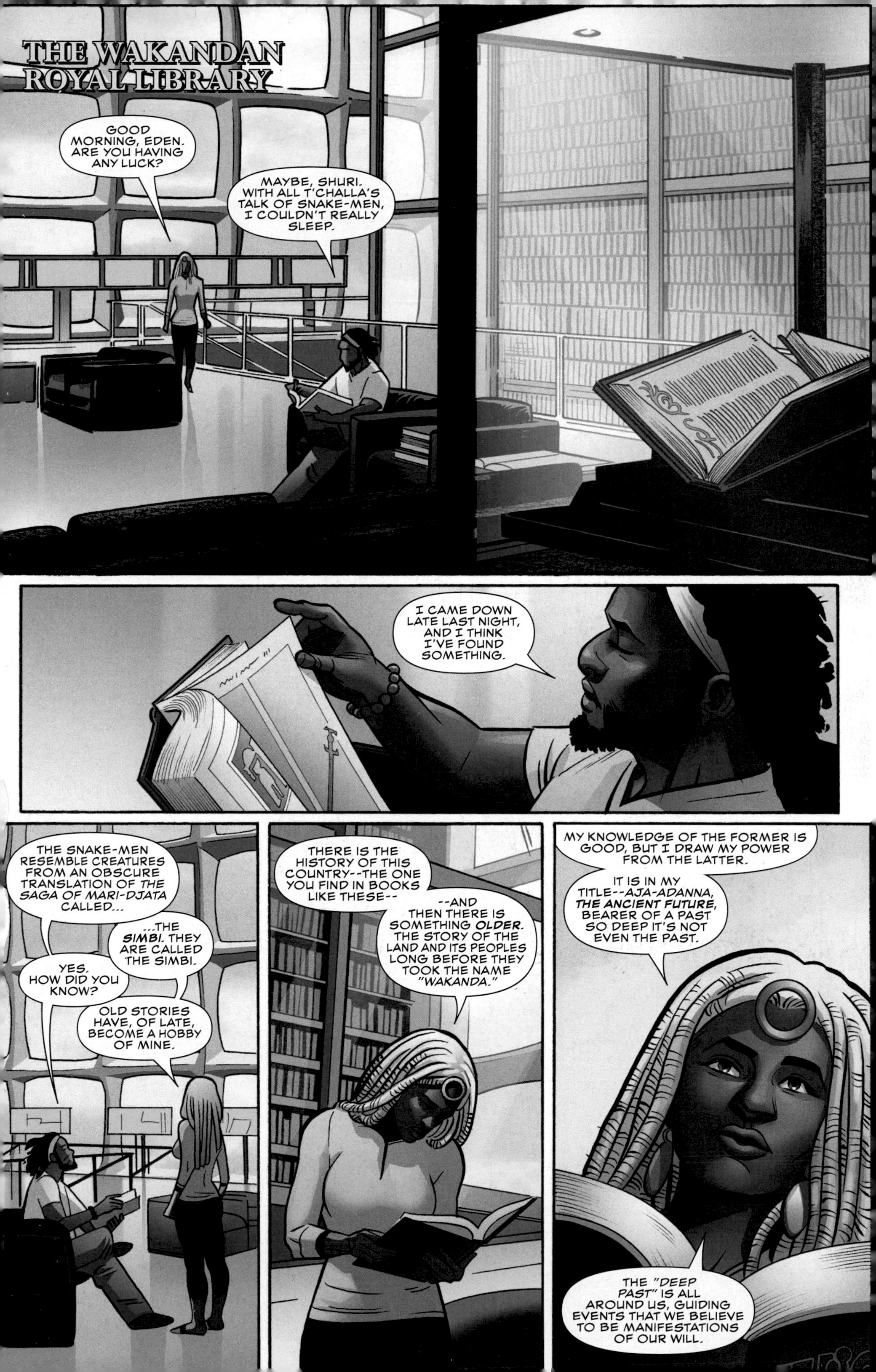

THE WAKANDAN ROYAL LIBRARY
GOOD MORNING, EDEN. ARE YOU HAVING ANY LUCK?
MAYBE, SHURI. WITH ALL T'CHALLA'S TALK OF SNAKE-MEN, I COULDN'T REALLY SLEEP.
I CAME DOWN LATE LAST NIGHT, AND I THINK I'VE FOUND SOMETHING.
THE SNAKE-MEN RESEMBLE CREATURES FROM AN OBSCURE TRANSLATION OF *THE SAGA OF MARI-DJATA* CALLED...
...THE *SIMBI.* THEY ARE CALLED THE SIMBI.
YES. HOW DID YOU KNOW?
OLD STORIES HAVE, OF LATE, BECOME A HOBBY OF MINE.
THERE IS THE HISTORY OF THIS COUNTRY--THE ONE YOU FIND IN BOOKS LIKE THESE--
--AND THEN THERE IS SOMETHING *OLDER.* THE STORY OF THE LAND AND ITS PEOPLES LONG BEFORE THEY TOOK THE NAME *"WAKANDA."*
MY KNOWLEDGE OF THE FORMER IS GOOD, BUT I DRAW MY POWER FROM THE LATTER.
IT IS IN MY TITLE--*AJA-ADANNA, THE ANCIENT FUTURE,* BEARER OF A PAST SO DEEP IT'S NOT EVEN THE PAST.
THE *"DEEP PAST"* IS ALL AROUND US, GUIDING EVENTS THAT WE BELIEVE TO BE MANIFESTATIONS OF OUR WILL.

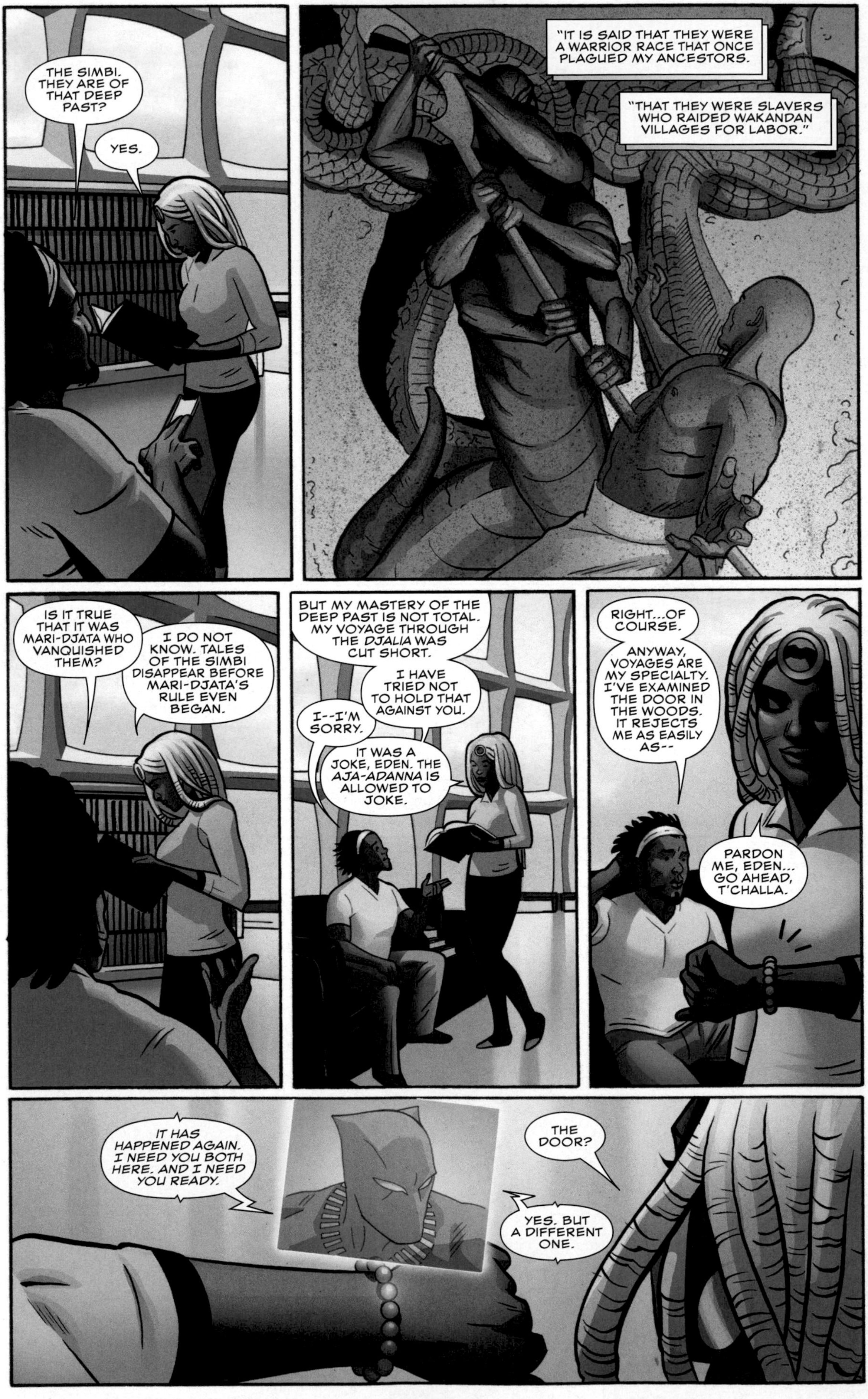
THE SIMBI. THEY ARE OF THAT DEEP PAST?
YES.
"IT IS SAID THAT THEY WERE A WARRIOR RACE THAT ONCE PLAGUED MY ANCESTORS.
"THAT THEY WERE SLAVERS WHO RAIDED WAKANDAN VILLAGES FOR LABOR."
IS IT TRUE THAT IT WAS MARI-DJATA WHO VANQUISHED THEM?
I DO NOT KNOW. TALES OF THE SIMBI DISAPPEAR BEFORE MARI-DJATA'S RULE EVEN BEGAN.
BUT MY MASTERY OF THE DEEP PAST IS NOT TOTAL. MY VOYAGE THROUGH THE DJALIA WAS CUT SHORT.
I HAVE TRIED NOT TO HOLD THAT AGAINST YOU.
I--I'M SORRY.
IT WAS A JOKE, EDEN. THE AJA-ADANNA IS ALLOWED TO JOKE.
RIGHT...OF COURSE.
ANYWAY, VOYAGES ARE MY SPECIALTY. I'VE EXAMINED THE DOOR IN THE WOODS. IT REJECTS ME AS EASILY AS--
PARDON ME, EDEN... GO AHEAD, T'CHALLA.
IT HAS HAPPENED AGAIN. I NEED YOU BOTH HERE. AND I NEED YOU READY.
THE DOOR?
YES. BUT A DIFFERENT ONE.

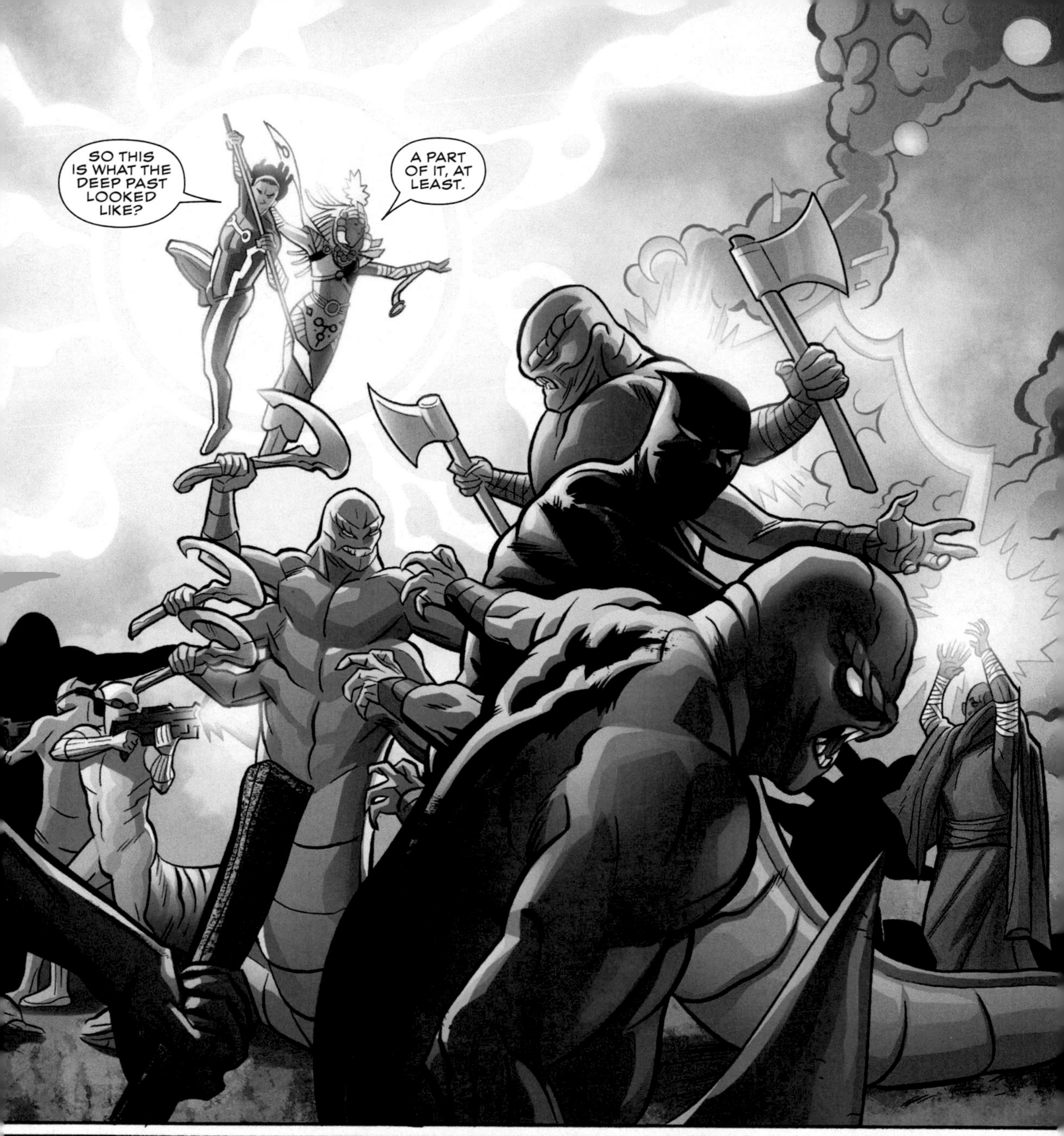
SO THIS IS WHAT THE DEEP PAST LOOKED LIKE?
A PART OF IT, AT LEAST.

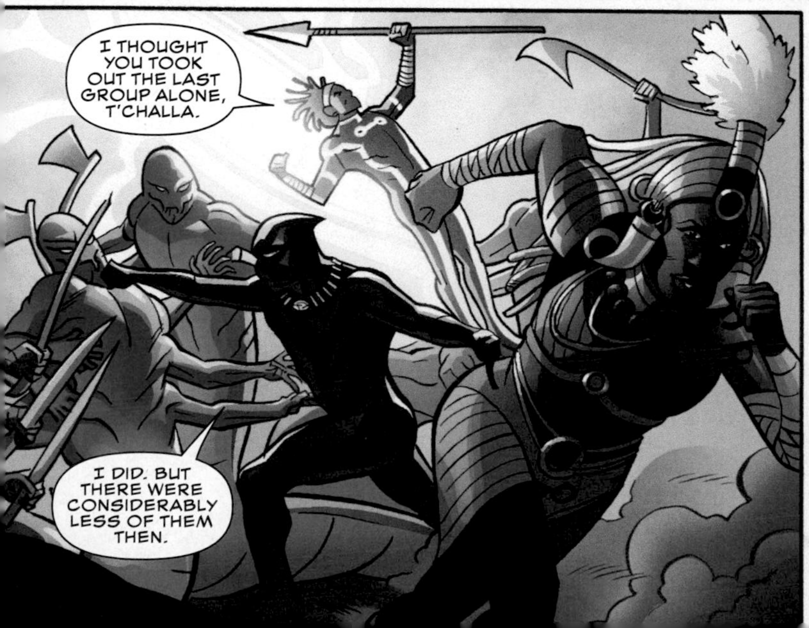
I THOUGHT YOU TOOK OUT THE LAST GROUP ALONE, T'CHALLA.
I DID. BUT THERE WERE CONSIDERABLY LESS OF THEM THEN.

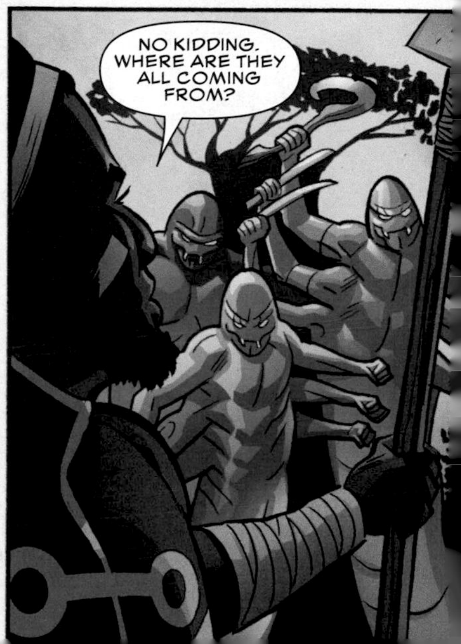
NO KIDDING. WHERE ARE THEY ALL COMING FROM?

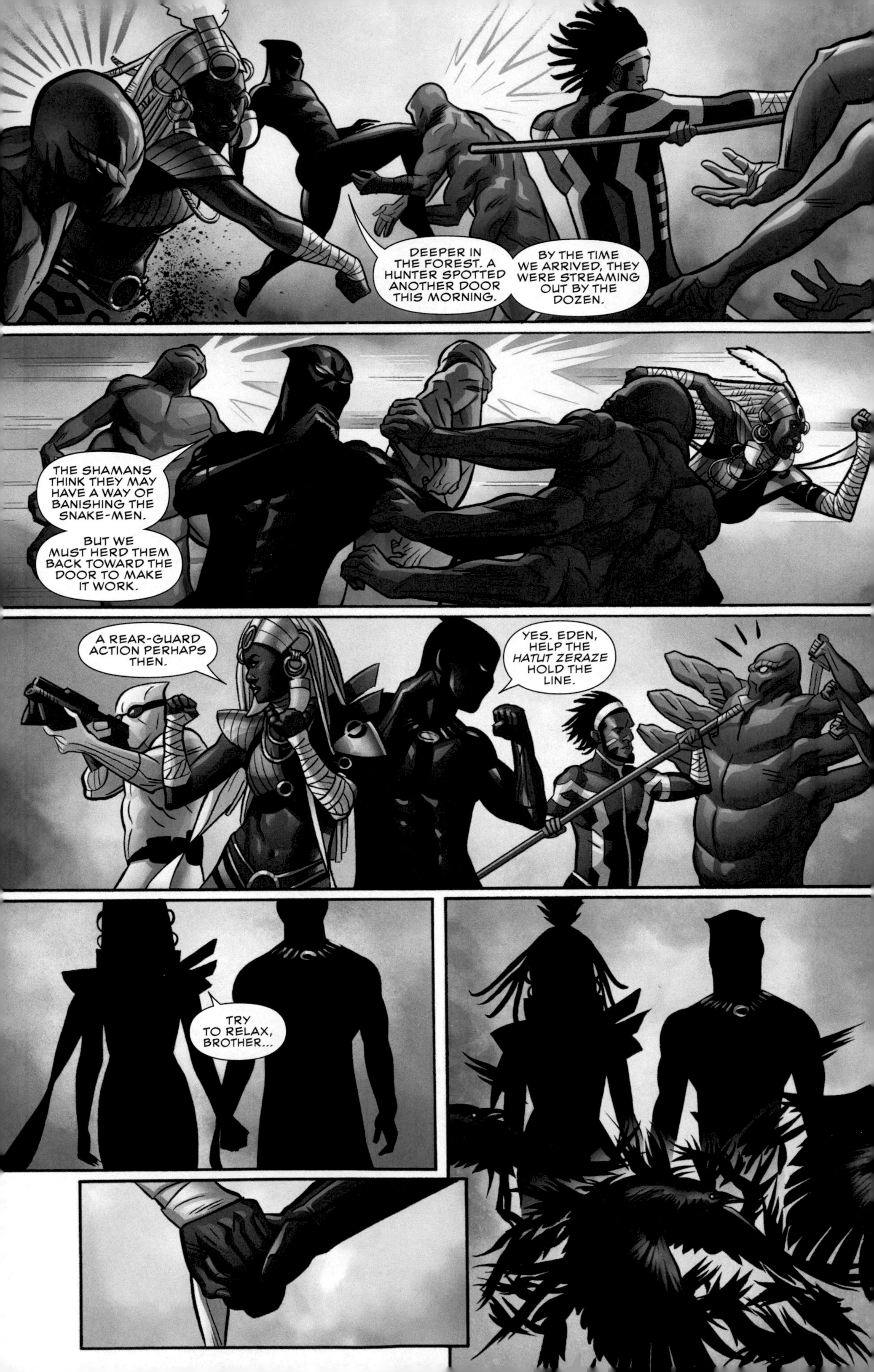

DEEPER IN THE FOREST. A HUNTER SPOTTED ANOTHER DOOR THIS MORNING.
BY THE TIME WE ARRIVED, THEY WERE STREAMING OUT BY THE DOZEN.
THE SHAMANS THINK THEY MAY HAVE A WAY OF BANISHING THE SNAKE-MEN.
BUT WE MUST HERD THEM BACK TOWARD THE DOOR TO MAKE IT WORK.
A REAR-GUARD ACTION PERHAPS THEN.
YES. EDEN, HELP THE *HATUT ZERAZE* HOLD THE LINE.
TRY TO RELAX, BROTHER...

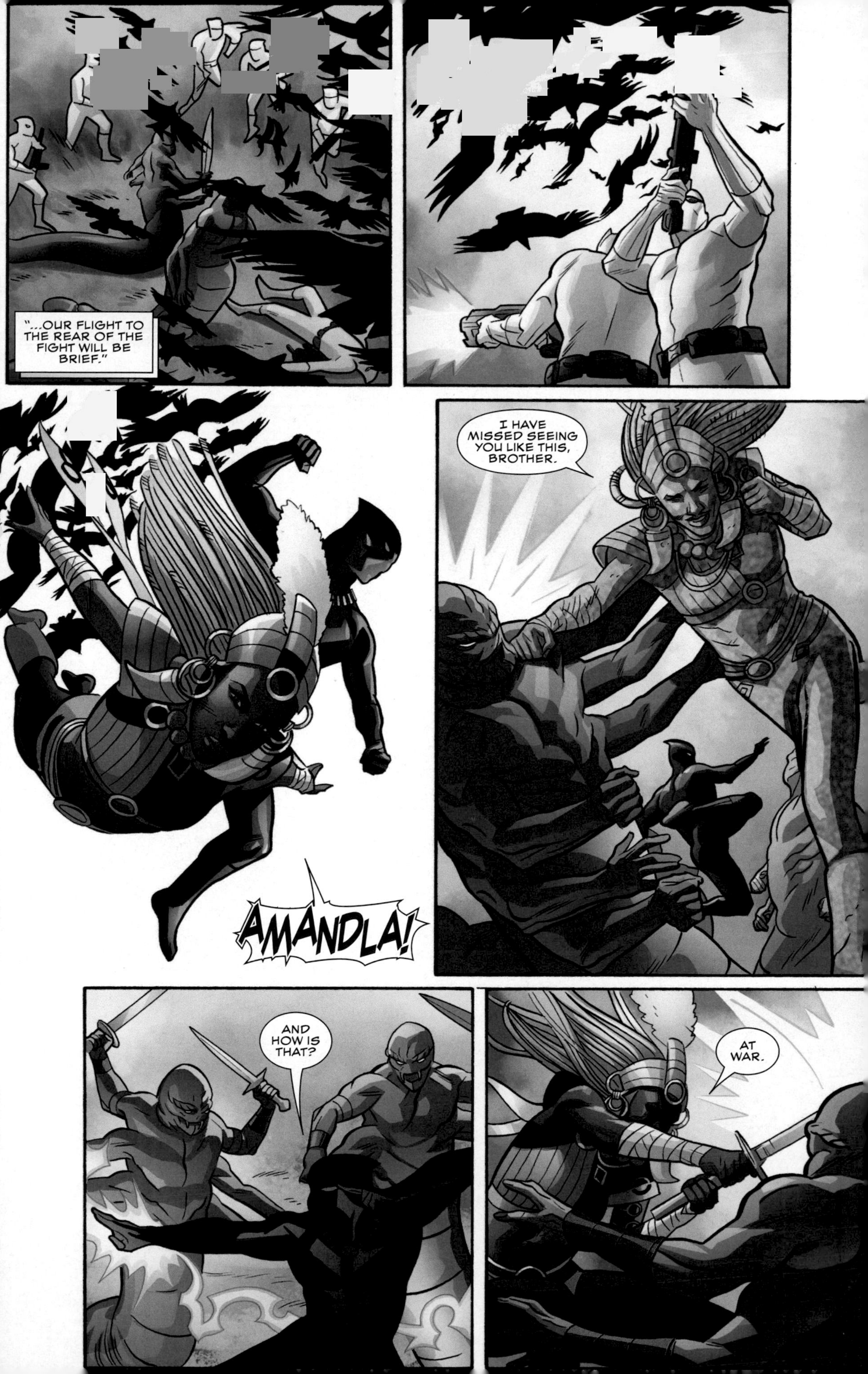
"...OUR FLIGHT TO THE REAR OF THE FIGHT WILL BE BRIEF."
AMANDLA!
I HAVE MISSED SEEING YOU LIKE THIS, BROTHER.
AND HOW IS THAT?
AT WAR.

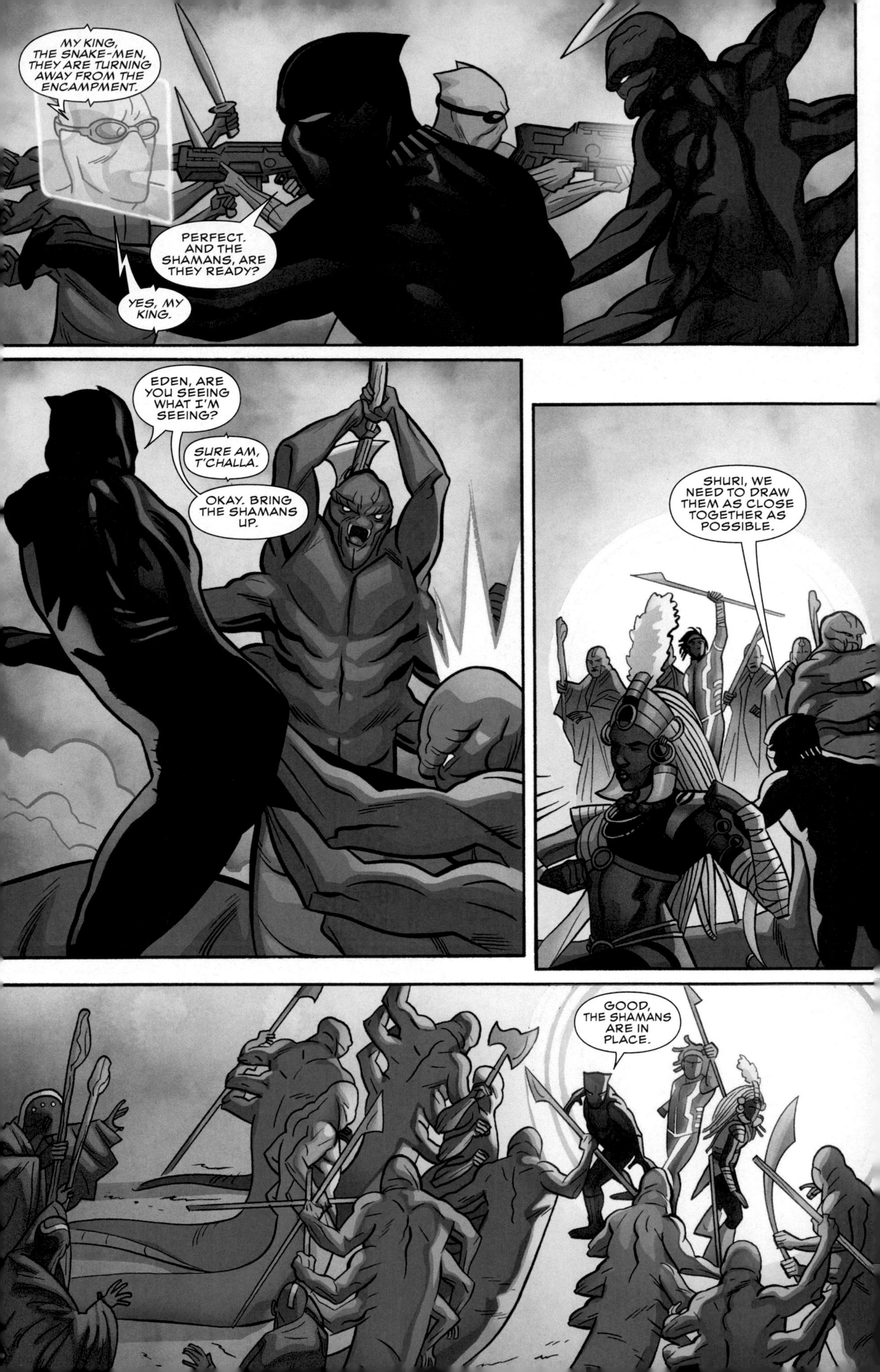

MY KING, THE SNAKE-MEN, THEY ARE TURNING AWAY FROM THE ENCAMPMENT.
PERFECT. AND THE SHAMANS, ARE THEY READY?
YES, MY KING.
EDEN, ARE YOU SEEING WHAT I'M SEEING?
SURE AM, T'CHALLA.
OKAY. BRING THE SHAMANS UP.
SHURI, WE NEED TO DRAW THEM AS CLOSE TOGETHER AS POSSIBLE.
GOOD, THE SHAMANS ARE IN PLACE.

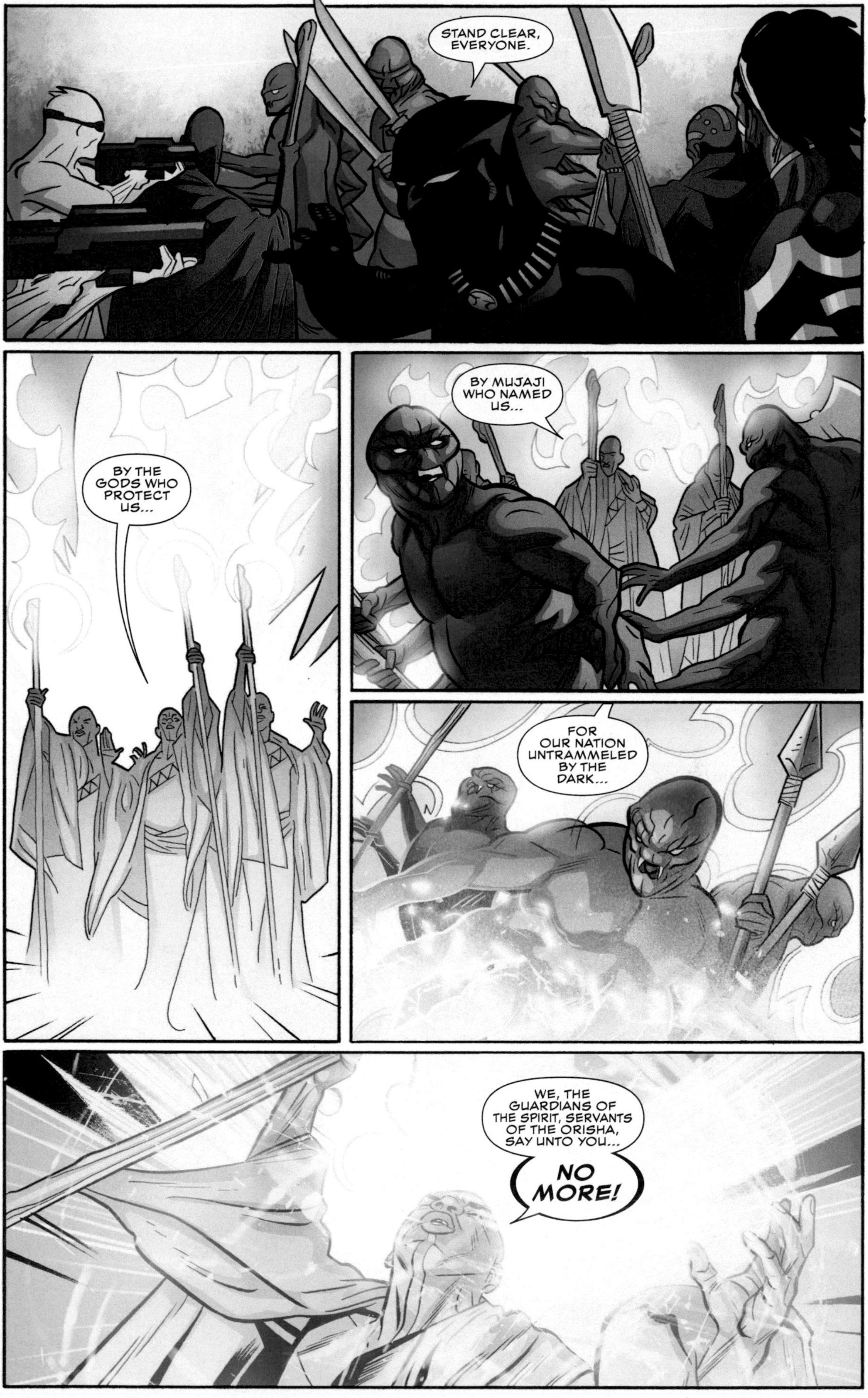
STAND CLEAR, EVERYONE.
BY THE GODS WHO PROTECT US...
BY MUJAJI WHO NAMED US...
FOR OUR NATION UNTRAMMELED BY THE DARK...
WE, THE GUARDIANS OF THE SPIRIT, SERVANTS OF THE ORISHA, SAY UNTO YOU...
NO MORE!

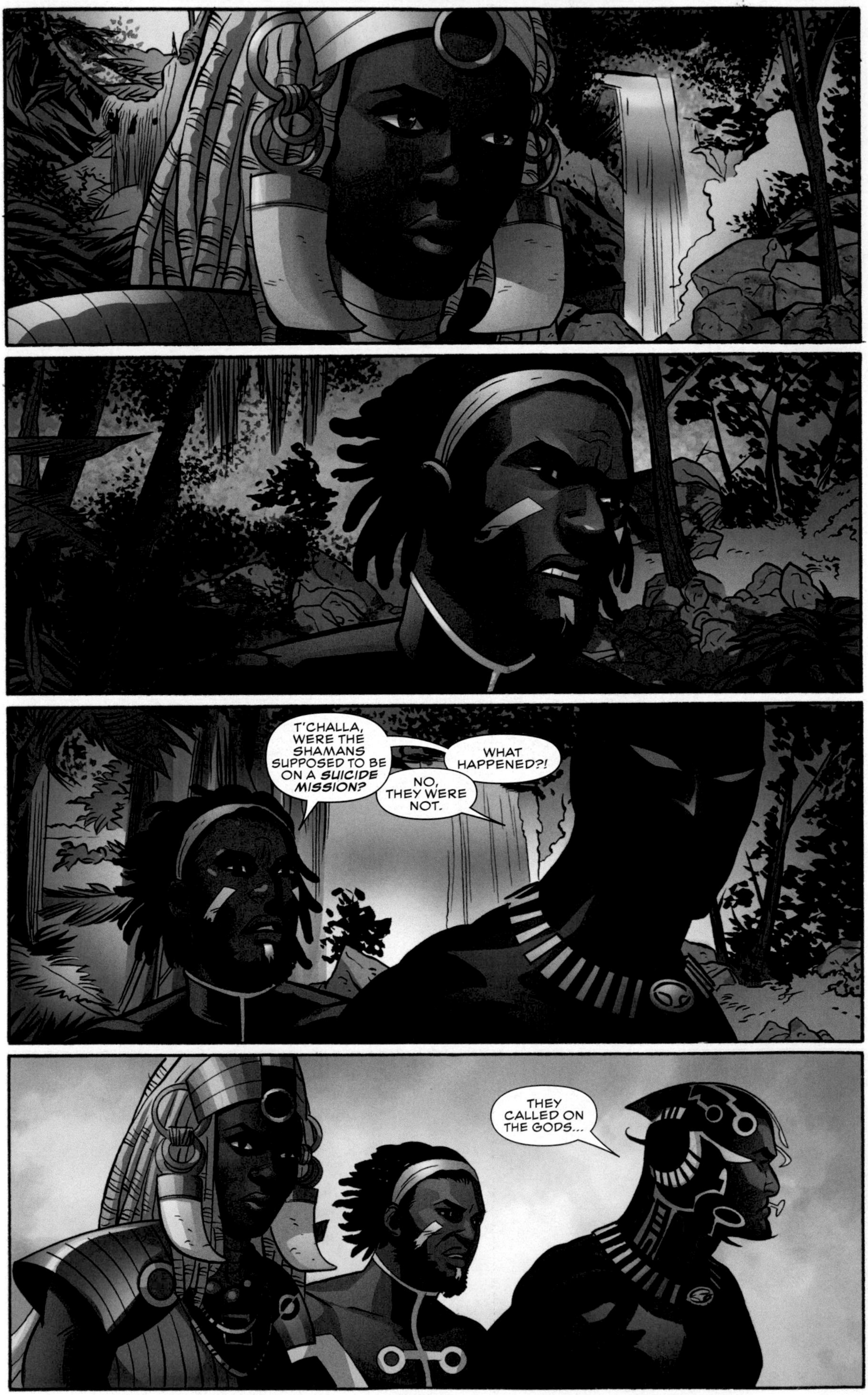
T'CHALLA, WERE THE SHAMANS SUPPOSED TO BE ON A *SUICIDE MISSION?*
WHAT HAPPENED?!
NO, THEY WERE NOT.
THEY CALLED ON THE GODS...

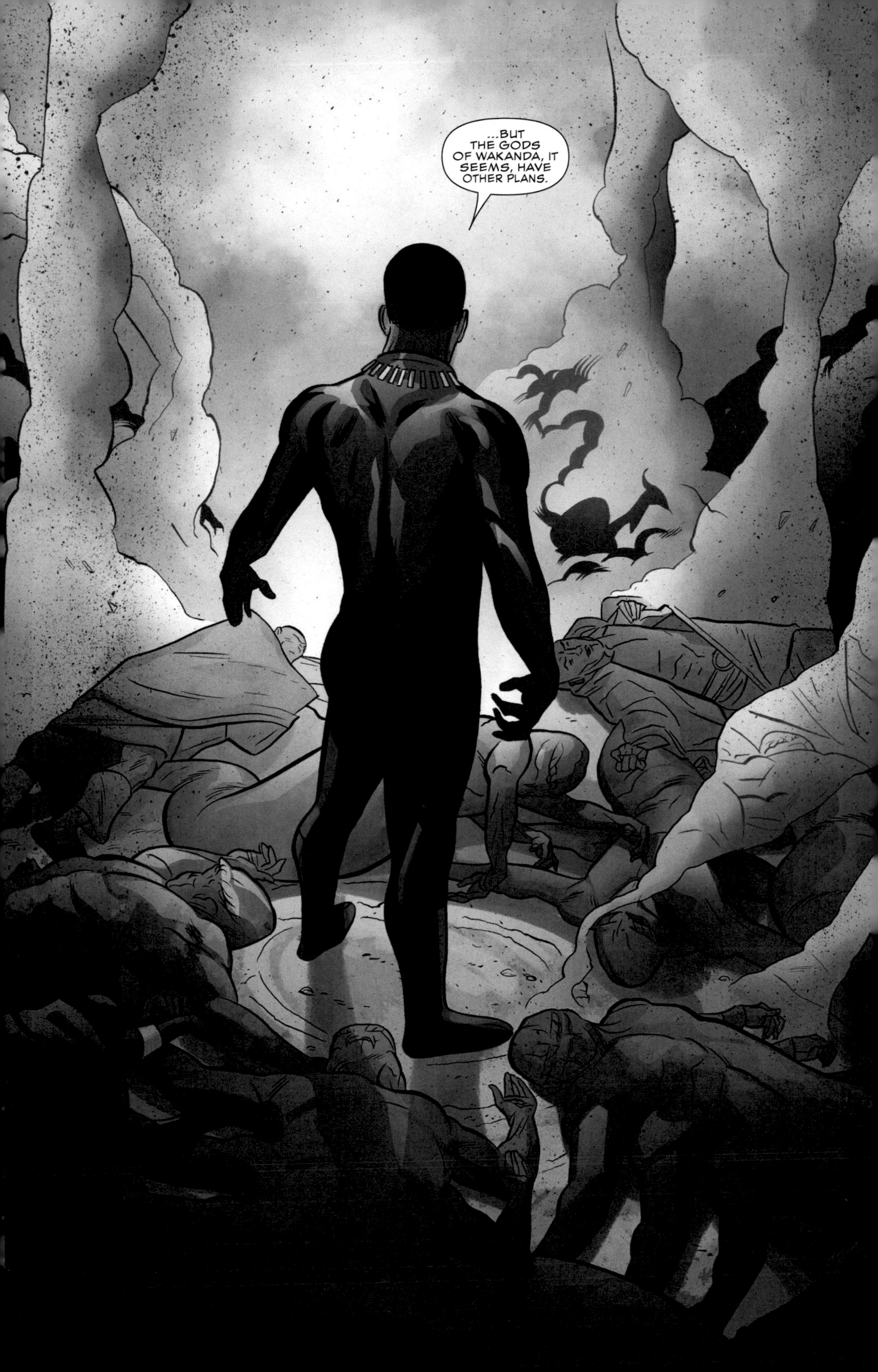
...BUT THE GODS OF WAKANDA, IT SEEMS, HAVE OTHER PLANS.

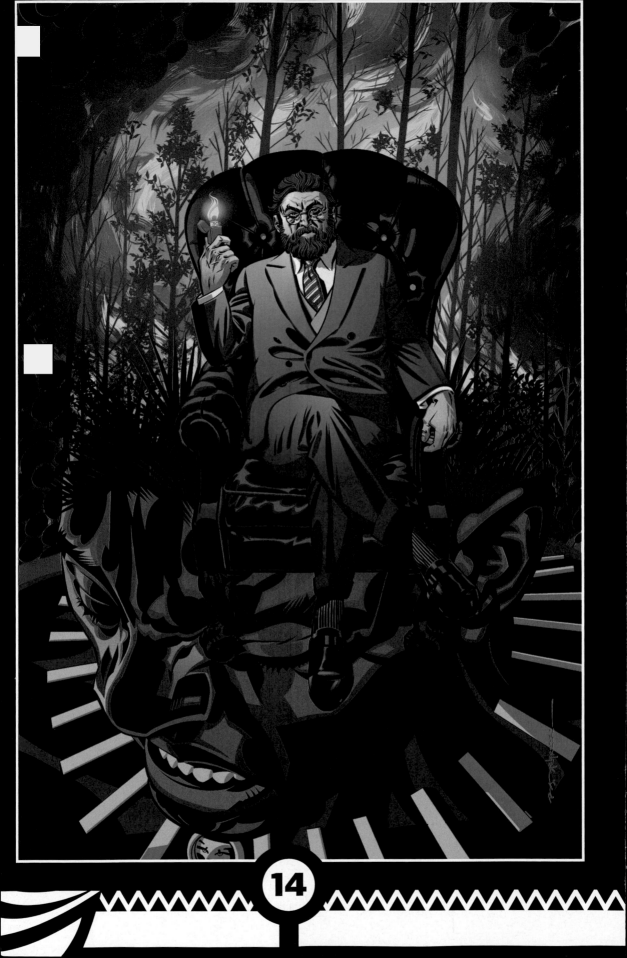

14

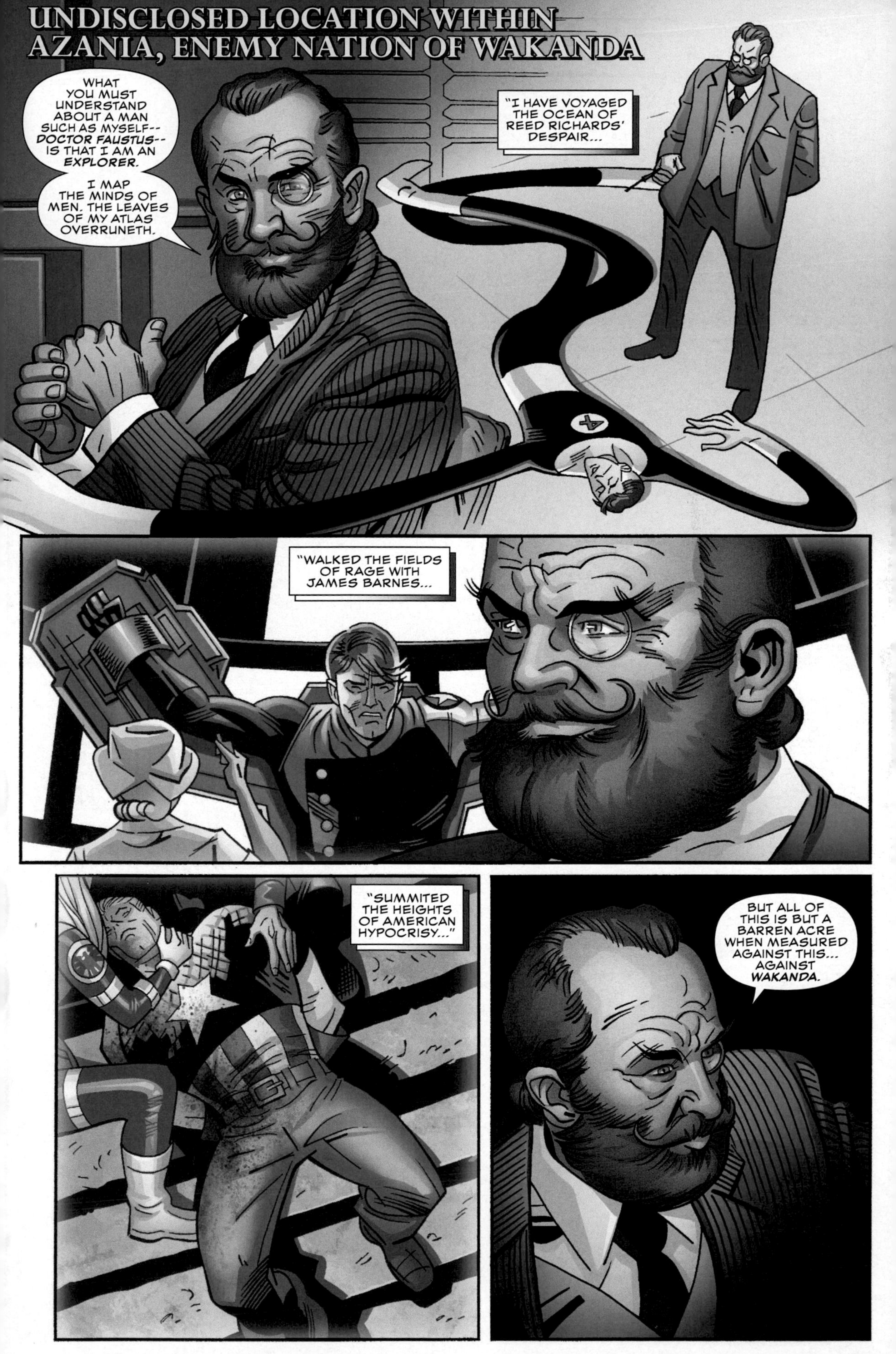
UNDISCLOSED LOCATION WITHIN AZANIA, ENEMY NATION OF WAKANDA
WHAT YOU MUST UNDERSTAND ABOUT A MAN SUCH AS MYSELF-- DOCTOR FAUSTUS-- IS THAT I AM AN EXPLORER.
I MAP THE MINDS OF MEN. THE LEAVES OF MY ATLAS OVERRUNETH.
"I HAVE VOYAGED THE OCEAN OF REED RICHARDS' DESPAIR...
"WALKED THE FIELDS OF RAGE WITH JAMES BARNES...
"SUMMITED THE HEIGHTS OF AMERICAN HYPOCRISY..."
BUT ALL OF THIS IS BUT A BARREN ACRE WHEN MEASURED AGAINST THIS... AGAINST WAKANDA.

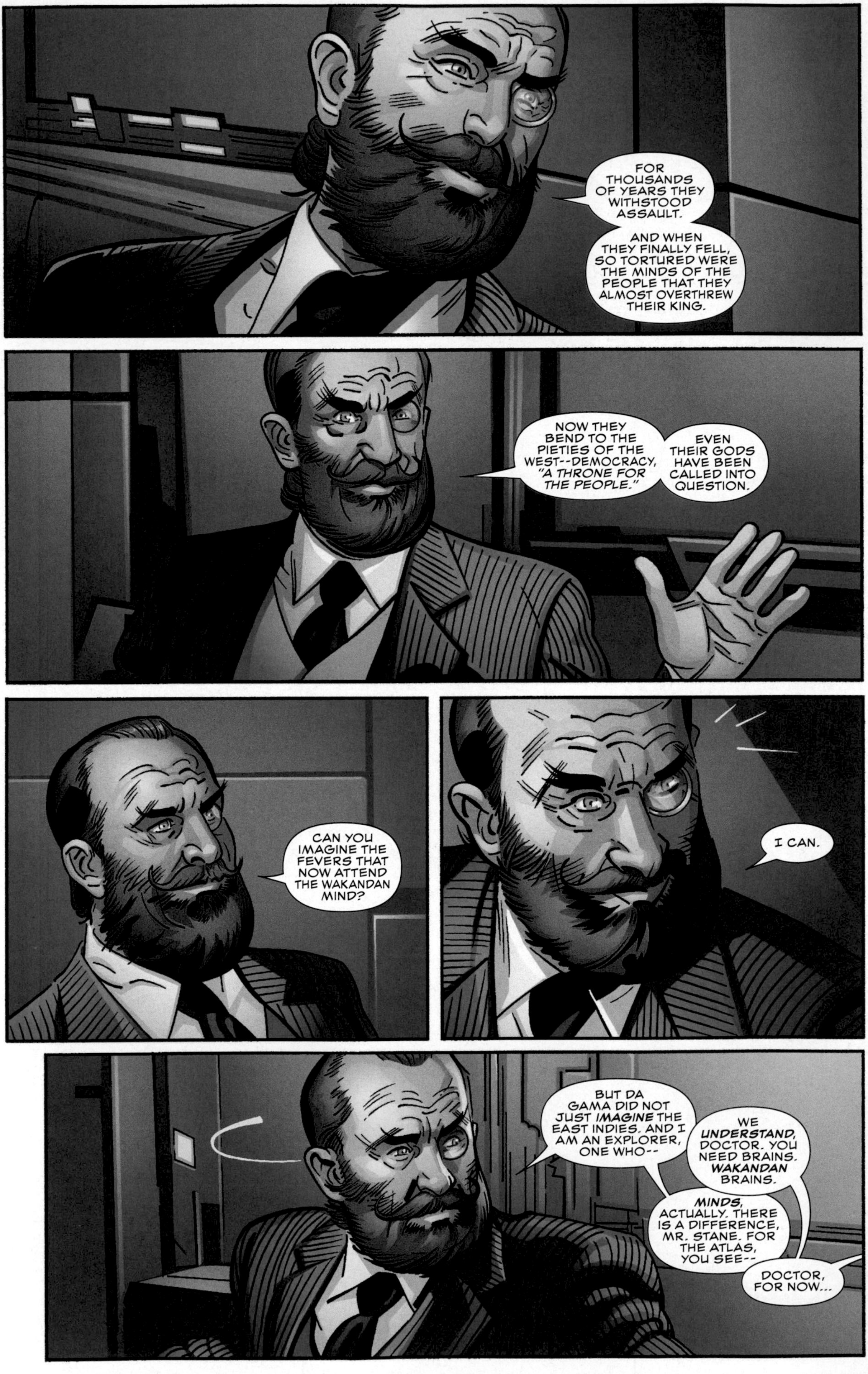
FOR THOUSANDS OF YEARS THEY WITHSTOOD ASSAULT.
AND WHEN THEY FINALLY FELL, SO TORTURED WERE THE MINDS OF THE PEOPLE THAT THEY ALMOST OVERTHREW THEIR KING.
NOW THEY BEND TO THE PIETIES OF THE WEST--DEMOCRACY, "A THRONE FOR THE PEOPLE."
EVEN THEIR GODS HAVE BEEN CALLED INTO QUESTION.
CAN YOU IMAGINE THE FEVERS THAT NOW ATTEND THE WAKANDAN MIND?
I CAN.
BUT DA GAMA DID NOT JUST IMAGINE THE EAST INDIES. AND I AM AN EXPLORER, ONE WHO--
WE UNDERSTAND, DOCTOR. YOU NEED BRAINS. WAKANDAN BRAINS.
MINDS, ACTUALLY. THERE IS A DIFFERENCE, MR. STANE. FOR THE ATLAS, YOU SEE--
DOCTOR, FOR NOW...

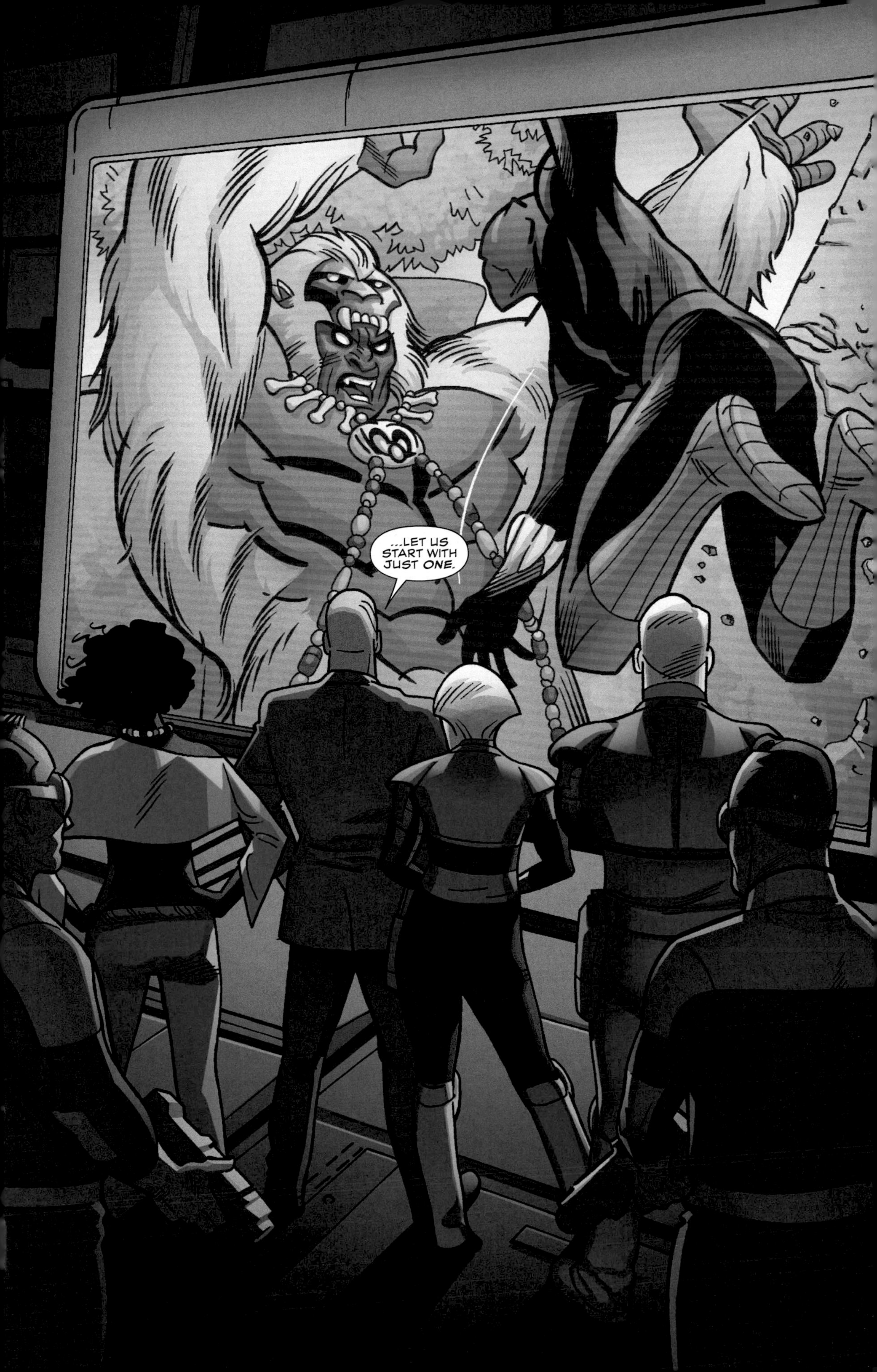
...LET US START WITH JUST ONE.

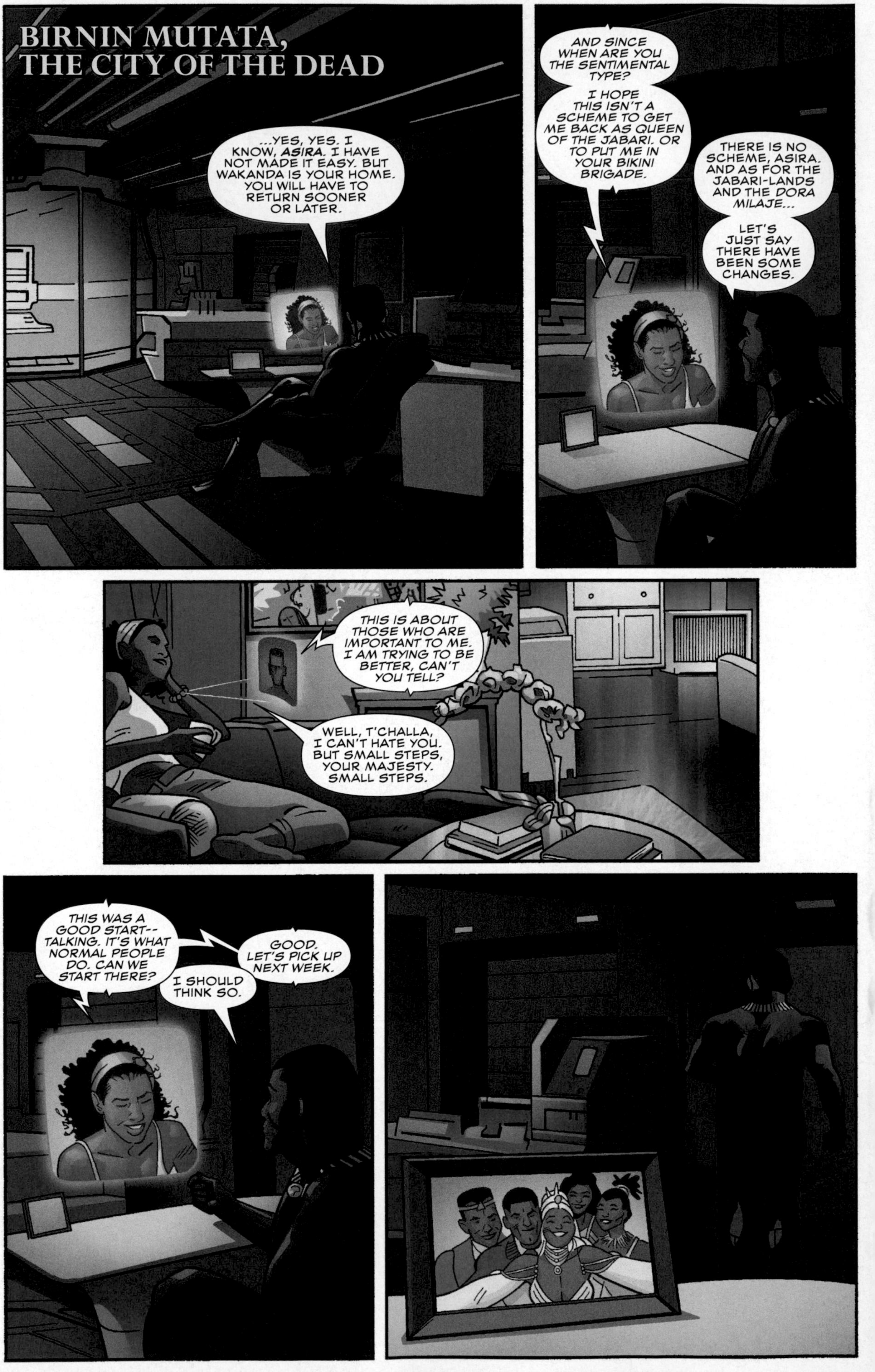
BIRNIN MUTATA, THE CITY OF THE DEAD
...YES, YES. I KNOW, ASIRA. I HAVE NOT MADE IT EASY. BUT WAKANDA IS YOUR HOME. YOU WILL HAVE TO RETURN SOONER OR LATER.
AND SINCE WHEN ARE YOU THE SENTIMENTAL TYPE?
I HOPE THIS ISN'T A SCHEME TO GET ME BACK AS QUEEN OF THE JABARI. OR TO PUT ME IN YOUR BIKINI BRIGADE.
THERE IS NO SCHEME, ASIRA. AND AS FOR THE JABARI-LANDS AND THE DORA MILAJE...
LET'S JUST SAY THERE HAVE BEEN SOME CHANGES.
THIS IS ABOUT THOSE WHO ARE IMPORTANT TO ME. I AM TRYING TO BE BETTER, CAN'T YOU TELL?
WELL, T'CHALLA, I CAN'T HATE YOU. BUT SMALL STEPS, YOUR MAJESTY. SMALL STEPS.
THIS WAS A GOOD START--TALKING. IT'S WHAT NORMAL PEOPLE DO. CAN WE START THERE?
I SHOULD THINK SO.
GOOD. LET'S PICK UP NEXT WEEK.

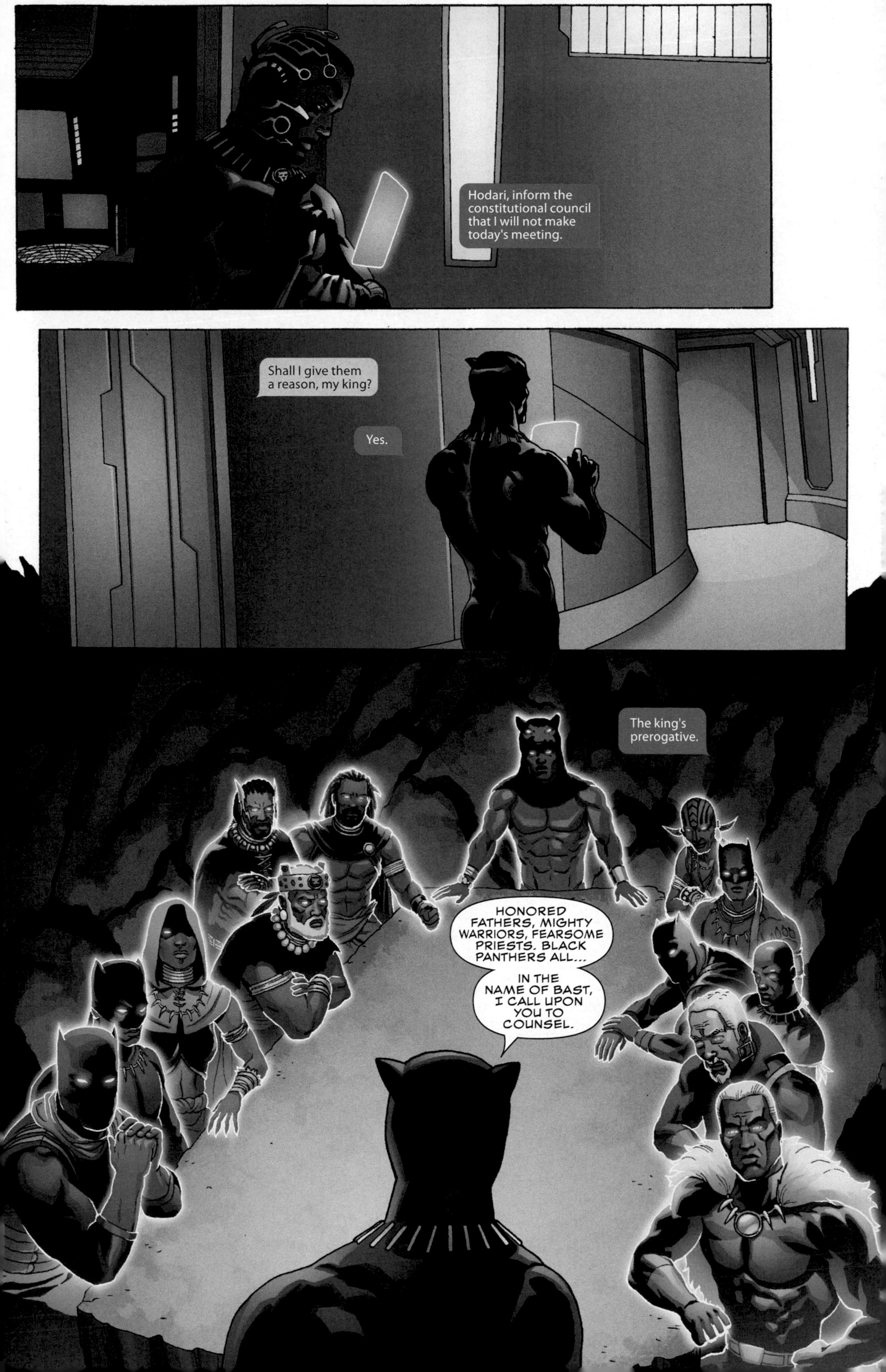
Hodari, inform the constitutional council that I will not make today's meeting.
Shall I give them a reason, my king?
Yes.
The king's prerogative.
HONORED FATHERS, MIGHTY WARRIORS, FEARSOME PRIESTS. BLACK PANTHERS ALL...
IN THE NAME OF BAST, I CALL UPON YOU TO COUNSEL.

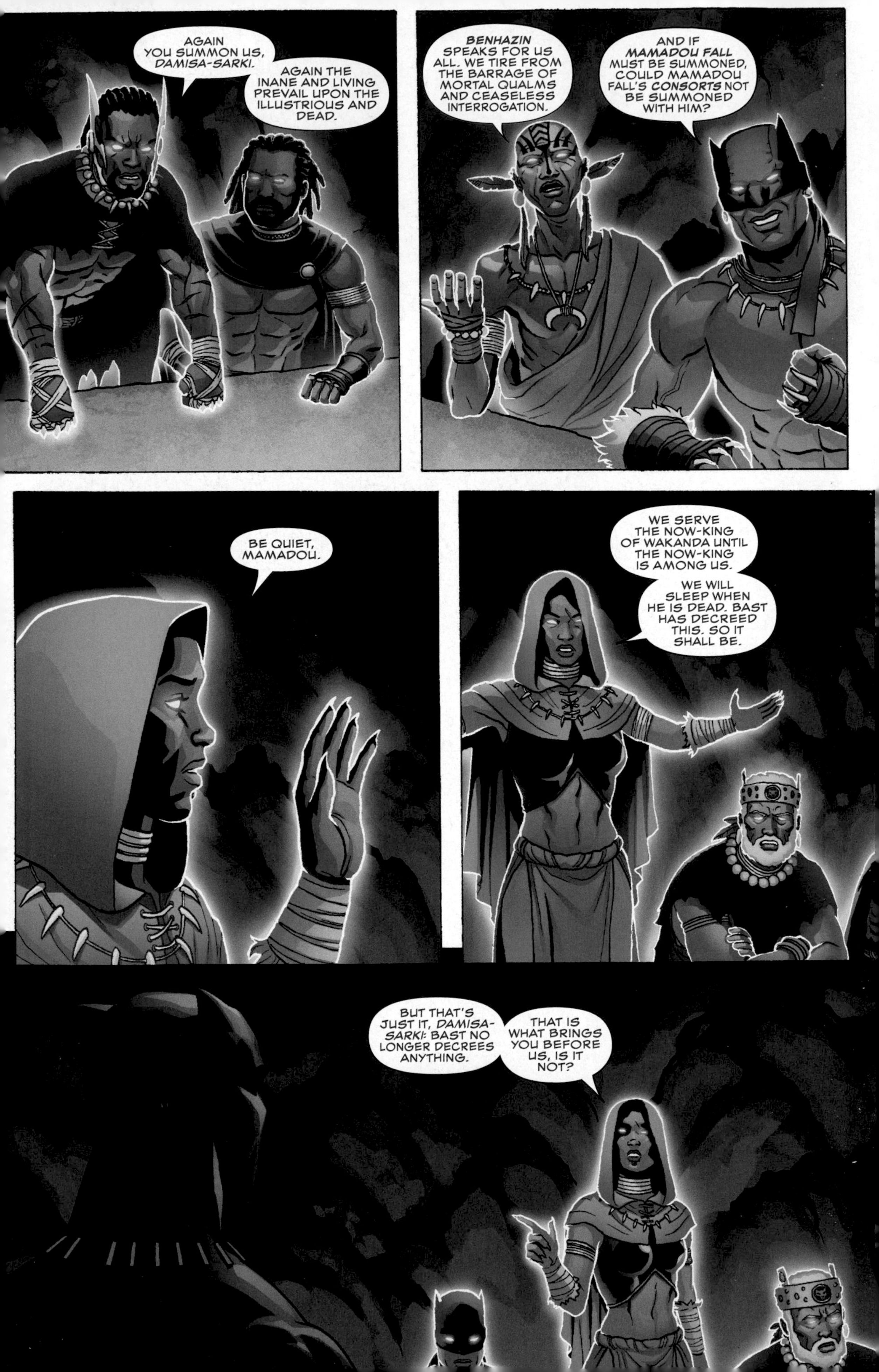
AGAIN YOU SUMMON US, DAMISA-SARKI.
AGAIN THE INANE AND LIVING PREVAIL UPON THE ILLUSTRIOUS AND DEAD.
BENHAZIN SPEAKS FOR US ALL. WE TIRE FROM THE BARRAGE OF MORTAL QUALMS AND CEASELESS INTERROGATION.
AND IF MAMADOU FALL MUST BE SUMMONED, COULD MAMADOU FALL'S CONSORTS NOT BE SUMMONED WITH HIM?
BE QUIET, MAMADOU.
WE SERVE THE NOW-KING OF WAKANDA UNTIL THE NOW-KING IS AMONG US.
WE WILL SLEEP WHEN HE IS DEAD. BAST HAS DECREED THIS. SO IT SHALL BE.
BUT THAT'S JUST IT, DAMISA-SARKI: BAST NO LONGER DECREES ANYTHING.
THAT IS WHAT BRINGS YOU BEFORE US, IS IT NOT?

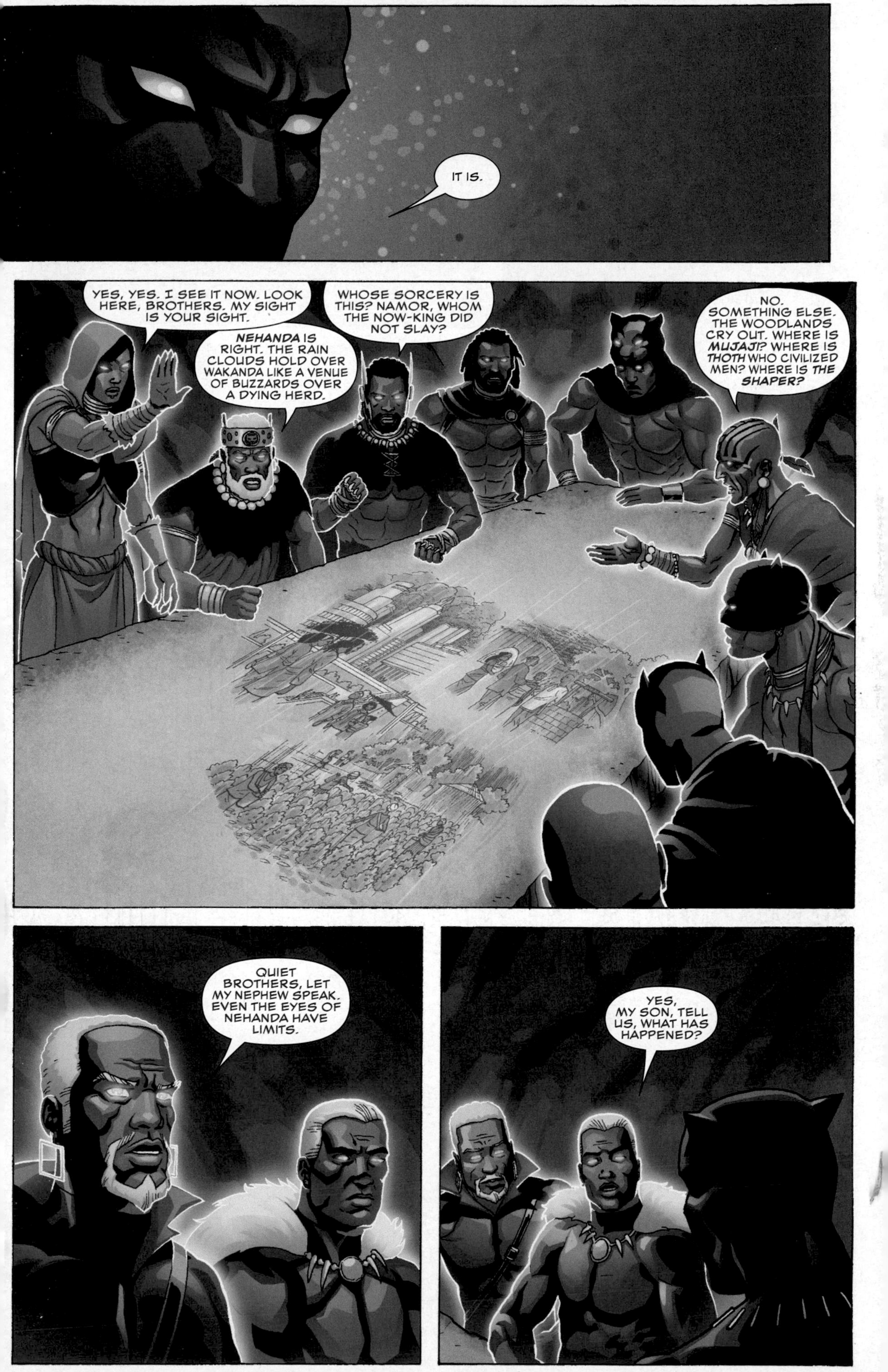

IT IS.
YES, YES. I SEE IT NOW. LOOK HERE, BROTHERS. MY SIGHT IS YOUR SIGHT.
NEHANDA IS RIGHT. THE RAIN CLOUDS HOLD OVER WAKANDA LIKE A VENUE OF BUZZARDS OVER A DYING HERD.
WHOSE SORCERY IS THIS? NAMOR, WHOM THE NOW-KING DID NOT SLAY?
NO. SOMETHING ELSE. THE WOODLANDS CRY OUT. WHERE IS MUJAJI? WHERE IS THOTH WHO CIVILIZED MEN? WHERE IS THE SHAPER?
QUIET BROTHERS, LET MY NEPHEW SPEAK. EVEN THE EYES OF NEHANDA HAVE LIMITS.
YES, MY SON, TELL US, WHAT HAS HAPPENED?

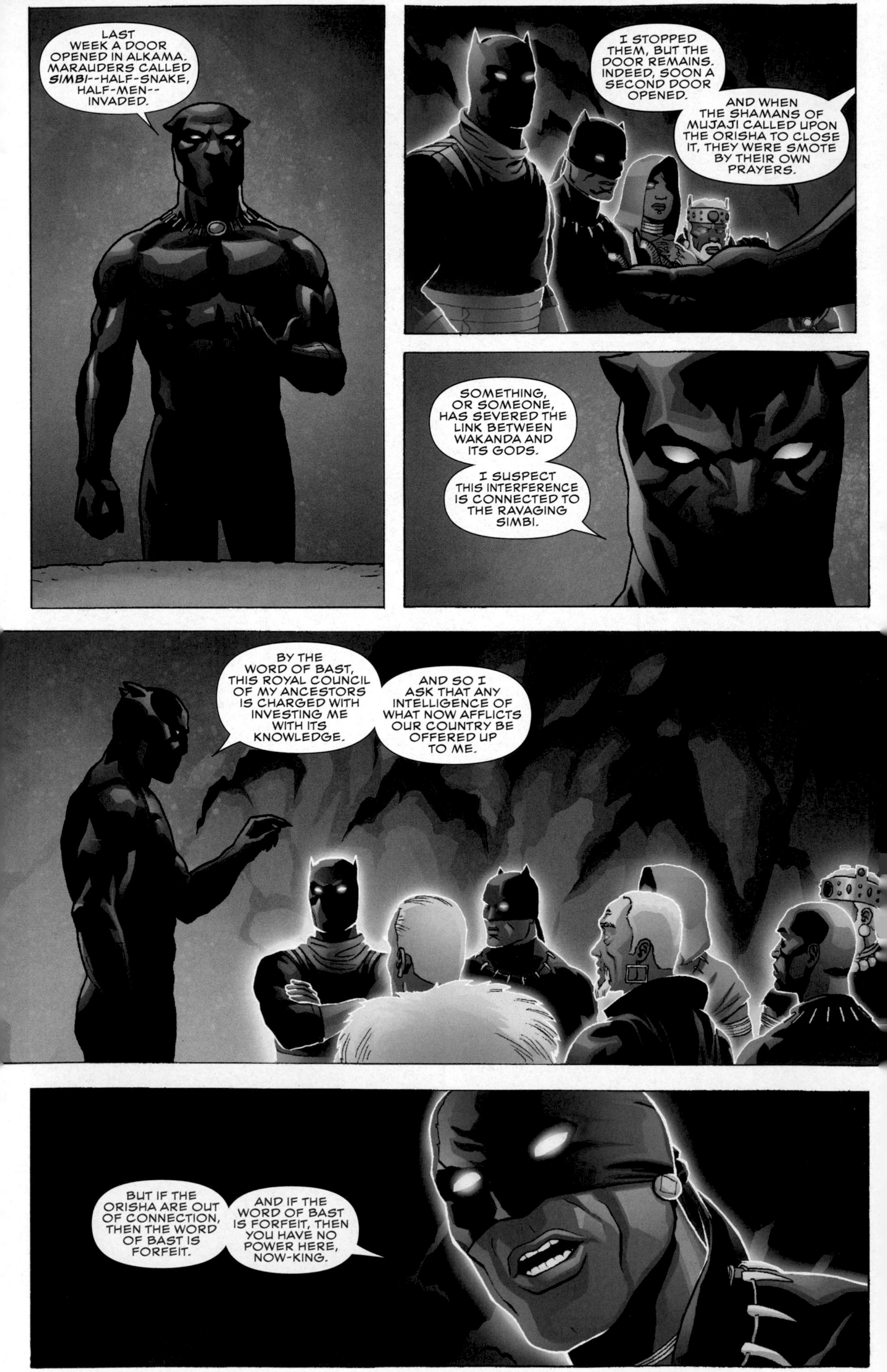
LAST WEEK A DOOR OPENED IN ALKAMA. MARAUDERS CALLED SIMBI--HALF-SNAKE, HALF-MEN--INVADED.
I STOPPED THEM, BUT THE DOOR REMAINS. INDEED, SOON A SECOND DOOR OPENED.
AND WHEN THE SHAMANS OF MUJAJI CALLED UPON THE ORISHA TO CLOSE IT, THEY WERE SMOTE BY THEIR OWN PRAYERS.
SOMETHING, OR SOMEONE, HAS SEVERED THE LINK BETWEEN WAKANDA AND ITS GODS.
I SUSPECT THIS INTERFERENCE IS CONNECTED TO THE RAVAGING SIMBI.
BY THE WORD OF BAST, THIS ROYAL COUNCIL OF MY ANCESTORS IS CHARGED WITH INVESTING ME WITH ITS KNOWLEDGE.
AND SO I ASK THAT ANY INTELLIGENCE OF WHAT NOW AFFLICTS OUR COUNTRY BE OFFERED UP TO ME.
BUT IF THE ORISHA ARE OUT OF CONNECTION, THEN THE WORD OF BAST IS FORFEIT.
AND IF THE WORD OF BAST IS FORFEIT, THEN YOU HAVE NO POWER HERE, NOW-KING.

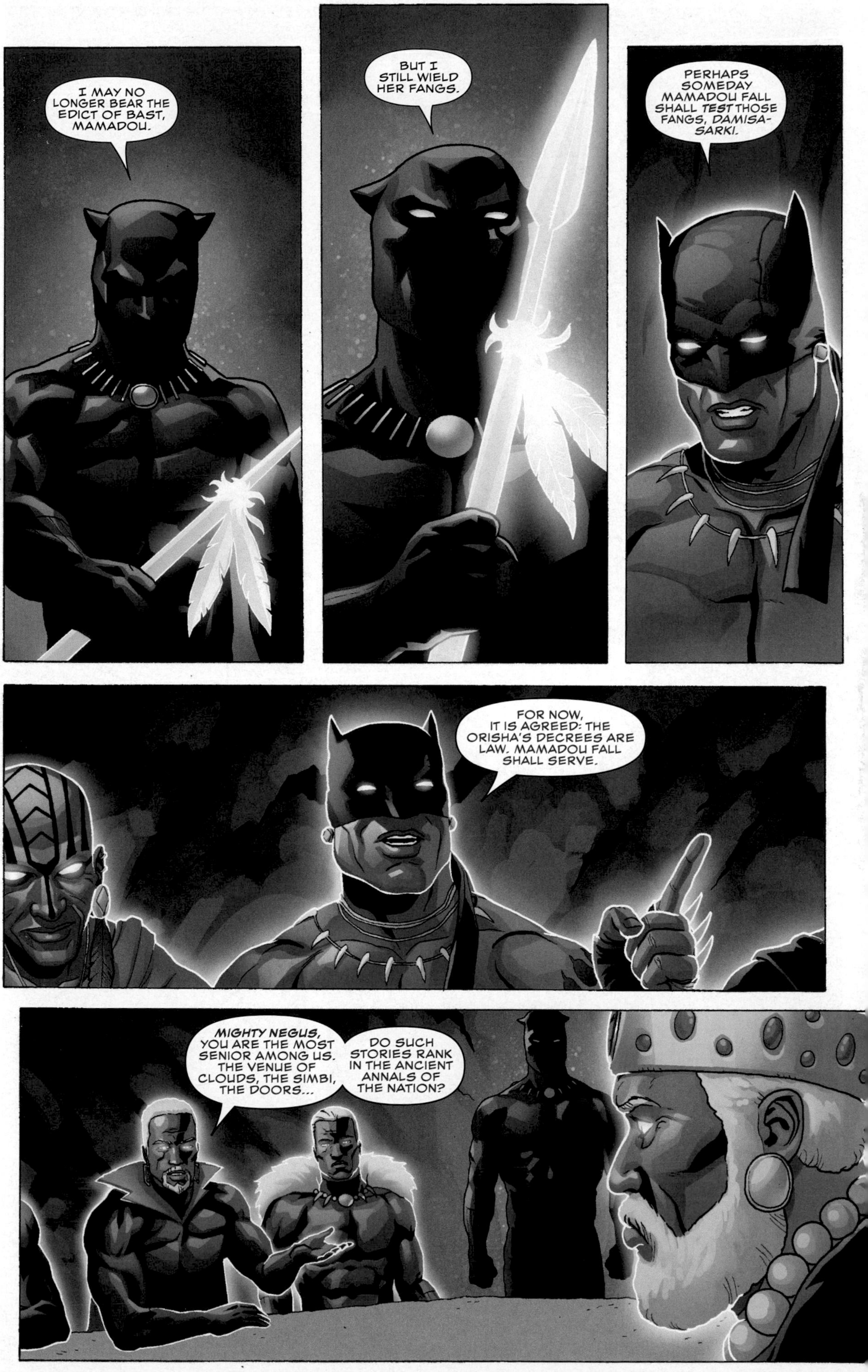
I MAY NO LONGER BEAR THE EDICT OF BAST, MAMADOU.
BUT I STILL WIELD HER FANGS.
PERHAPS SOMEDAY MAMADOU FALL SHALL *TEST* THOSE FANGS, *DAMISA-SARKI.*
FOR NOW, IT IS AGREED: THE ORISHA'S DECREES ARE LAW. MAMADOU FALL SHALL SERVE.
MIGHTY NEGUS, YOU ARE THE MOST SENIOR AMONG US. THE VENUE OF CLOUDS, THE SIMBI, THE DOORS...
DO SUCH STORIES RANK IN THE ANCIENT ANNALS OF THE NATION?

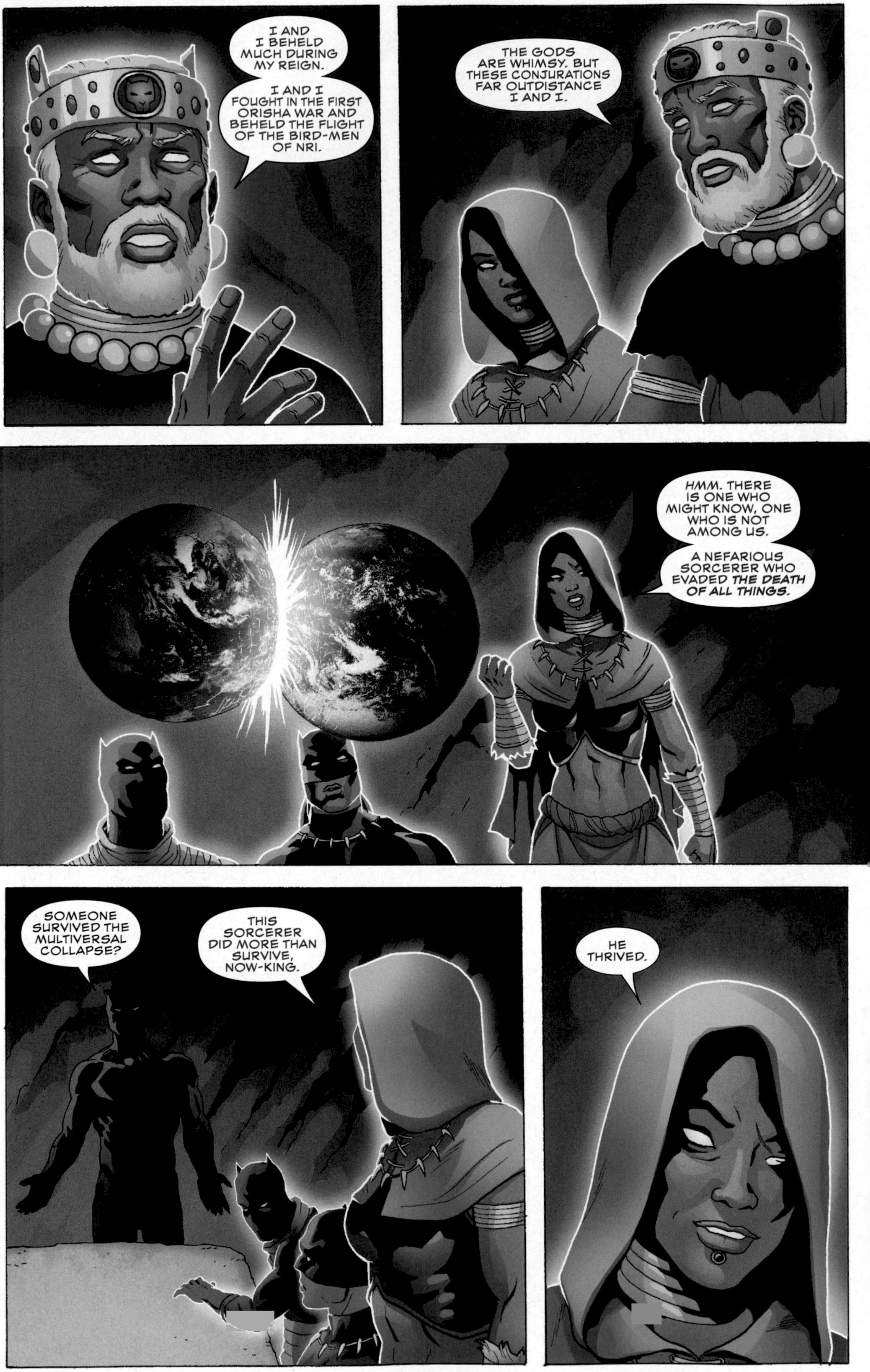
I AND I BEHELD MUCH DURING MY REIGN.
I AND I FOUGHT IN THE FIRST ORISHA WAR AND BEHELD THE FLIGHT OF THE BIRD-MEN OF NRI.
THE GODS ARE WHIMSY. BUT THESE CONJURATIONS FAR OUTDISTANCE I AND I.
HMM. THERE IS ONE WHO MIGHT KNOW, ONE WHO IS NOT AMONG US.
A NEFARIOUS SORCERER WHO EVADED ***THE DEATH OF ALL THINGS.***
SOMEONE SURVIVED THE MULTIVERSAL COLLAPSE?
THIS SORCERER DID MORE THAN SURVIVE, NOW-KING.
HE THRIVED.

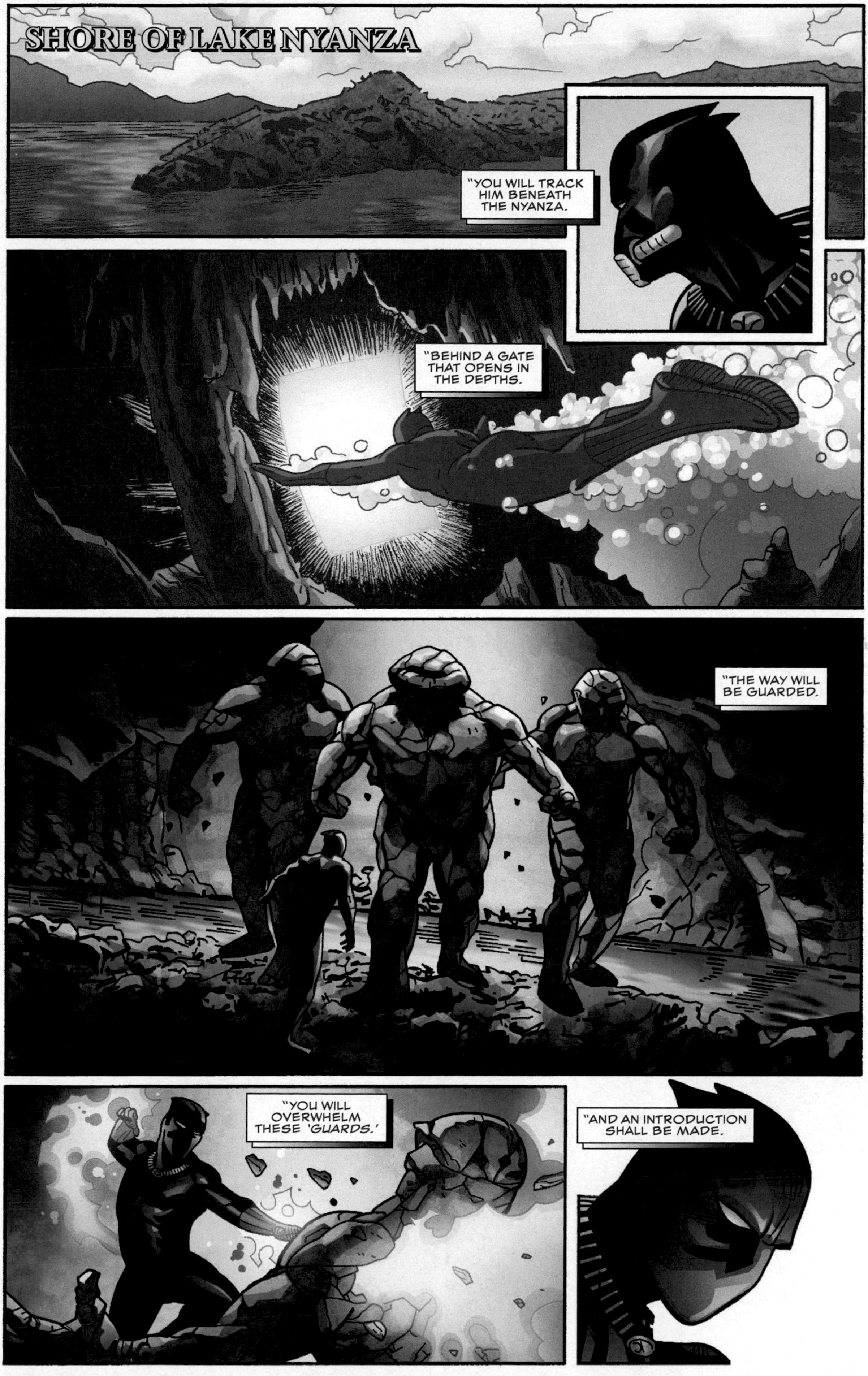
SHORE OF LAKE NYANZA
"YOU WILL TRACK HIM BENEATH THE NYANZA.
"BEHIND A GATE THAT OPENS IN THE DEPTHS.
"THE WAY WILL BE GUARDED.
"YOU WILL OVERWHELM THESE 'GUARDS.'
"AND AN INTRODUCTION SHALL BE MADE.

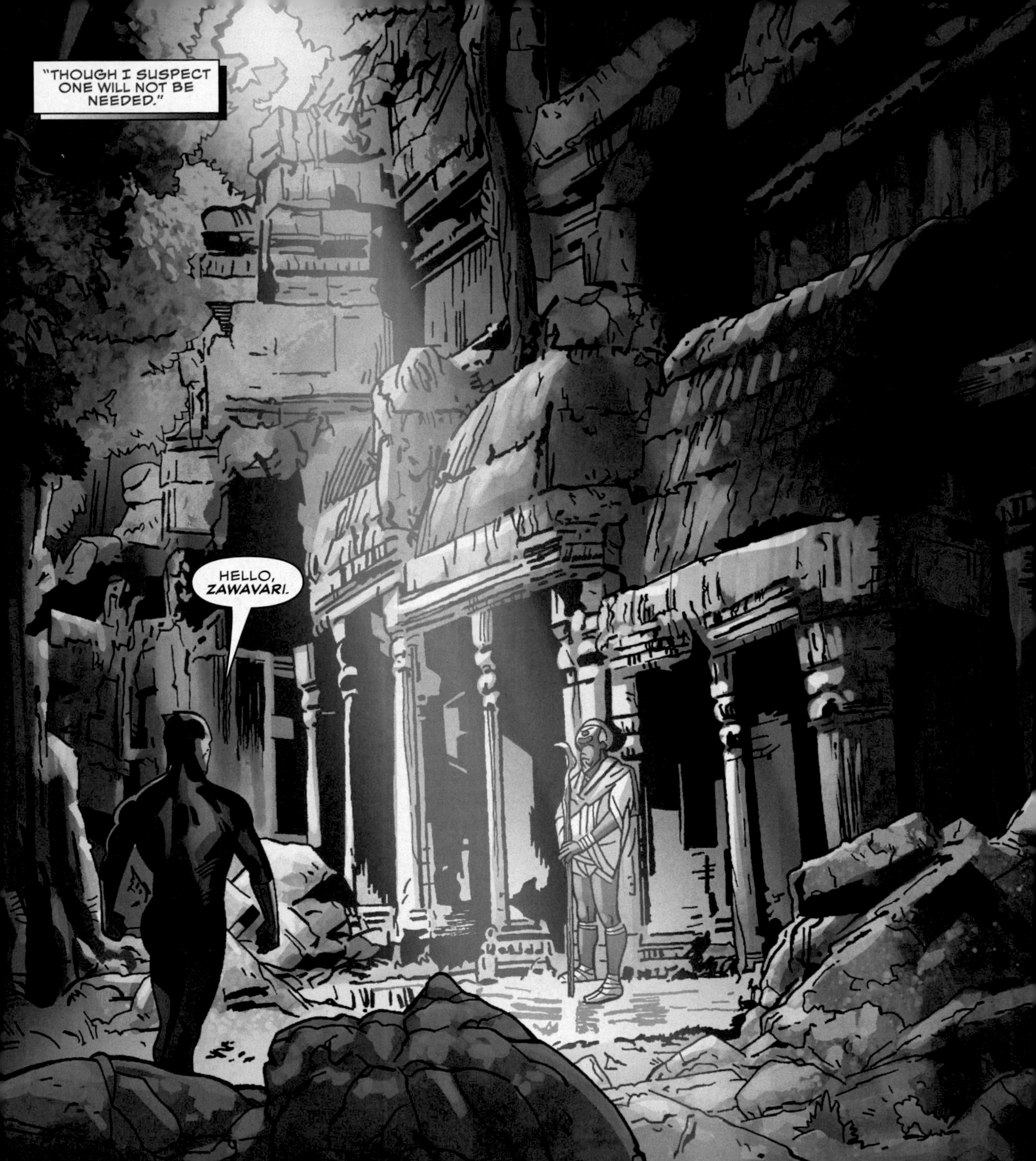
"THOUGH I SUSPECT ONE WILL NOT BE NEEDED."
HELLO, ZAWAVARI.

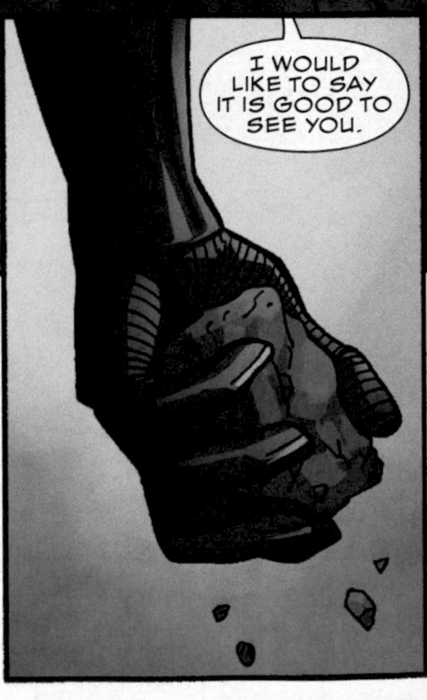
I WOULD LIKE TO SAY IT IS GOOD TO SEE YOU.

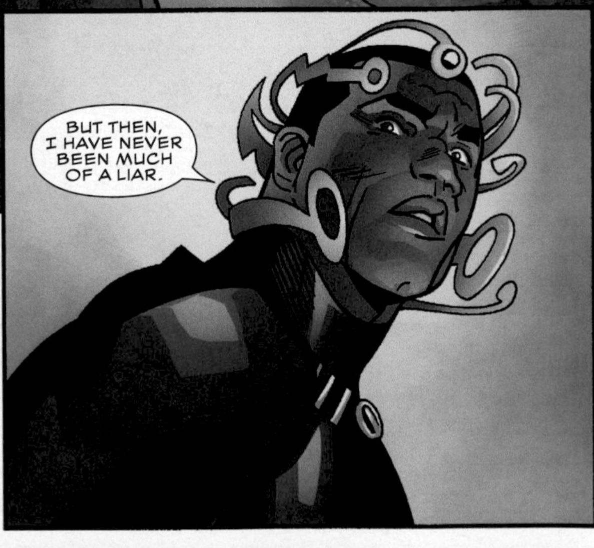
BUT THEN, I HAVE NEVER BEEN MUCH OF A LIAR.

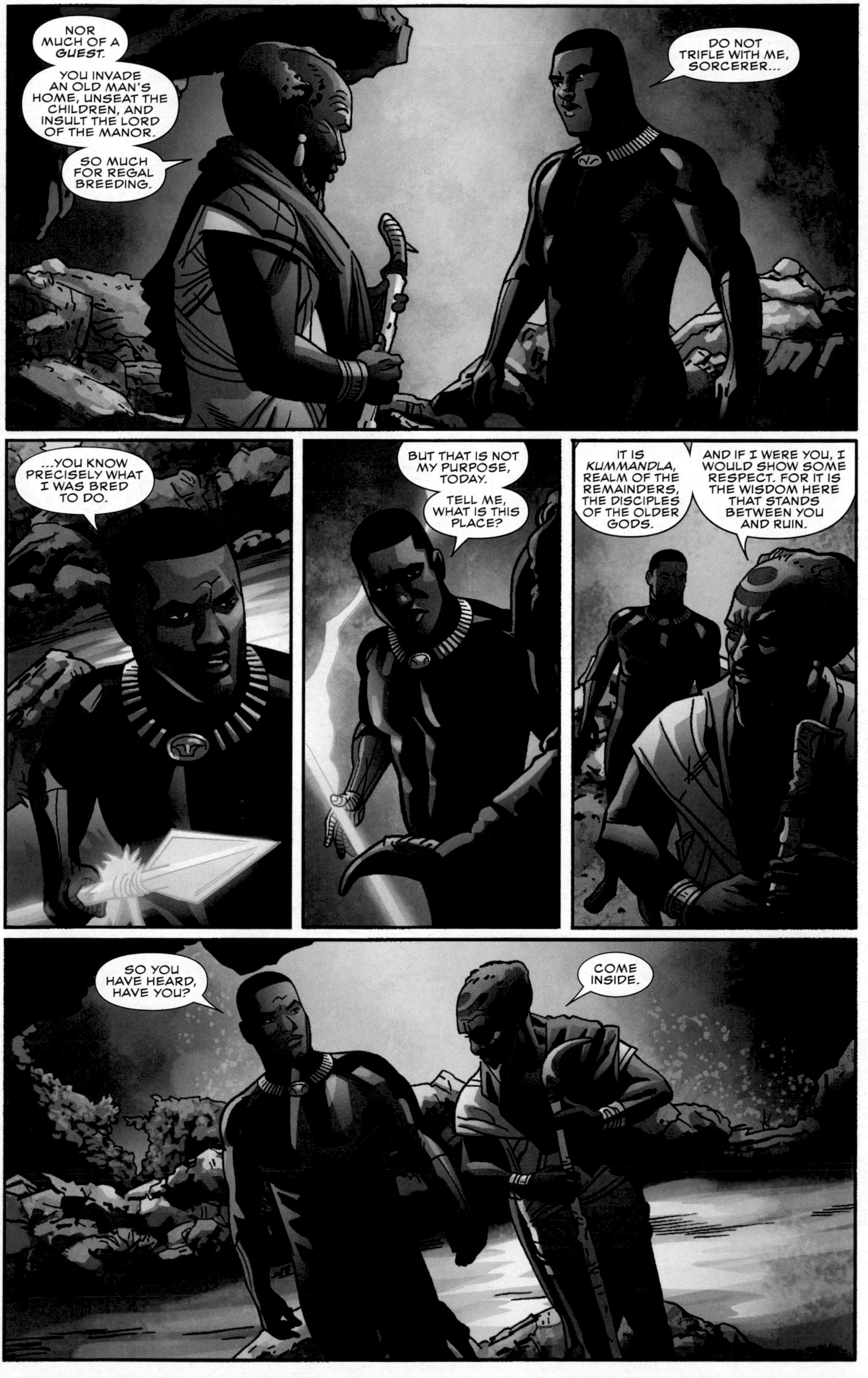
NOR MUCH OF A *GUEST*.
YOU INVADE AN OLD MAN'S HOME, UNSEAT THE CHILDREN, AND INSULT THE LORD OF THE MANOR.
SO MUCH FOR REGAL BREEDING.
DO NOT TRIFLE WITH ME, SORCERER...
...YOU KNOW PRECISELY WHAT I WAS BRED TO DO.
BUT THAT IS NOT MY PURPOSE, TODAY.
TELL ME, WHAT IS THIS PLACE?
IT IS *KUMMANDLA*, REALM OF THE REMAINDERS, THE DISCIPLES OF THE OLDER GODS.
AND IF I WERE YOU, I WOULD SHOW SOME RESPECT. FOR IT IS THE WISDOM HERE THAT STANDS BETWEEN YOU AND RUIN.
SO YOU HAVE HEARD, HAVE YOU?
COME INSIDE.

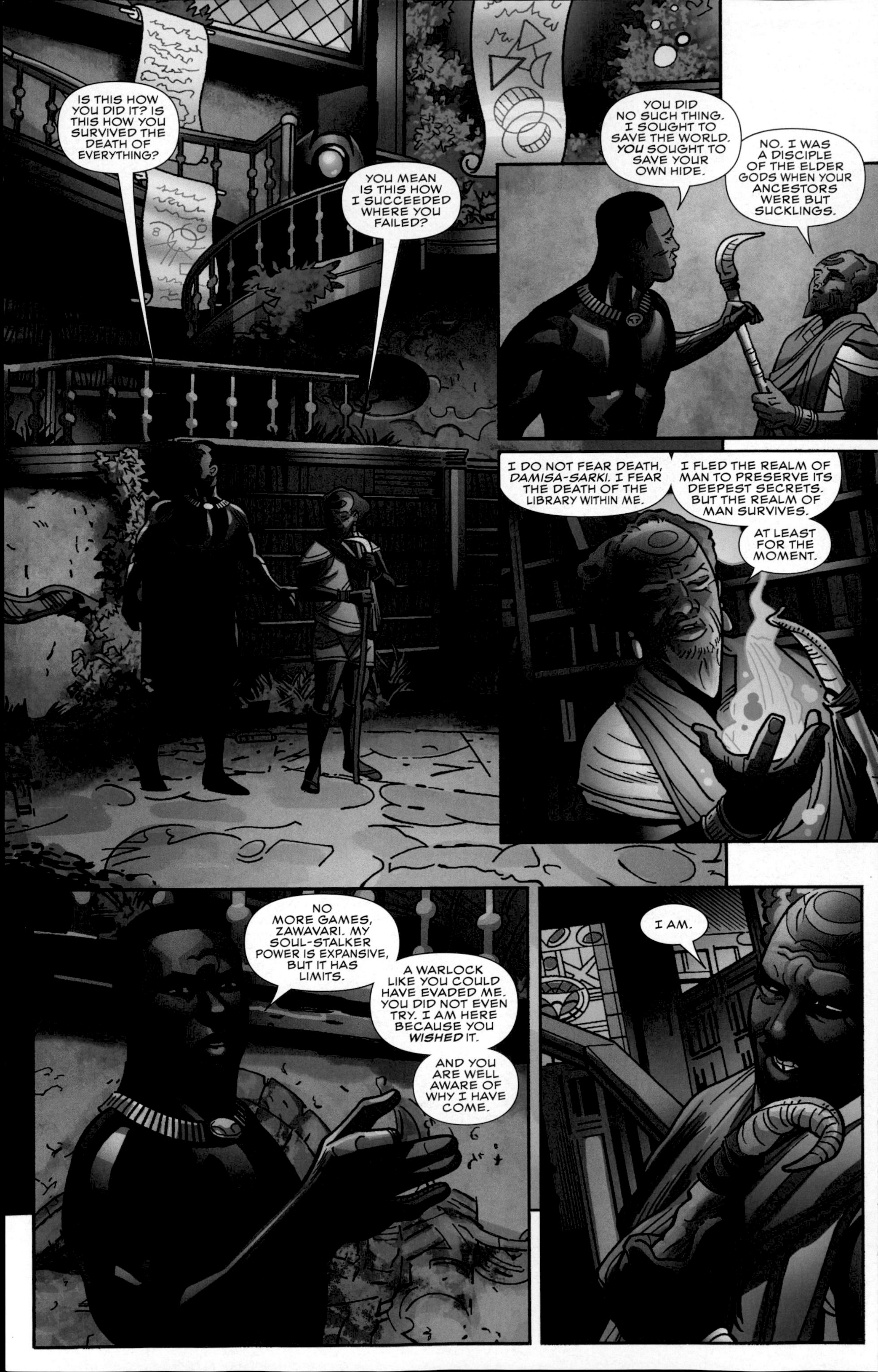
IS THIS HOW YOU DID IT? IS THIS HOW YOU SURVIVED THE DEATH OF EVERYTHING?
YOU MEAN IS THIS HOW I SUCCEEDED WHERE YOU FAILED?
YOU DID NO SUCH THING. I SOUGHT TO SAVE THE WORLD. *YOU* SOUGHT TO SAVE YOUR OWN HIDE.
NO. I WAS A DISCIPLE OF THE ELDER GODS WHEN YOUR ANCESTORS WERE BUT SUCKLINGS.
I DO NOT FEAR DEATH, *DAMISA-SARKI*. I FEAR THE DEATH OF THE LIBRARY WITHIN ME.
I FLED THE REALM OF MAN TO PRESERVE ITS DEEPEST SECRETS. BUT THE REALM OF MAN SURVIVES.
AT LEAST FOR THE MOMENT.
NO MORE GAMES, ZAWAVARI. MY SOUL-STALKER POWER IS EXPANSIVE, BUT IT HAS LIMITS.
A WARLOCK LIKE YOU COULD HAVE EVADED ME. YOU DID NOT EVEN TRY. I AM HERE BECAUSE YOU *WISHED* IT.
AND YOU ARE WELL AWARE OF WHY I HAVE COME.
I AM.

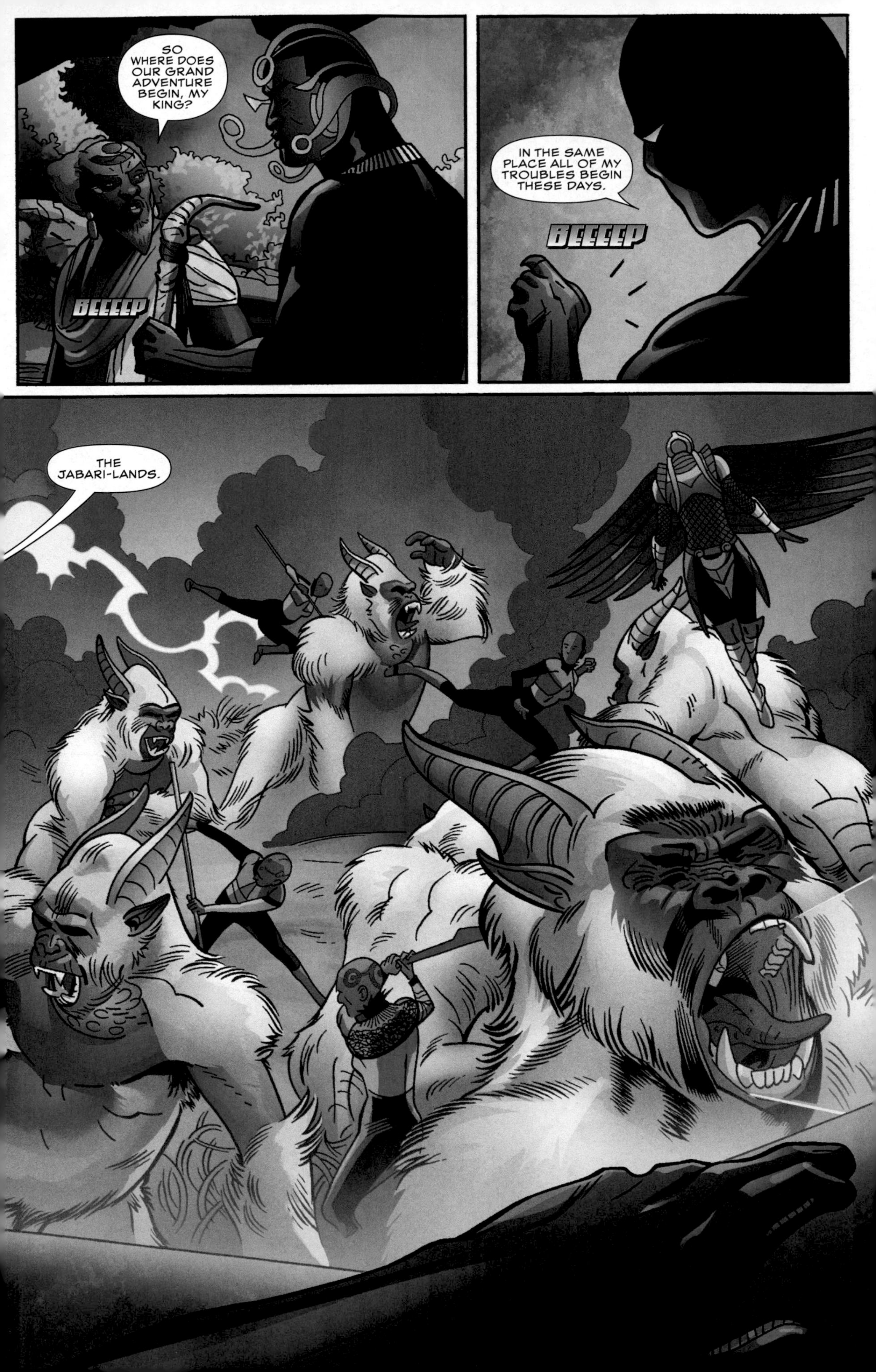
SO WHERE DOES OUR GRAND ADVENTURE BEGIN, MY KING?
BEEEEP
IN THE SAME PLACE ALL OF MY TROUBLES BEGIN THESE DAYS.
BEEEEP
THE JABARI-LANDS.

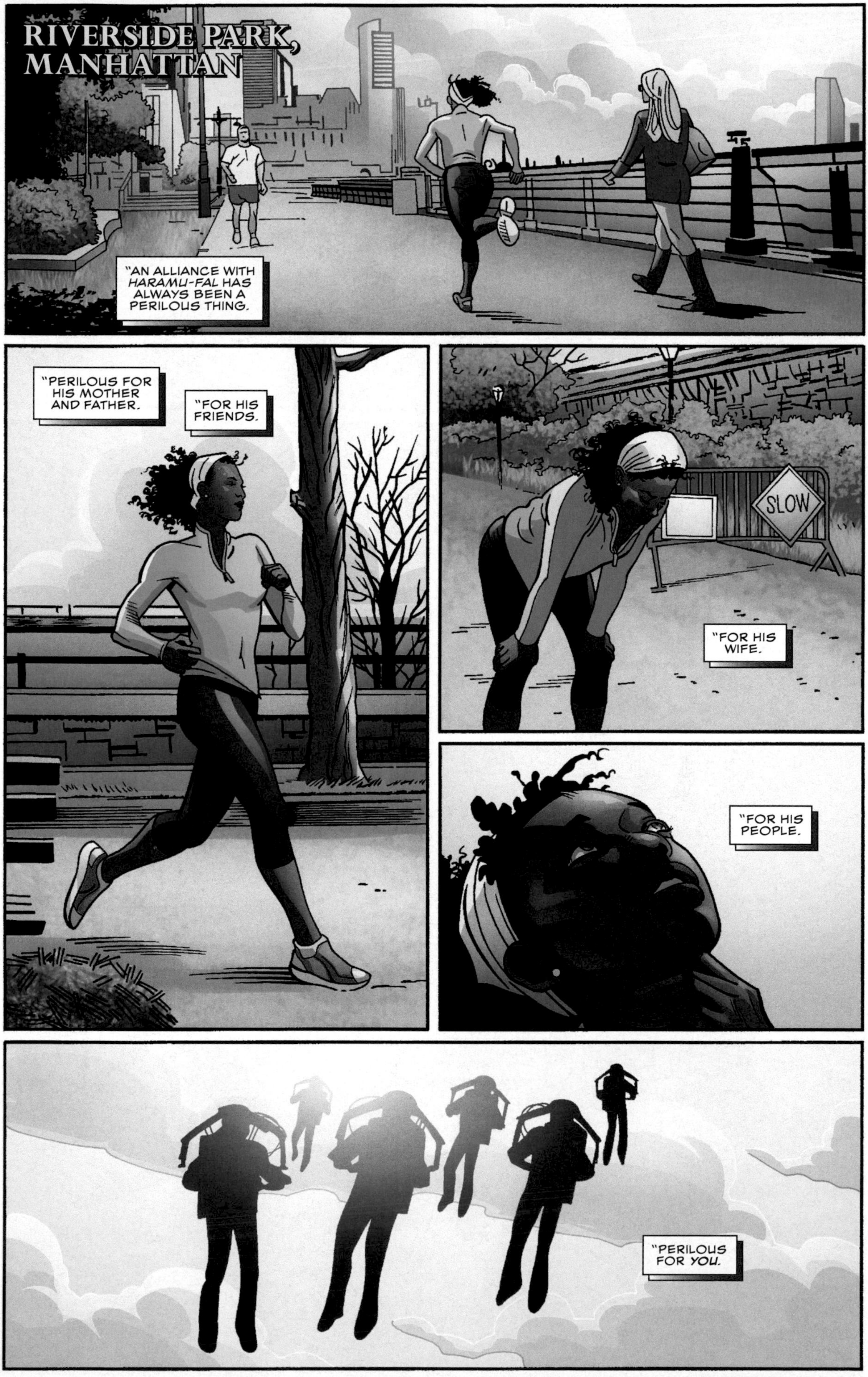
RIVERSIDE PARK, MANHATTAN
"AN ALLIANCE WITH HARAMU-FAL HAS ALWAYS BEEN A PERILOUS THING.
"PERILOUS FOR HIS MOTHER AND FATHER.
"FOR HIS FRIENDS.
SLOW
"FOR HIS WIFE.
"FOR HIS PEOPLE.
"PERILOUS FOR YOU.

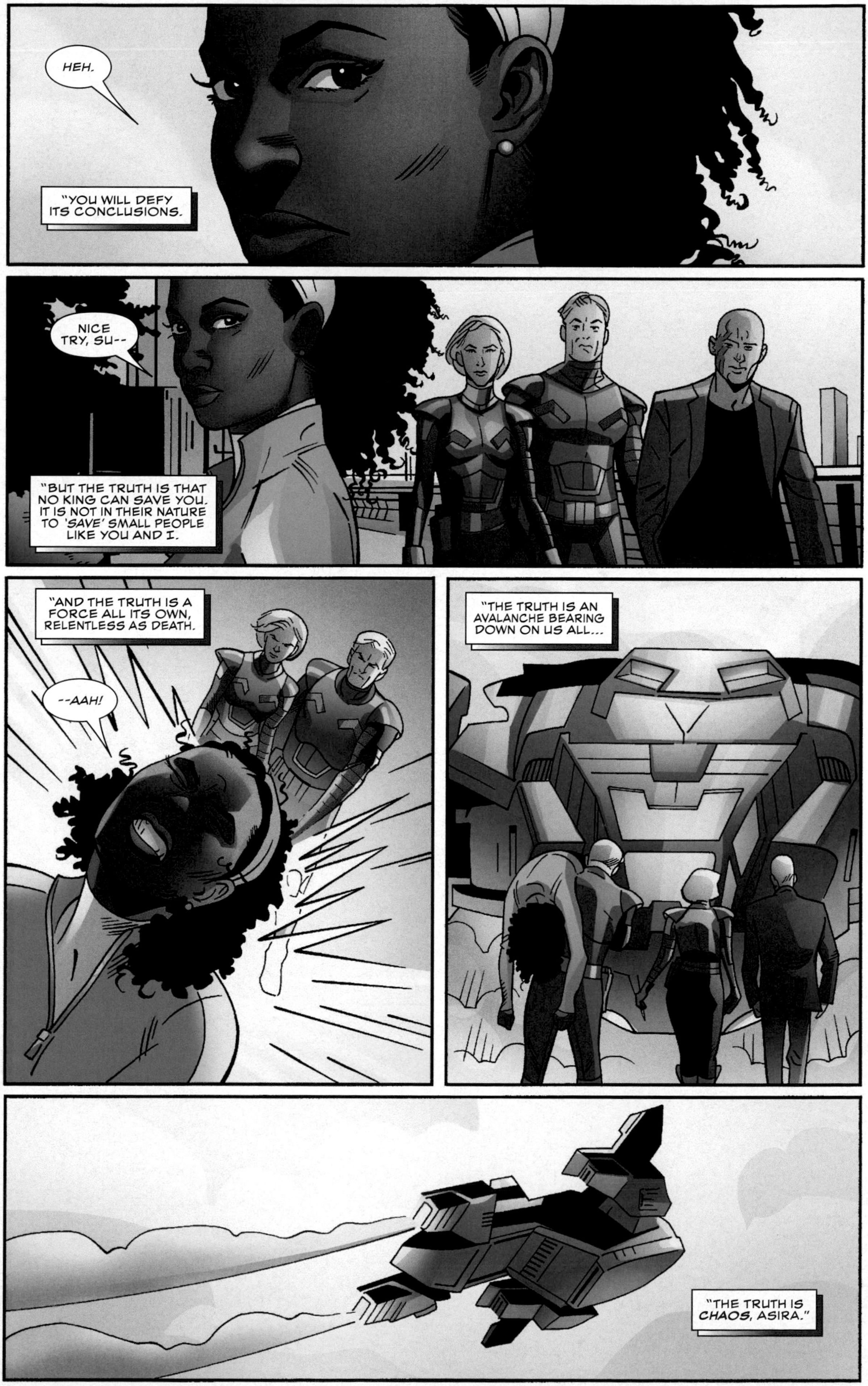
HEH.
"YOU WILL DEFY ITS CONCLUSIONS.
NICE TRY, SU--
"BUT THE TRUTH IS THAT NO KING CAN SAVE YOU. IT IS NOT IN THEIR NATURE TO 'SAVE' SMALL PEOPLE LIKE YOU AND I.
"AND THE TRUTH IS A FORCE ALL ITS OWN, RELENTLESS AS DEATH.
--AAH!
"THE TRUTH IS AN AVALANCHE BEARING DOWN ON US ALL...
"THE TRUTH IS CHAOS, ASIRA."

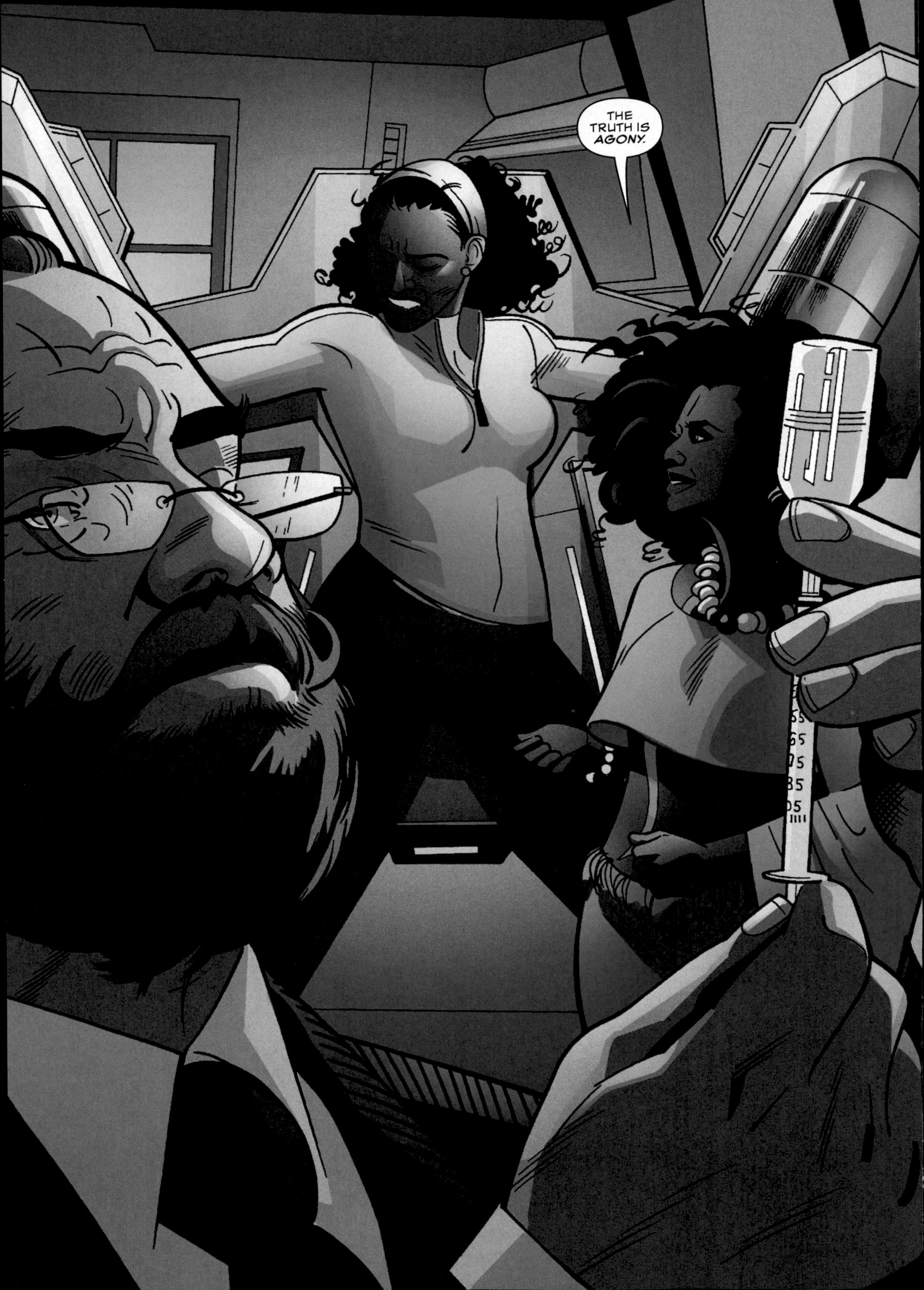
THE TRUTH IS AGONY.

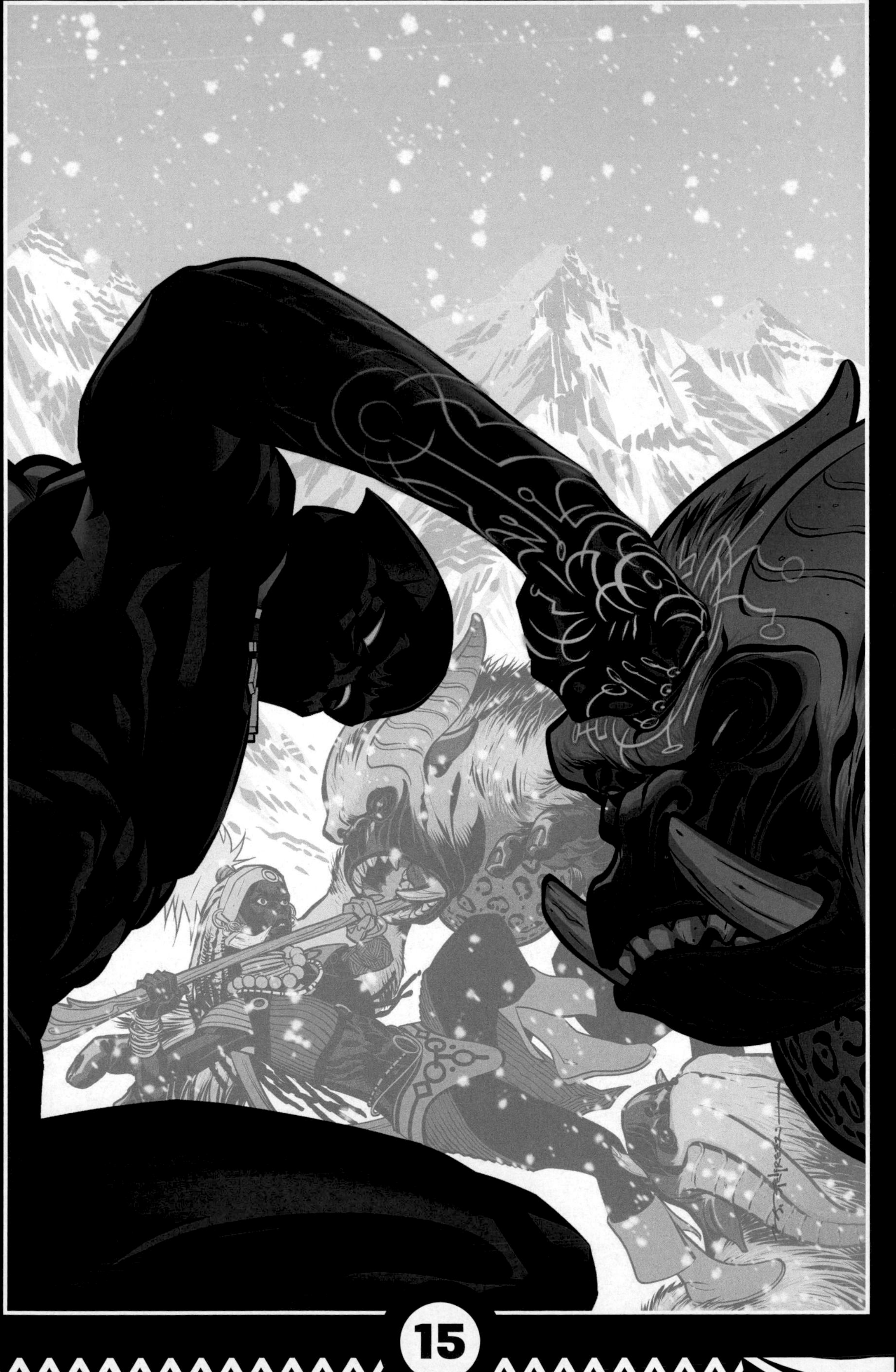

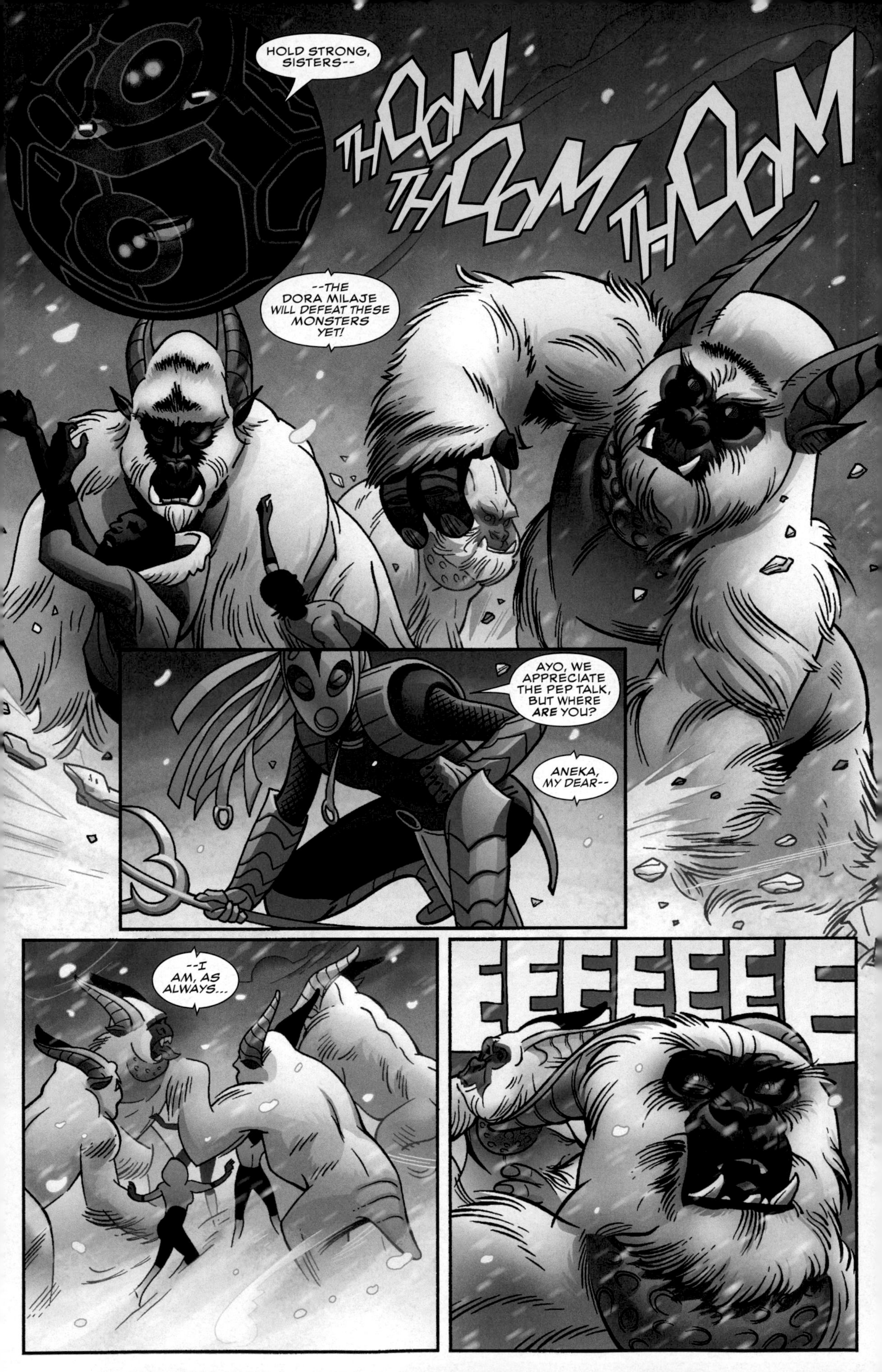
HOLD STRONG, SISTERS--
THOOM THOOM THOOM
--THE DORA MILAJE WILL DEFEAT THESE MONSTERS YET!
AYO, WE APPRECIATE THE PEP TALK, BUT WHERE ARE YOU?
ANEKA, MY DEAR--
--I AM, AS ALWAYS...
EEEEEE

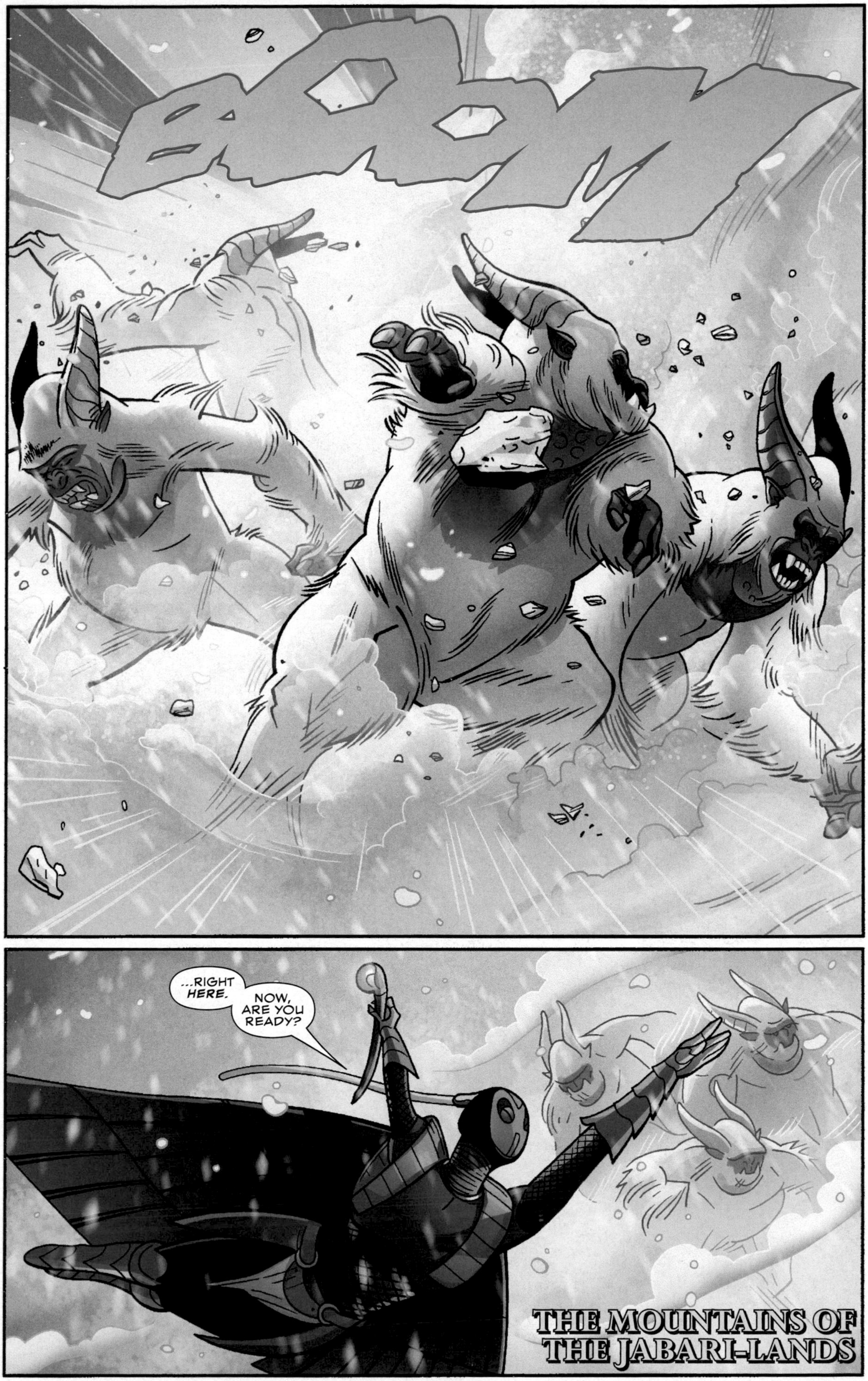
BOOM
...RIGHT HERE.
NOW, ARE YOU READY?
THE MOUNTAINS OF THE JABARI-LANDS

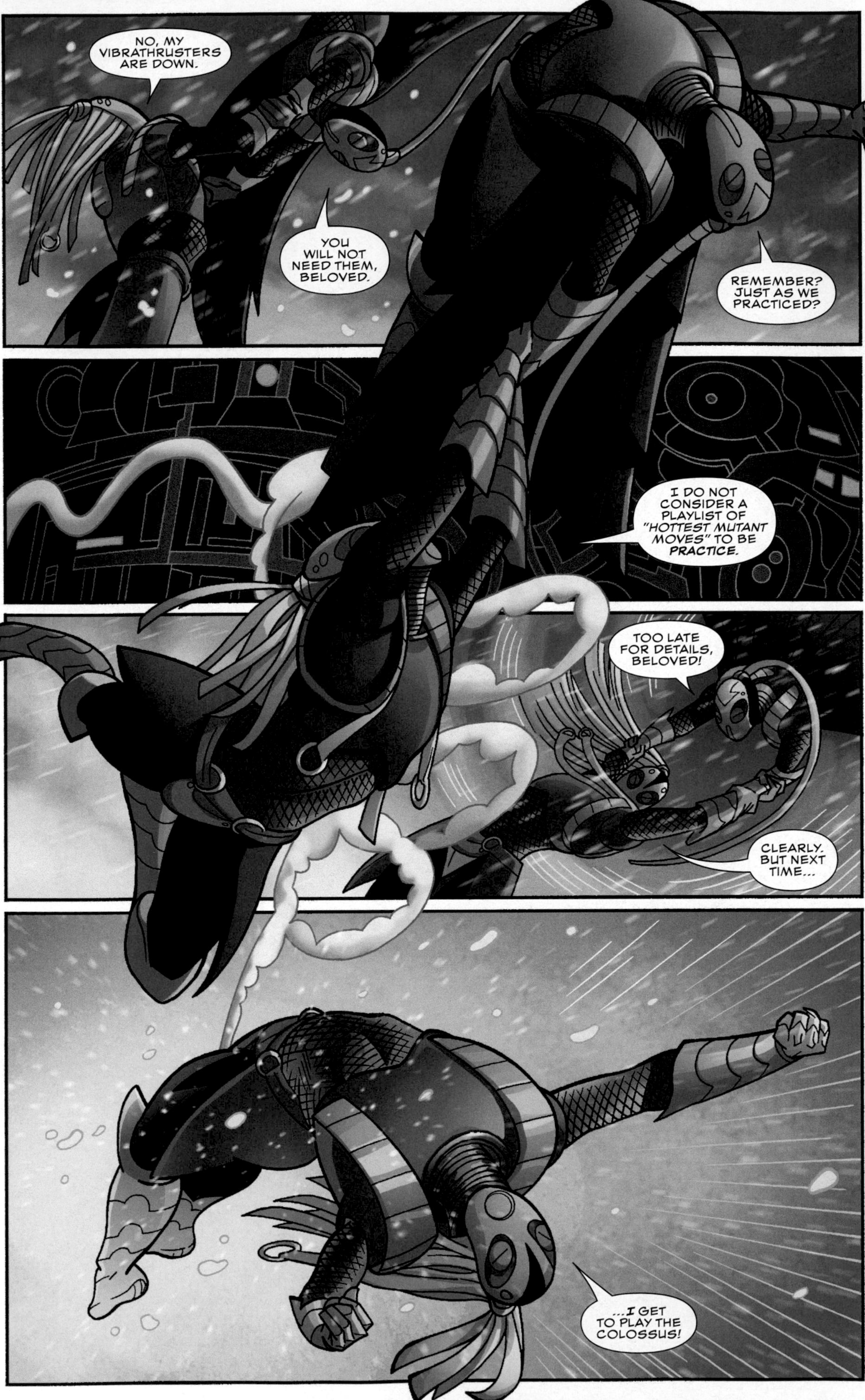
NO, MY VIBRATHRUSTERS ARE DOWN.
YOU WILL NOT NEED THEM, BELOVED.
REMEMBER? JUST AS WE PRACTICED?
I DO NOT CONSIDER A PLAYLIST OF "HOTTEST MUTANT MOVES" TO BE PRACTICE.
TOO LATE FOR DETAILS, BELOVED!
CLEARLY. BUT NEXT TIME...
...I GET TO PLAY THE COLOSSUS!

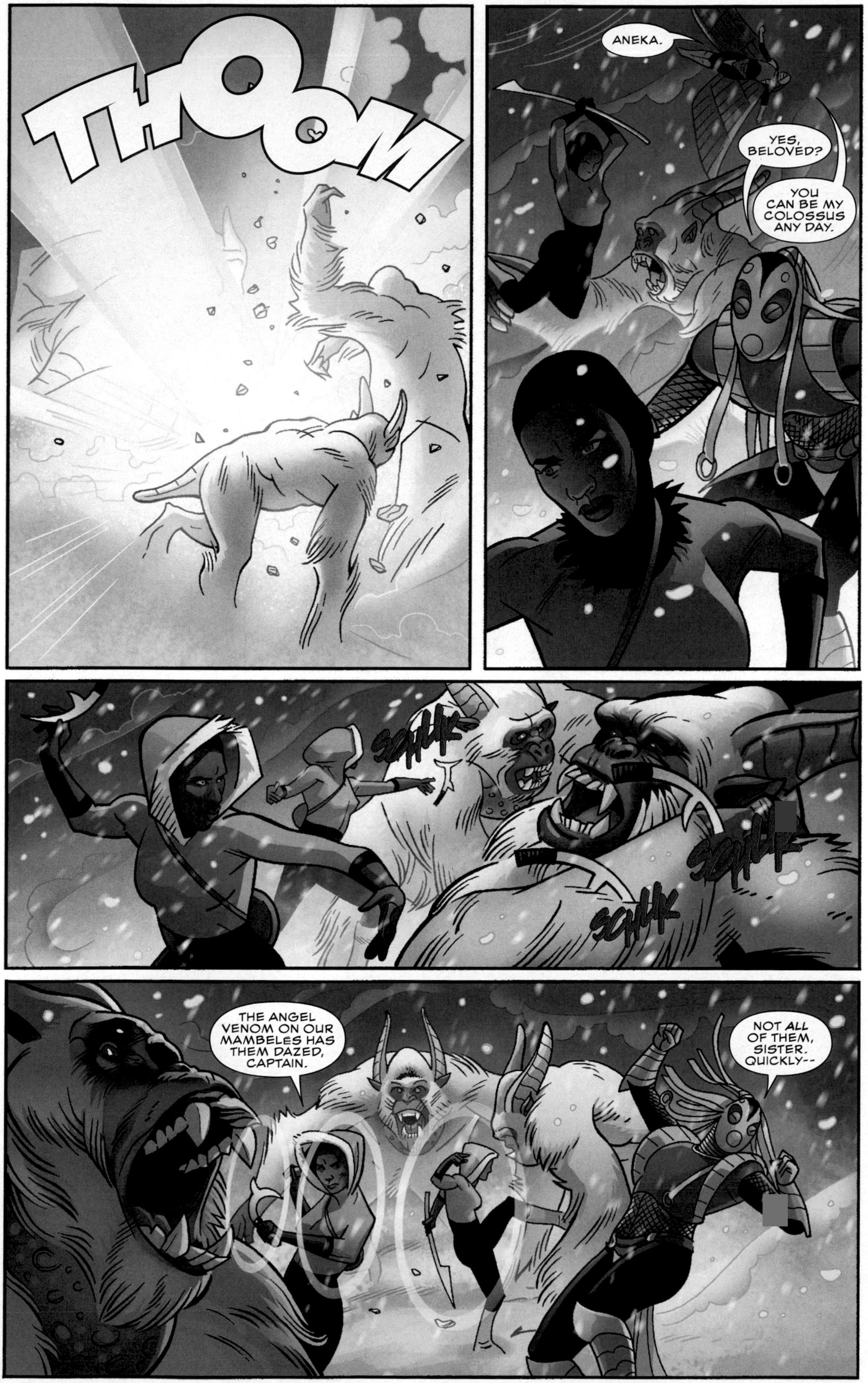
THOOM
ANEKA.
YES, BELOVED?
YOU CAN BE MY COLOSSUS ANY DAY.
SCHLUK
SCHLUK
SCHLUK
THE ANGEL VENOM ON OUR MAMBELES HAS THEM DAZED, CAPTAIN.
NOT *ALL* OF THEM, SISTER. QUICKLY--

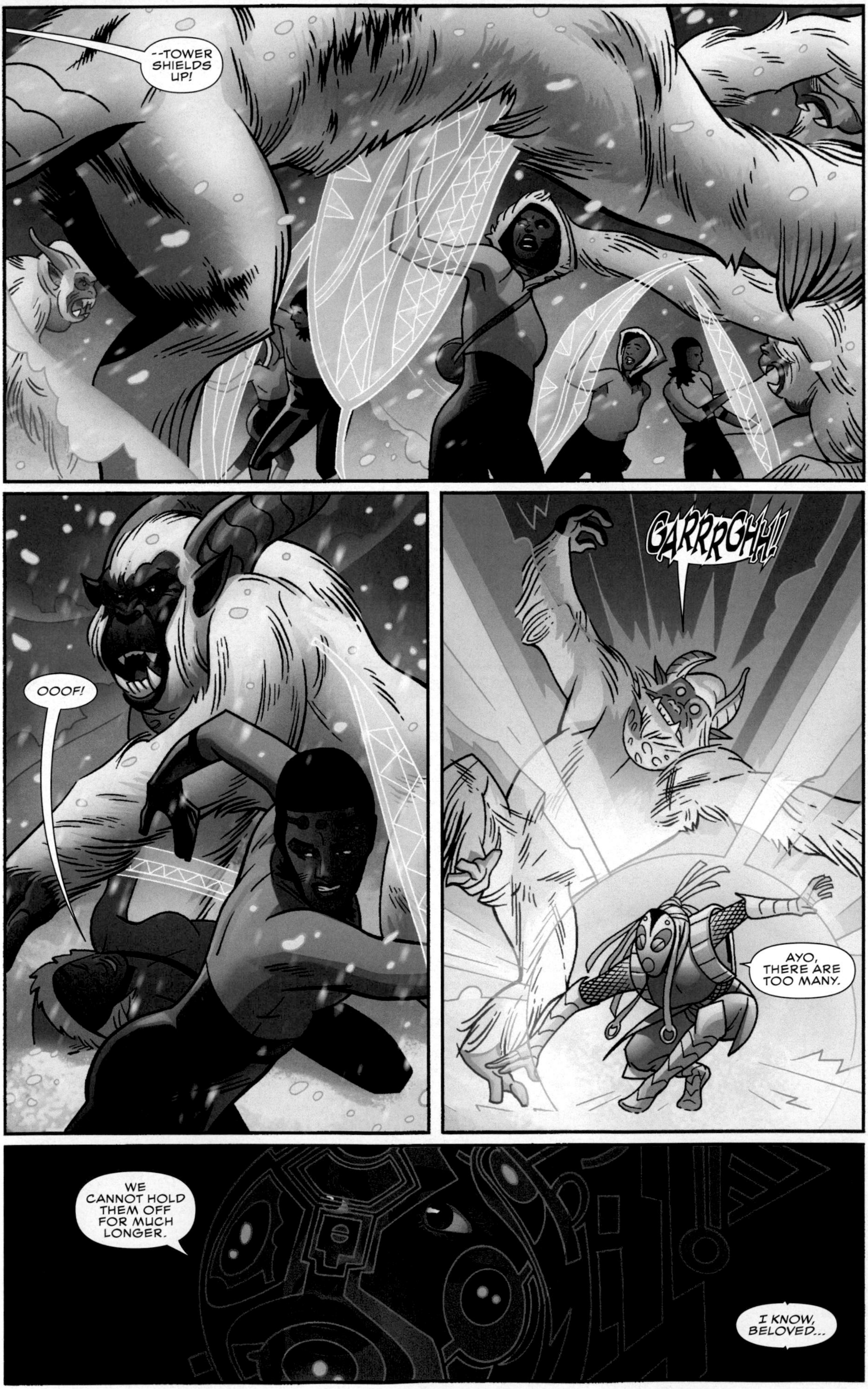
--TOWER SHIELDS UP!
OOOF!
GARRRGHH!
AYO, THERE ARE TOO MANY.
WE CANNOT HOLD THEM OFF FOR MUCH LONGER.
I KNOW, BELOVED...

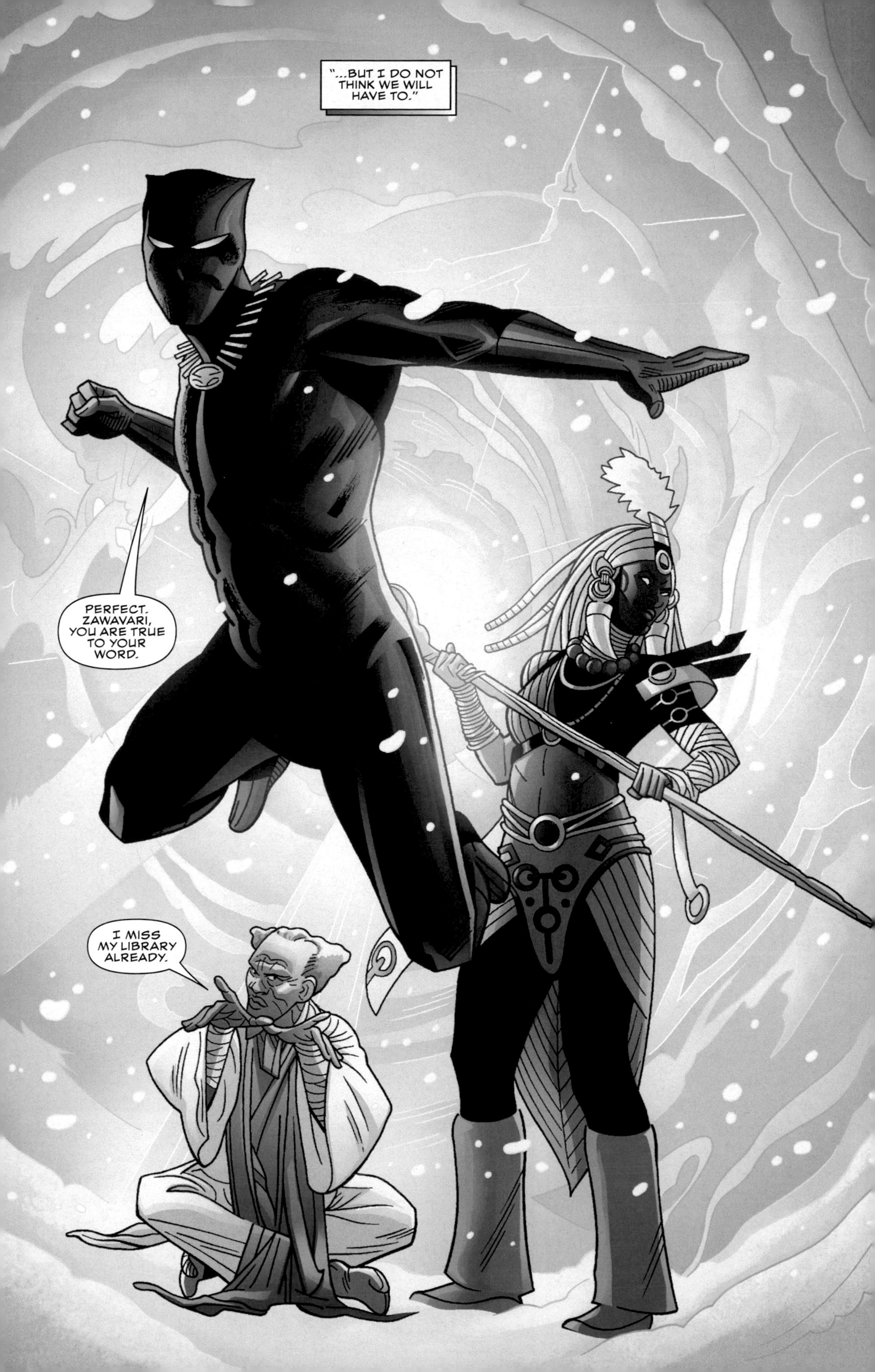
"...BUT I DO NOT THINK WE WILL HAVE TO."
PERFECT. ZAWAVARI, YOU ARE TRUE TO YOUR WORD.
I MISS MY LIBRARY ALREADY.

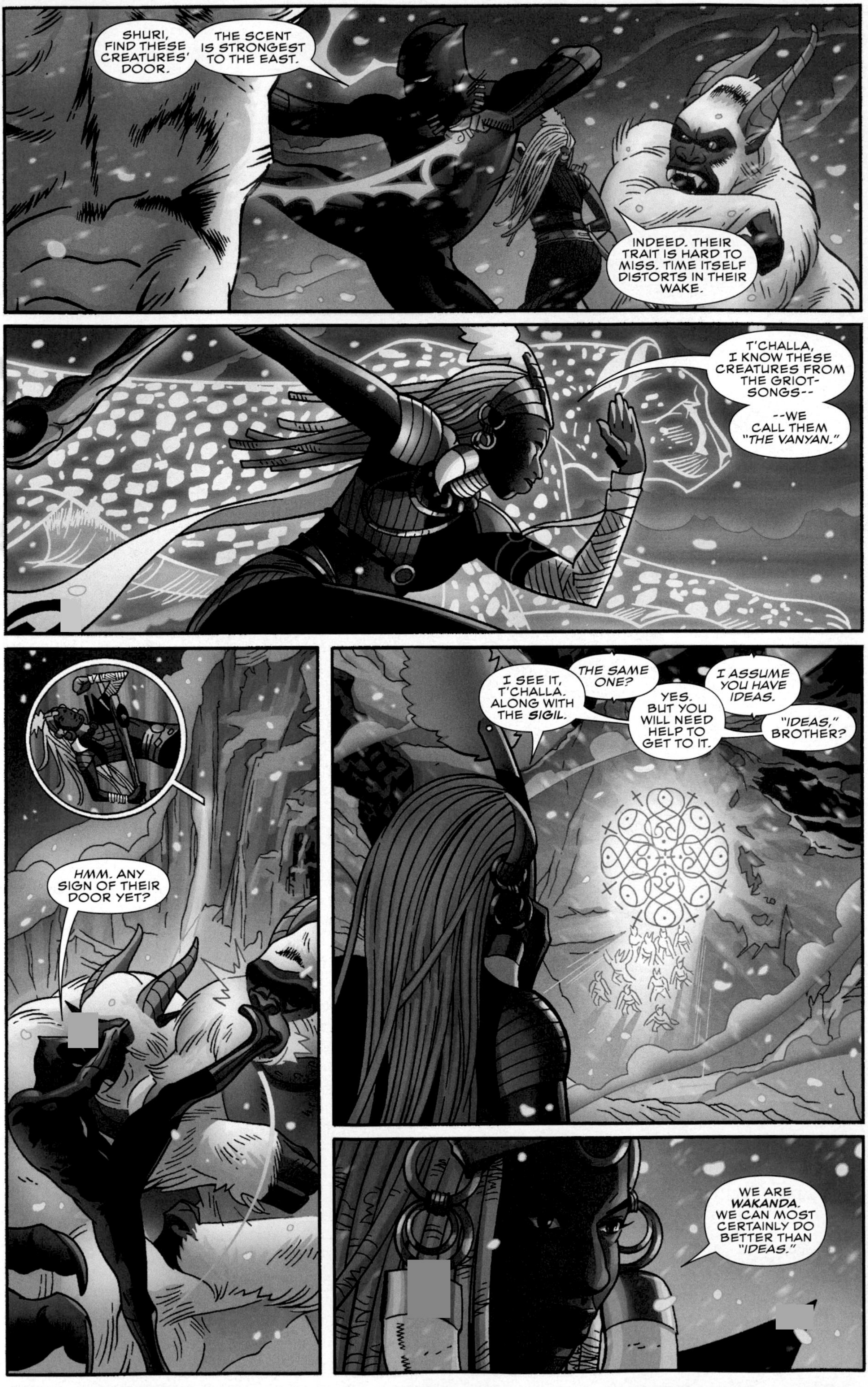
SHURI, FIND THESE CREATURES' DOOR.
THE SCENT IS STRONGEST TO THE EAST.
INDEED. THEIR TRAIT IS HARD TO MISS. TIME ITSELF DISTORTS IN THEIR WAKE.
T'CHALLA, I KNOW THESE CREATURES FROM THE GRIOT-SONGS--
--WE CALL THEM *"THE VANYAN."*
HMM. ANY SIGN OF THEIR DOOR YET?
I SEE IT, T'CHALLA. ALONG WITH THE **SIGIL.**
THE SAME ONE?
YES. BUT YOU WILL NEED HELP TO GET TO IT.
I ASSUME YOU HAVE IDEAS.
"IDEAS," BROTHER?
WE ARE **WAKANDA.** WE CAN MOST CERTAINLY DO BETTER THAN *"IDEAS."*

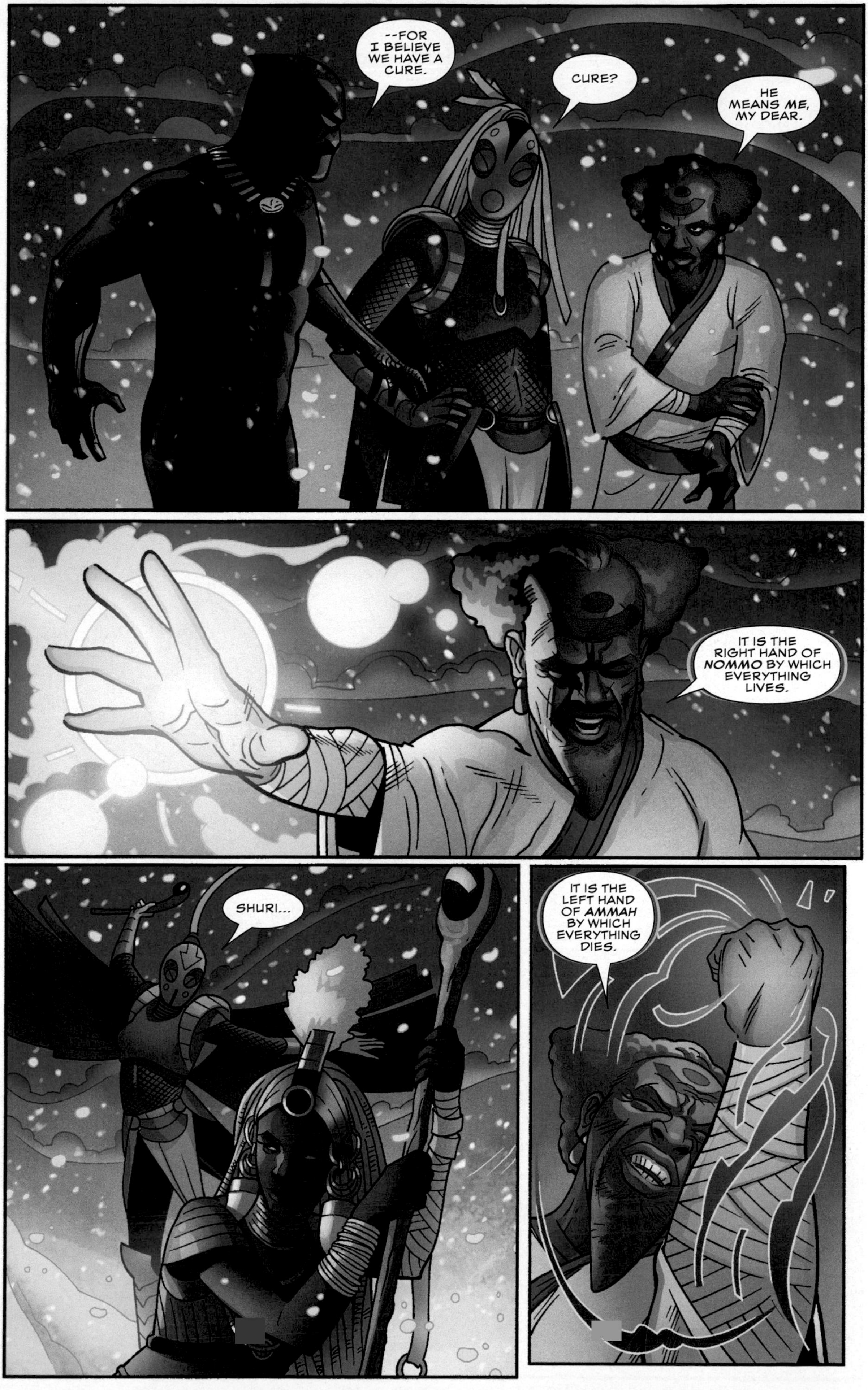
--FOR I BELIEVE WE HAVE A CURE.
CURE?
HE MEANS *ME*, MY DEAR.
IT IS THE RIGHT HAND OF *NOMMO* BY WHICH EVERYTHING LIVES.
SHURI...
IT IS THE LEFT HAND OF *AMMAH* BY WHICH EVERYTHING DIES.

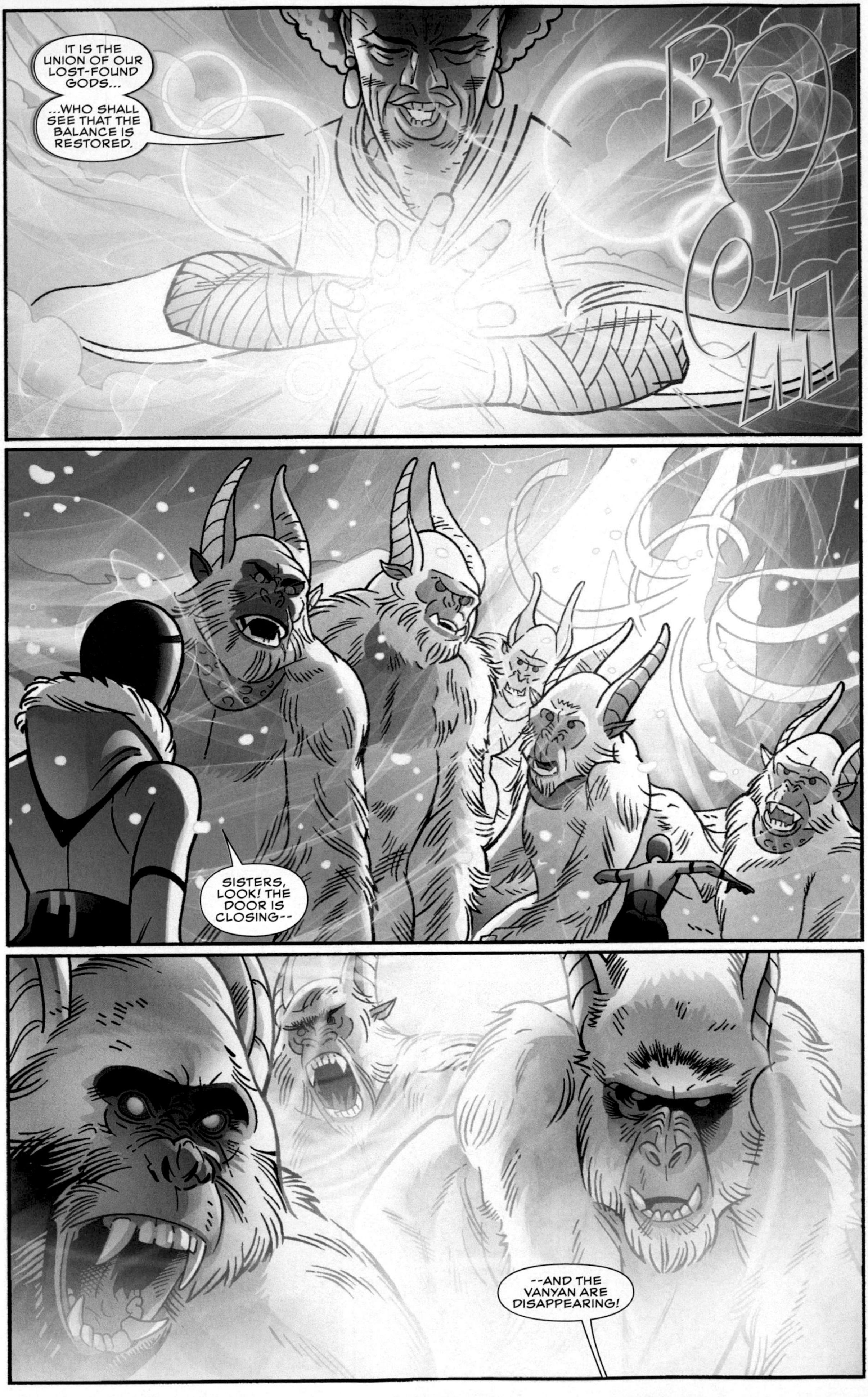
IT IS THE UNION OF OUR LOST-FOUND GODS...
...WHO SHALL SEE THAT THE BALANCE IS RESTORED.
BOOM
SISTERS, LOOK! THE DOOR IS CLOSING--
--AND THE VANYAN ARE DISAPPEARING!

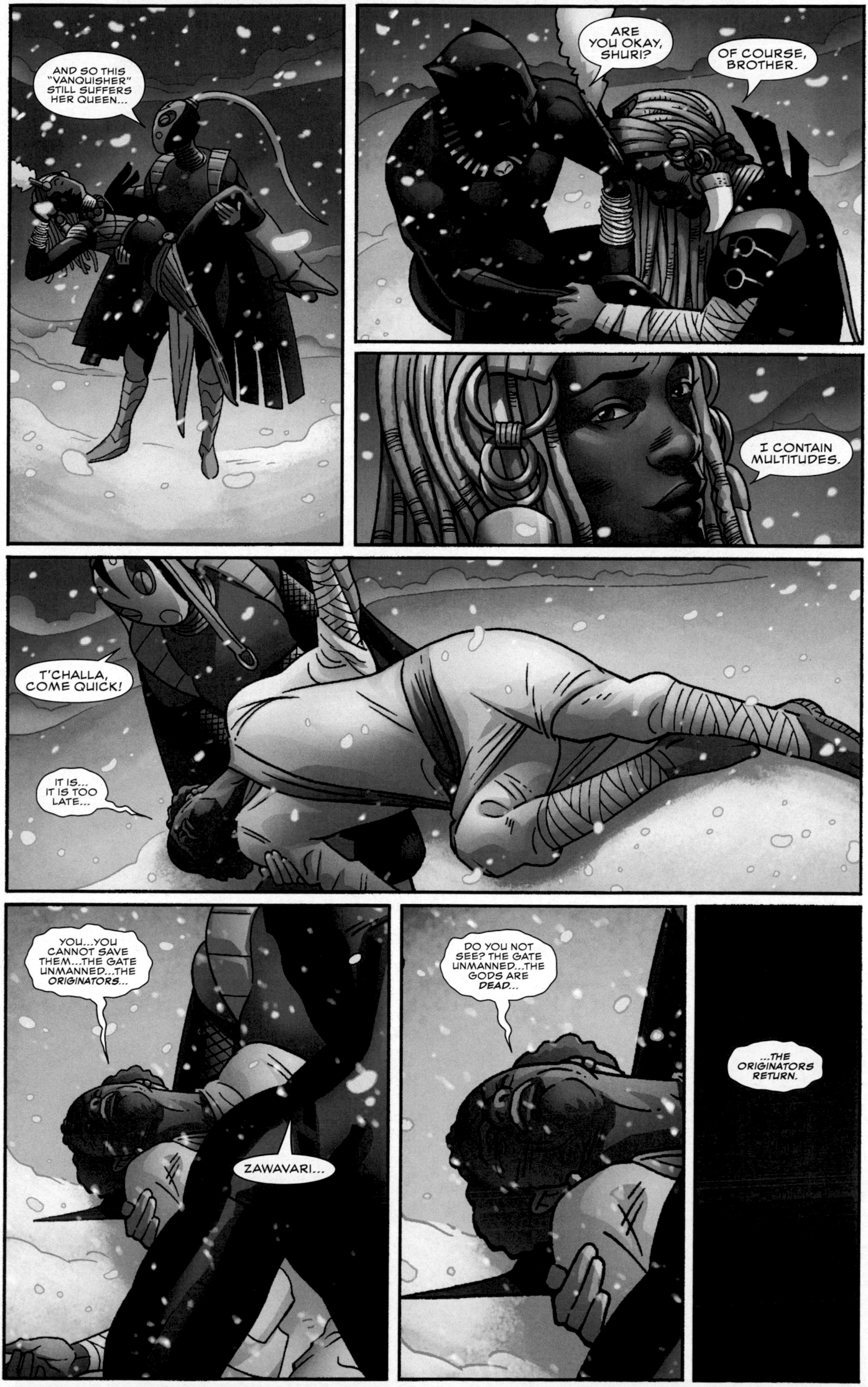
AND SO THIS "VANQUISHER" STILL SUFFERS HER QUEEN...
ARE YOU OKAY, SHURI?
OF COURSE, BROTHER.
I CONTAIN MULTITUDES.
T'CHALLA, COME QUICK!
IT IS... IT IS TOO LATE...
YOU...YOU CANNOT SAVE THEM...THE GATE UNMANNED...THE ORIGINATORS...
ZAWAVARI...
DO YOU NOT SEE? THE GATE UNMANNED...THE GODS ARE DEAD...
...THE ORIGINATORS RETURN.

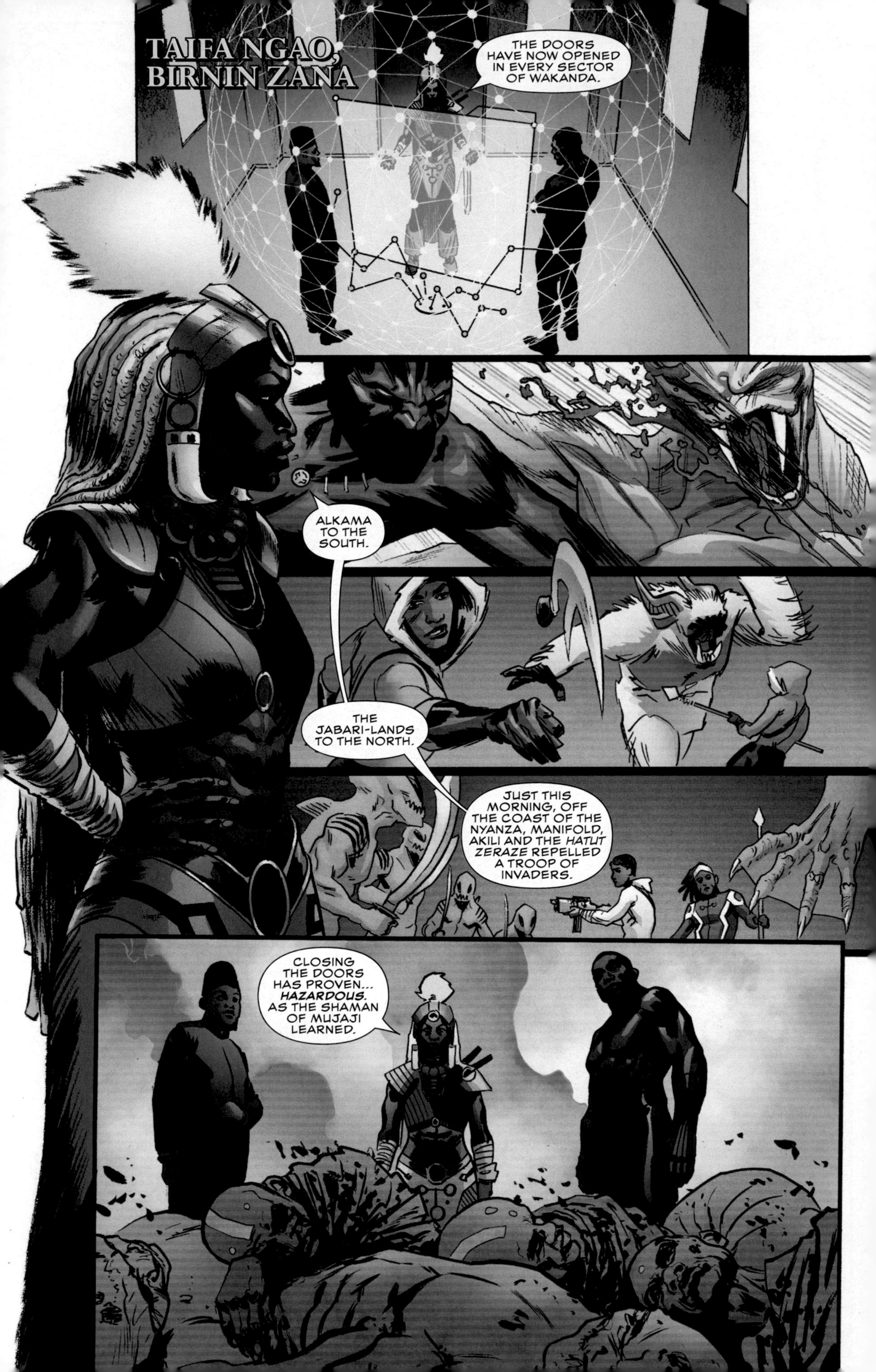
TAIFA NGAO, BIRNIN ZANA
THE DOORS HAVE NOW OPENED IN EVERY SECTOR OF WAKANDA.
ALKAMA TO THE SOUTH.
THE JABARI-LANDS TO THE NORTH.
JUST THIS MORNING, OFF THE COAST OF THE NYANZA, MANIFOLD, AKILI AND THE *HATUT ZERAZE* REPELLED A TROOP OF INVADERS.
CLOSING THE DOORS HAS PROVEN... ***HAZARDOUS.*** AS THE SHAMAN OF MUJAJI LEARNED.

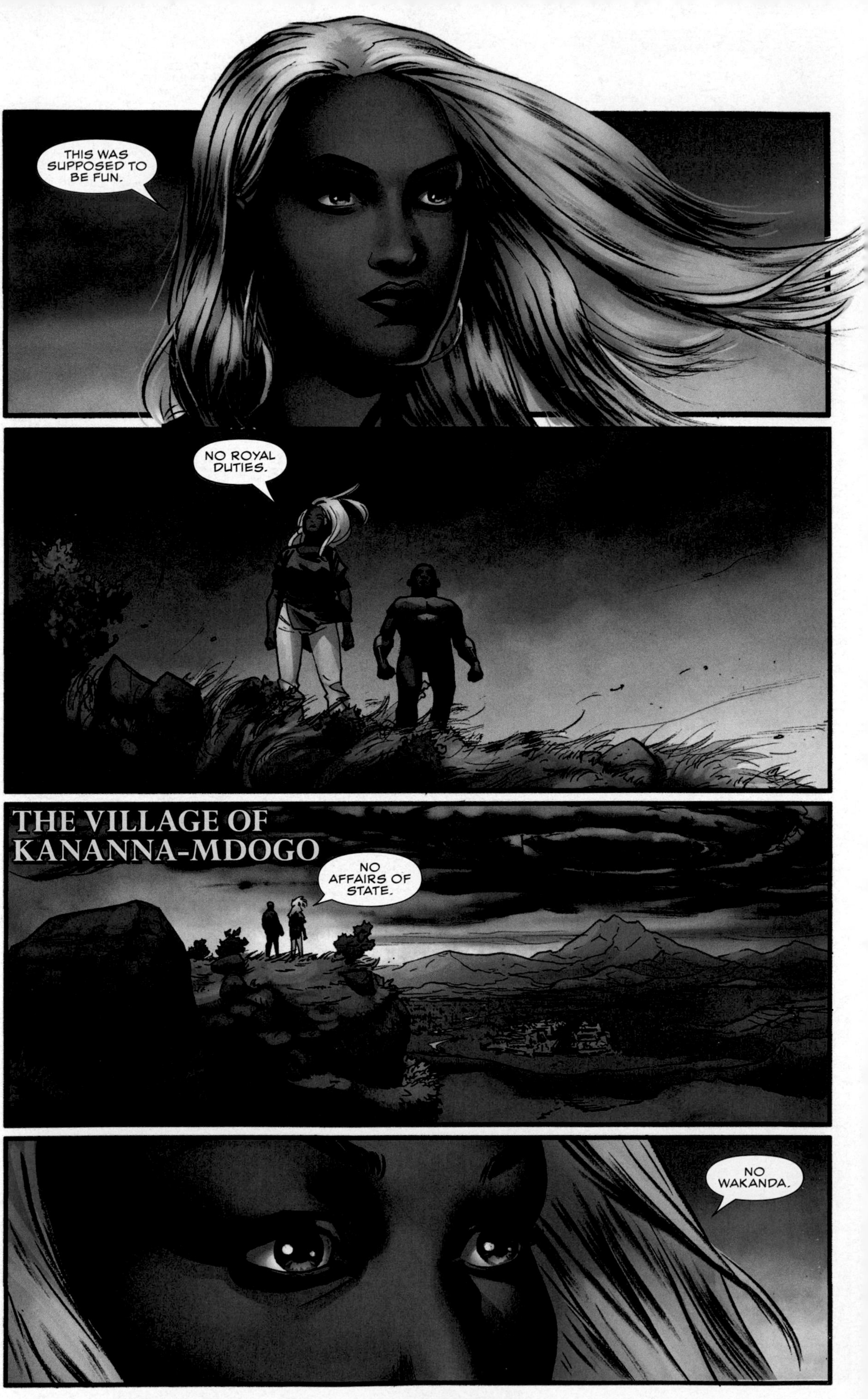
THIS WAS SUPPOSED TO BE FUN.
NO ROYAL DUTIES.
THE VILLAGE OF KANANNA-MDOGO
NO AFFAIRS OF STATE.
NO WAKANDA.

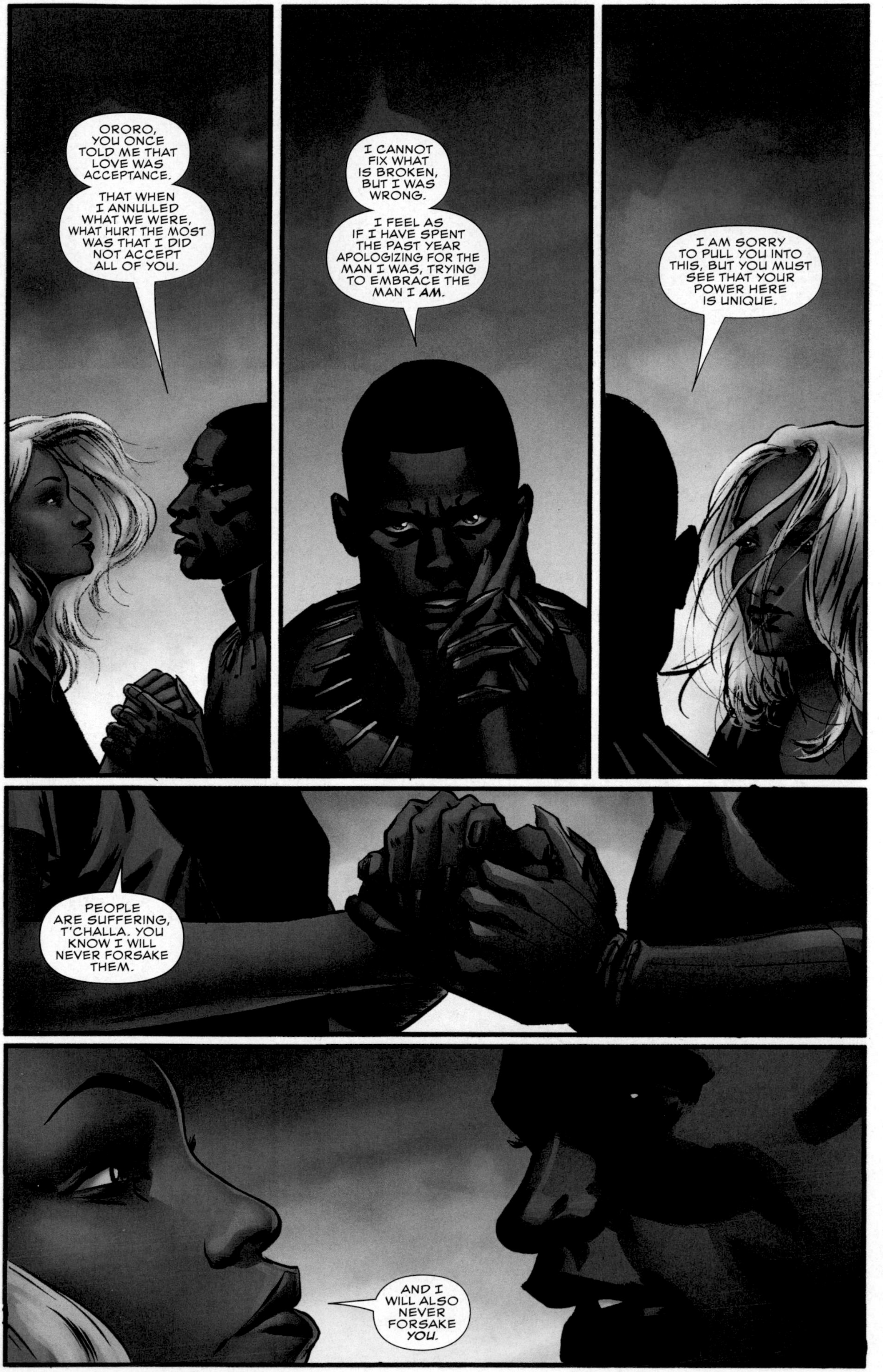
ORORO, YOU ONCE TOLD ME THAT LOVE WAS ACCEPTANCE.
THAT WHEN I ANNULLED WHAT WE WERE, WHAT HURT THE MOST WAS THAT I DID NOT ACCEPT ALL OF YOU.
I CANNOT FIX WHAT IS BROKEN, BUT I WAS WRONG.
I FEEL AS IF I HAVE SPENT THE PAST YEAR APOLOGIZING FOR THE MAN I WAS, TRYING TO EMBRACE THE MAN I *AM*.
I AM SORRY TO PULL YOU INTO THIS, BUT YOU MUST SEE THAT YOUR POWER HERE IS UNIQUE.
PEOPLE ARE SUFFERING, T'CHALLA. YOU KNOW I WILL NEVER FORSAKE THEM.
AND I WILL ALSO NEVER FORSAKE *YOU*.

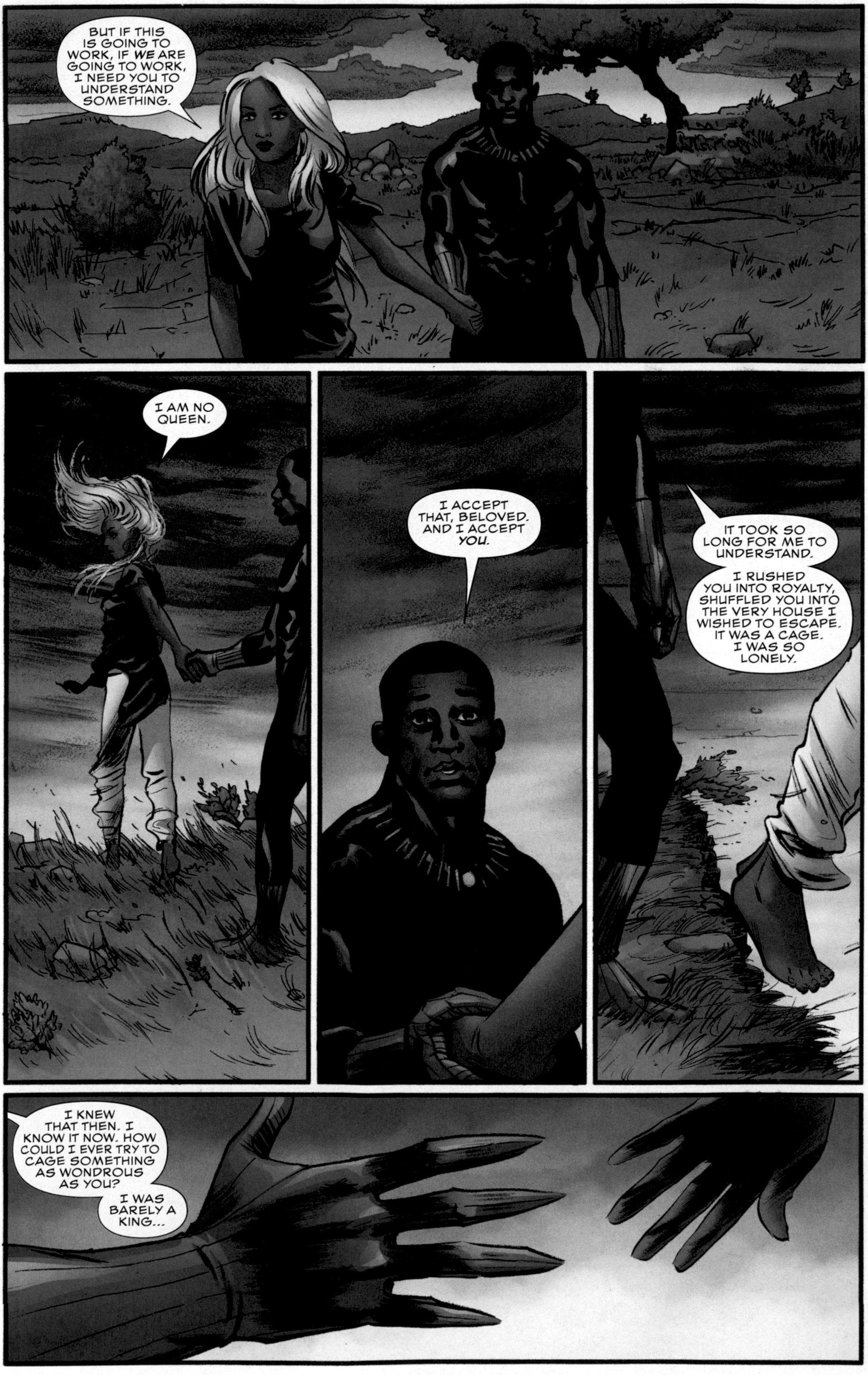
BUT IF THIS IS GOING TO WORK, IF *WE* ARE GOING TO WORK, I NEED YOU TO UNDERSTAND SOMETHING.
I AM NO QUEEN.
I ACCEPT THAT, BELOVED. AND I ACCEPT *YOU.*
IT TOOK SO LONG FOR ME TO UNDERSTAND.
I RUSHED YOU INTO ROYALTY, SHUFFLED YOU INTO THE VERY HOUSE I WISHED TO ESCAPE. IT WAS A CAGE. I WAS SO LONELY.
I KNEW THAT THEN. I KNOW IT NOW. HOW COULD I EVER TRY TO CAGE SOMETHING AS WONDROUS AS YOU?
I WAS BARELY A KING...

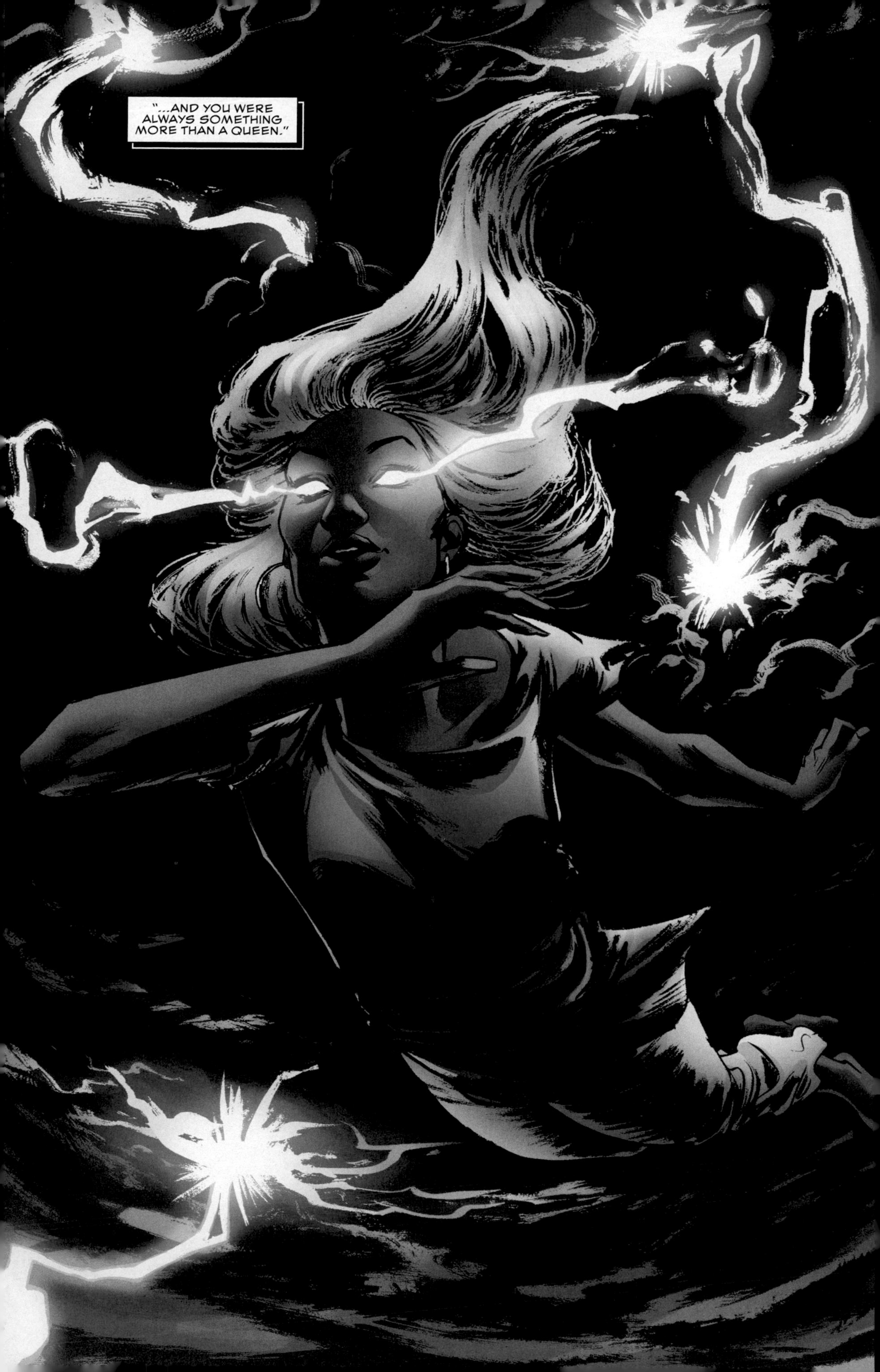
"...AND YOU WERE ALWAYS SOMETHING MORE THAN A QUEEN."

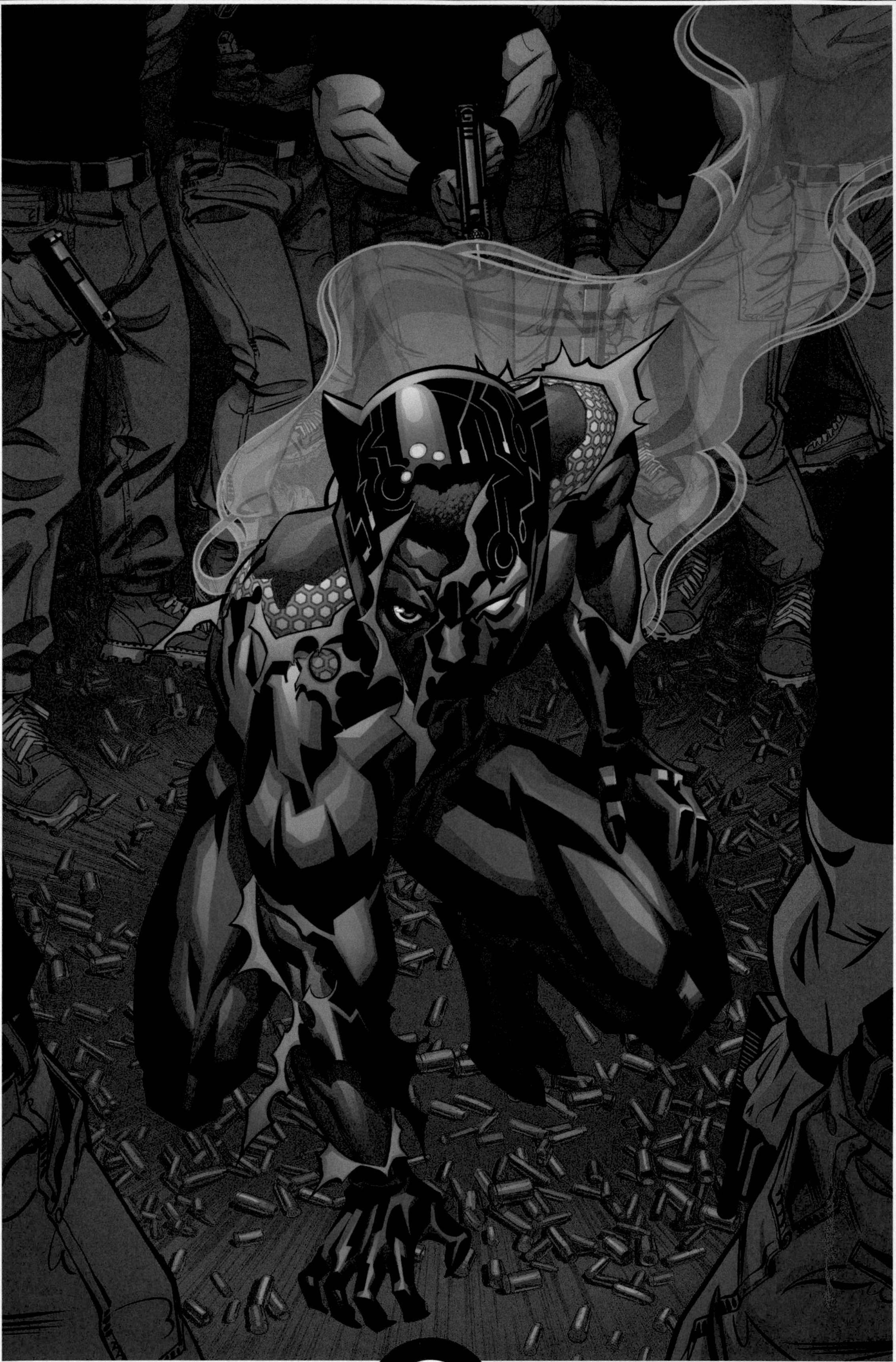

16

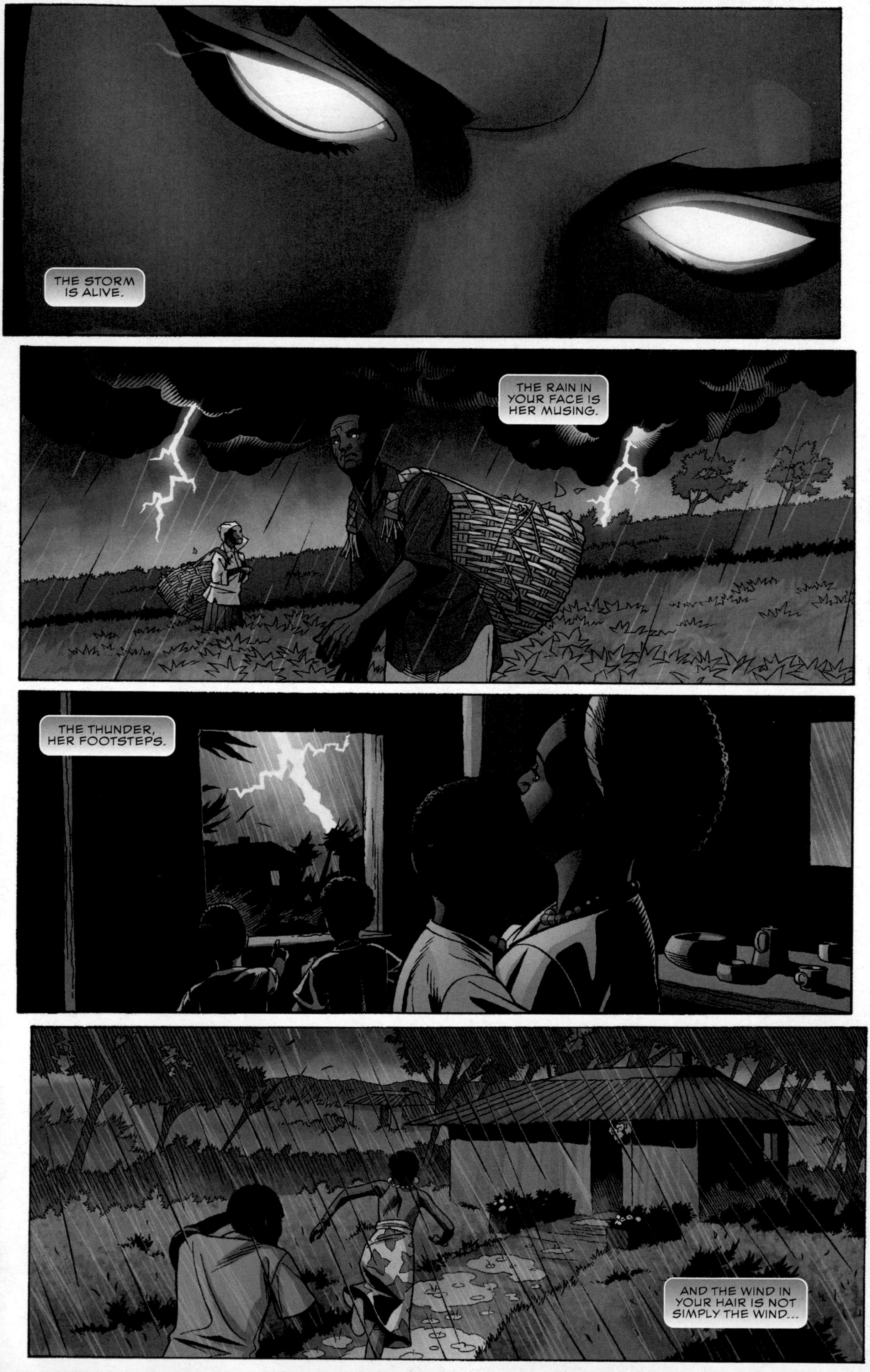
THE STORM IS ALIVE.
THE RAIN IN YOUR FACE IS HER MUSING.
THE THUNDER, HER FOOTSTEPS.
AND THE WIND IN YOUR HAIR IS NOT SIMPLY THE WIND...

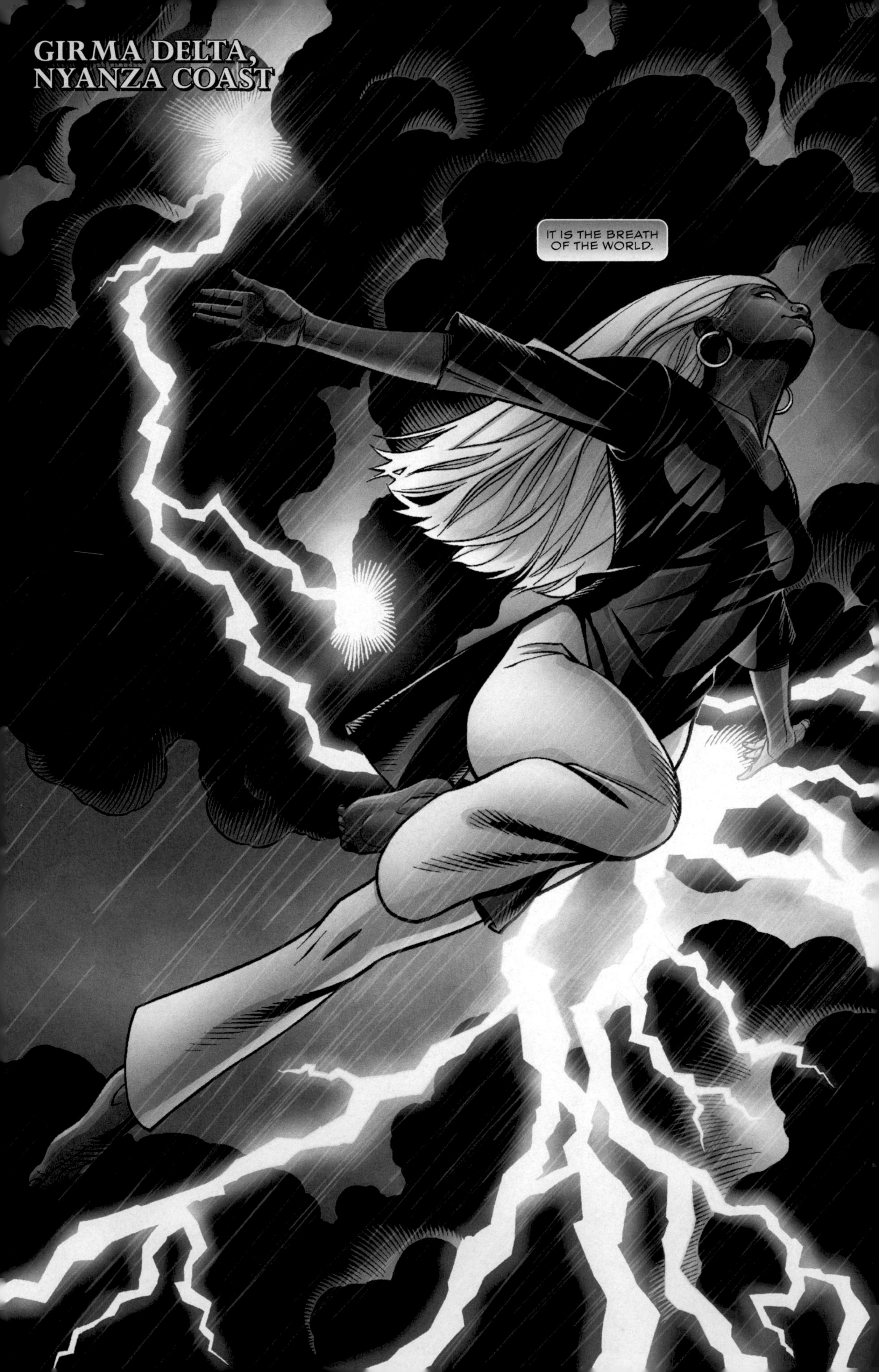
GIRMA DELTA, NYANZA COAST
IT IS THE BREATH OF THE WORLD.

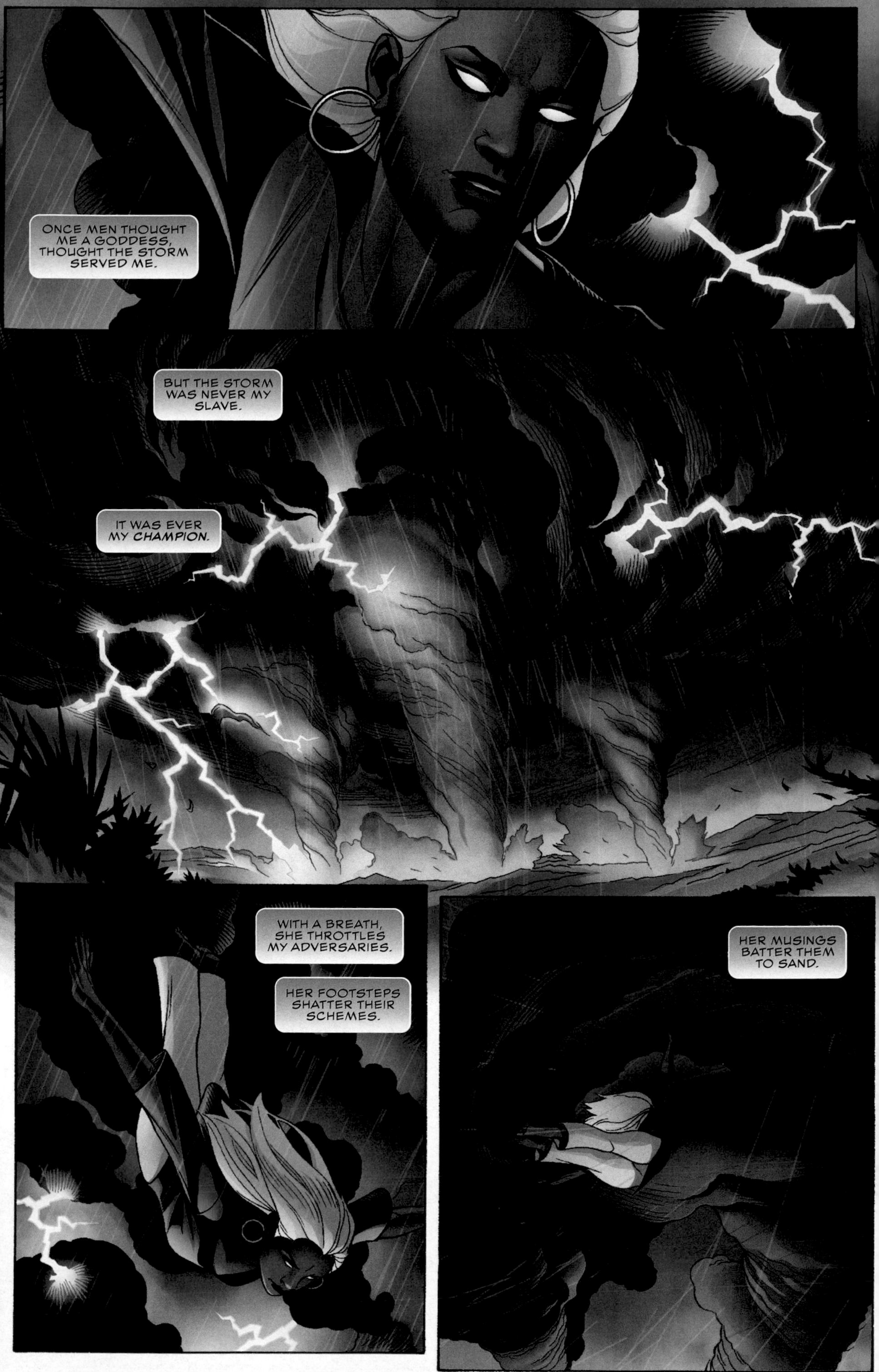
ONCE MEN THOUGHT ME A GODDESS, THOUGHT THE STORM SERVED ME.
BUT THE STORM WAS NEVER MY SLAVE.
IT WAS EVER MY CHAMPION.
WITH A BREATH, SHE THROTTLES MY ADVERSARIES.
HER FOOTSTEPS SHATTER THEIR SCHEMES.
HER MUSINGS BATTER THEM TO SAND.

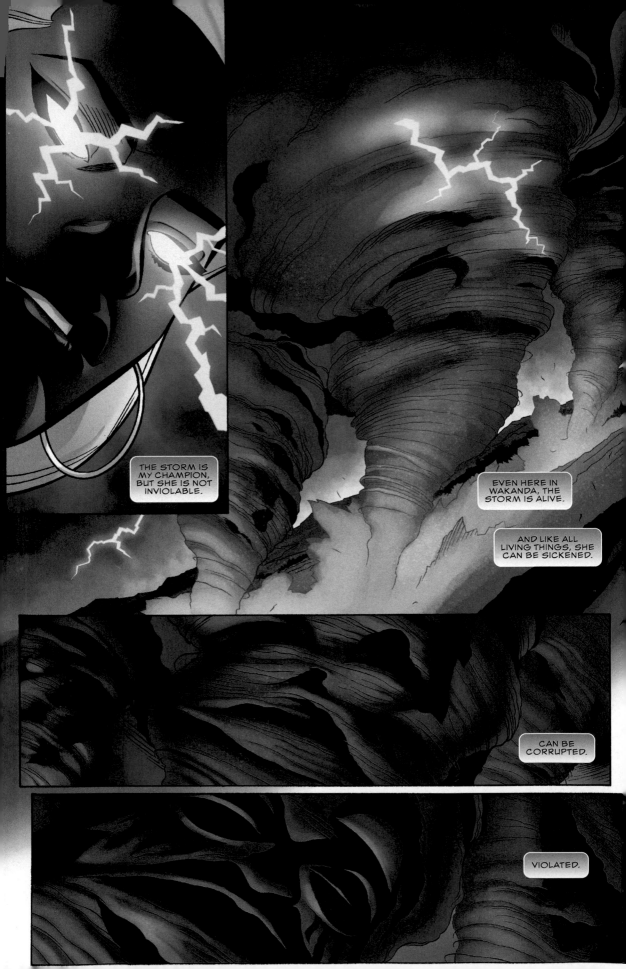

THE STORM IS MY CHAMPION, BUT SHE IS NOT INVIOLABLE.

EVEN HERE IN WAKANDA, THE STORM IS ALIVE.

AND LIKE ALL LIVING THINGS, SHE CAN BE SICKENED.

CAN BE CORRUPTED.

VIOLATED.

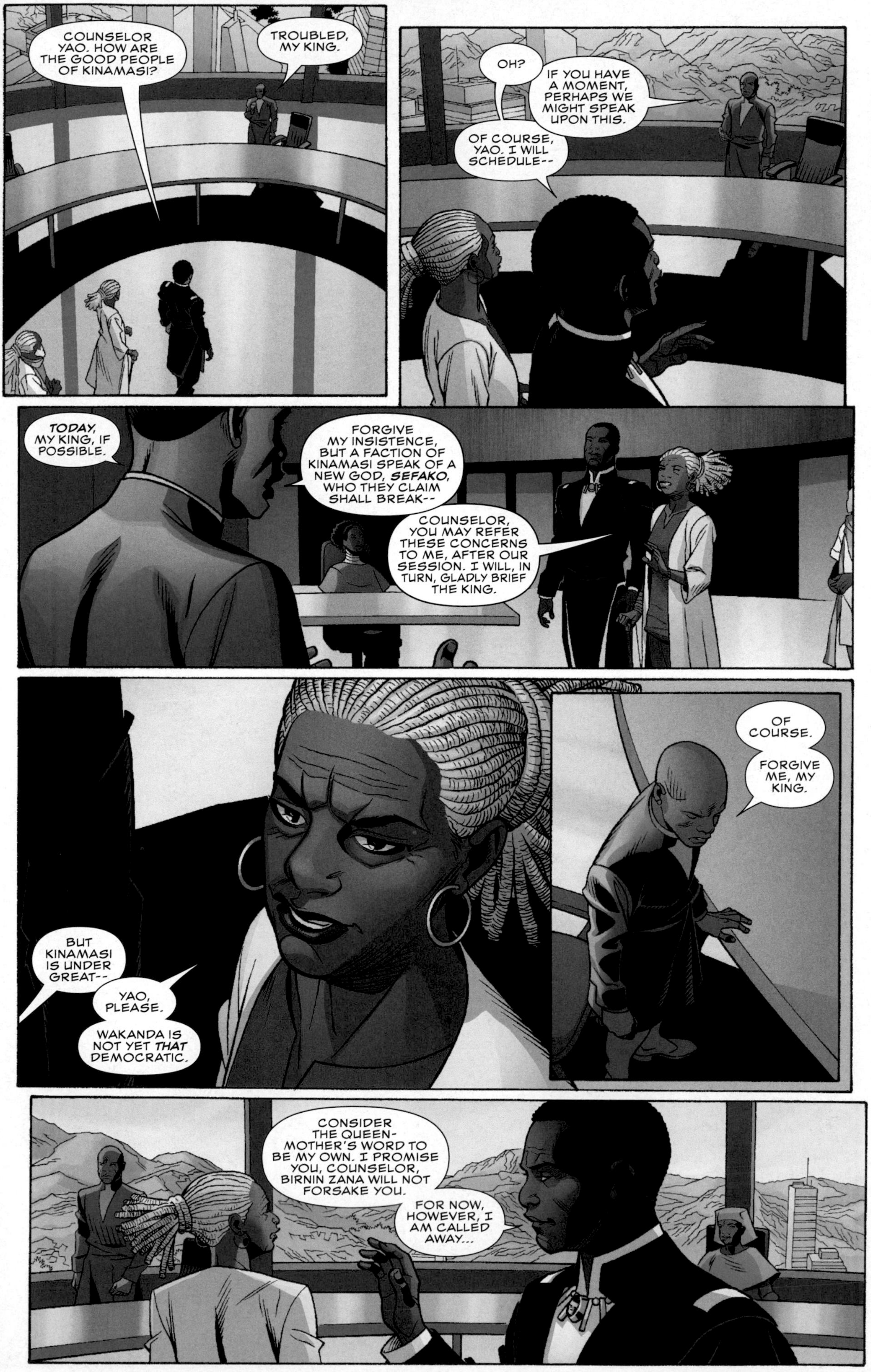
COUNSELOR YAO. HOW ARE THE GOOD PEOPLE OF KINAMASI?
TROUBLED, MY KING.
OH?
IF YOU HAVE A MOMENT, PERHAPS WE MIGHT SPEAK UPON THIS.
OF COURSE, YAO. I WILL SCHEDULE--
TODAY, MY KING, IF POSSIBLE.
FORGIVE MY INSISTENCE, BUT A FACTION OF KINAMASI SPEAK OF A NEW GOD, ***SEFAKO***, WHO THEY CLAIM SHALL BREAK--
COUNSELOR, YOU MAY REFER THESE CONCERNS TO ME, AFTER OUR SESSION. I WILL, IN TURN, GLADLY BRIEF THE KING.
BUT KINAMASI IS UNDER GREAT--
YAO, PLEASE.
WAKANDA IS NOT YET *THAT* DEMOCRATIC.
OF COURSE.
FORGIVE ME, MY KING.
CONSIDER THE QUEEN-MOTHER'S WORD TO BE MY OWN. I PROMISE YOU, COUNSELOR, BIRNIN ZANA WILL NOT FORSAKE YOU.
FOR NOW, HOWEVER, I AM CALLED AWAY...

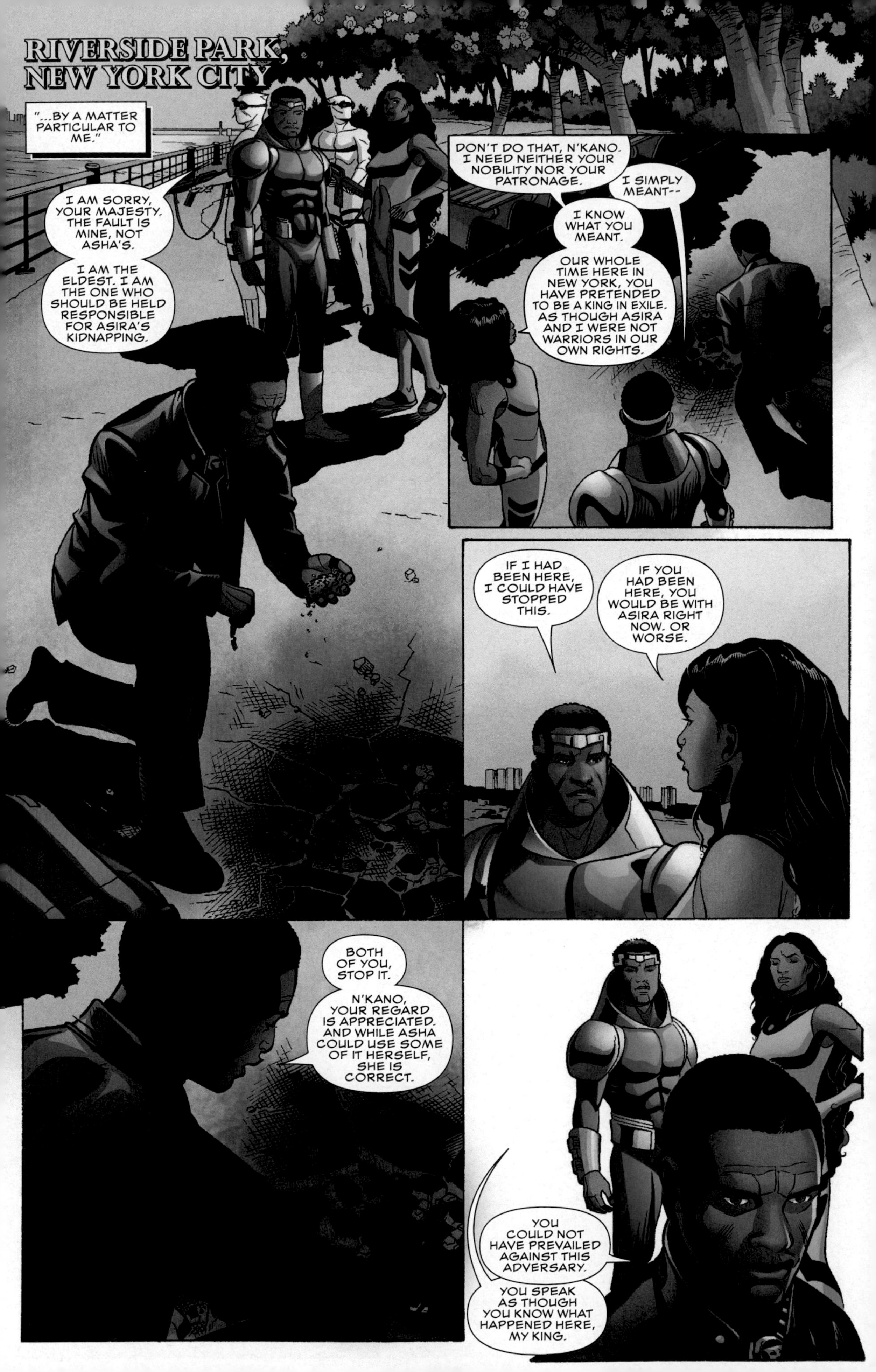
RIVERSIDE PARK, NEW YORK CITY
"...BY A MATTER PARTICULAR TO ME."
I AM SORRY, YOUR MAJESTY. THE FAULT IS MINE, NOT ASHA'S.
I AM THE ELDEST. I AM THE ONE WHO SHOULD BE HELD RESPONSIBLE FOR ASIRA'S KIDNAPPING.
DON'T DO THAT, N'KANO. I NEED NEITHER YOUR NOBILITY NOR YOUR PATRONAGE.
I SIMPLY MEANT--
I KNOW WHAT YOU MEANT.
OUR WHOLE TIME HERE IN NEW YORK, YOU HAVE PRETENDED TO BE A KING IN EXILE. AS THOUGH ASIRA AND I WERE NOT WARRIORS IN OUR OWN RIGHTS.
IF I HAD BEEN HERE, I COULD HAVE STOPPED THIS.
IF YOU HAD BEEN HERE, YOU WOULD BE WITH ASIRA RIGHT NOW. OR WORSE.
BOTH OF YOU, STOP IT.
N'KANO, YOUR REGARD IS APPRECIATED. AND WHILE ASHA COULD USE SOME OF IT HERSELF, SHE IS CORRECT.
YOU COULD NOT HAVE PREVAILED AGAINST THIS ADVERSARY.
YOU SPEAK AS THOUGH YOU KNOW WHAT HAPPENED HERE, MY KING.

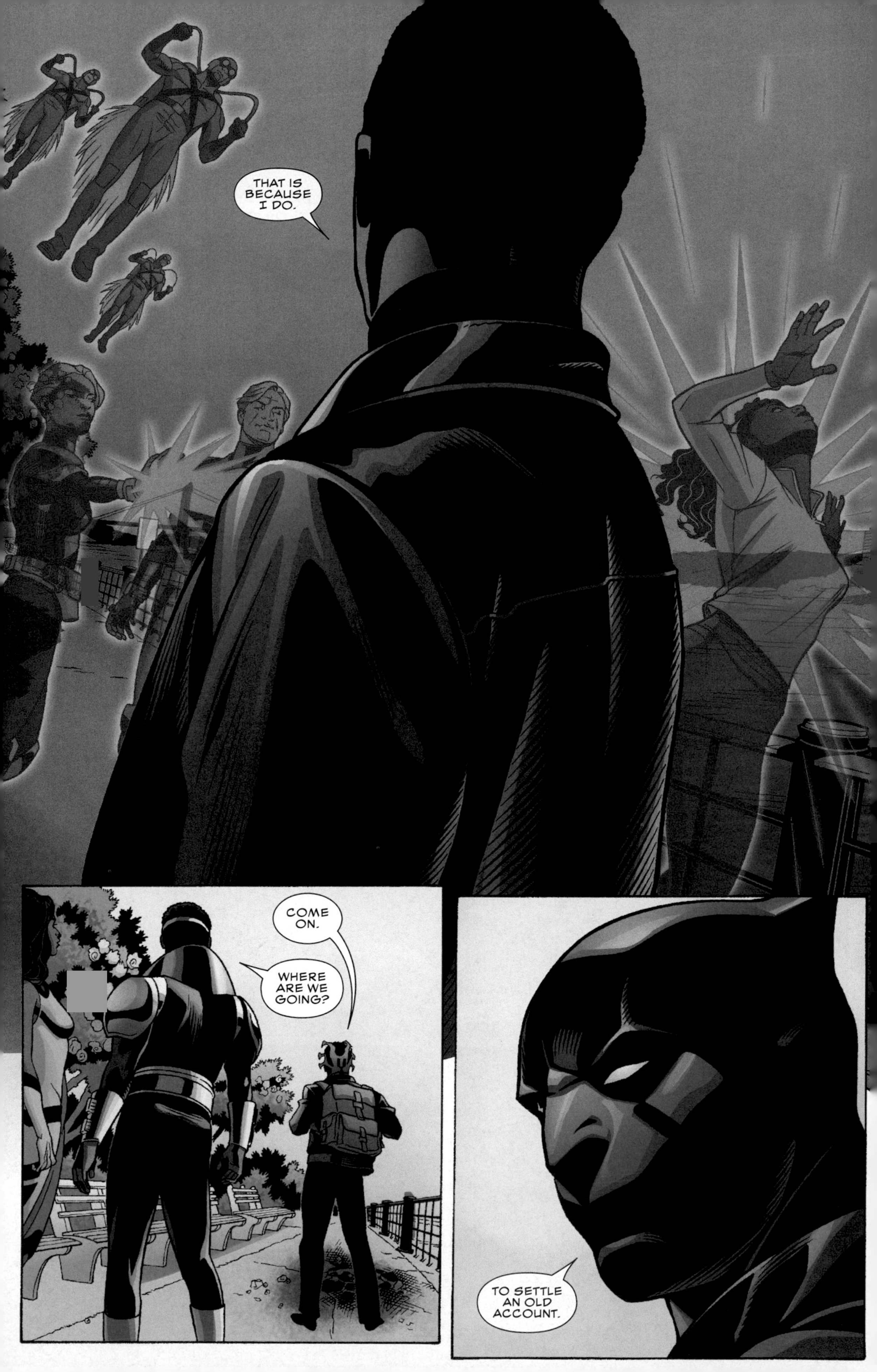
THAT IS BECAUSE I DO.
COME ON.
WHERE ARE WE GOING?
TO SETTLE AN OLD ACCOUNT.

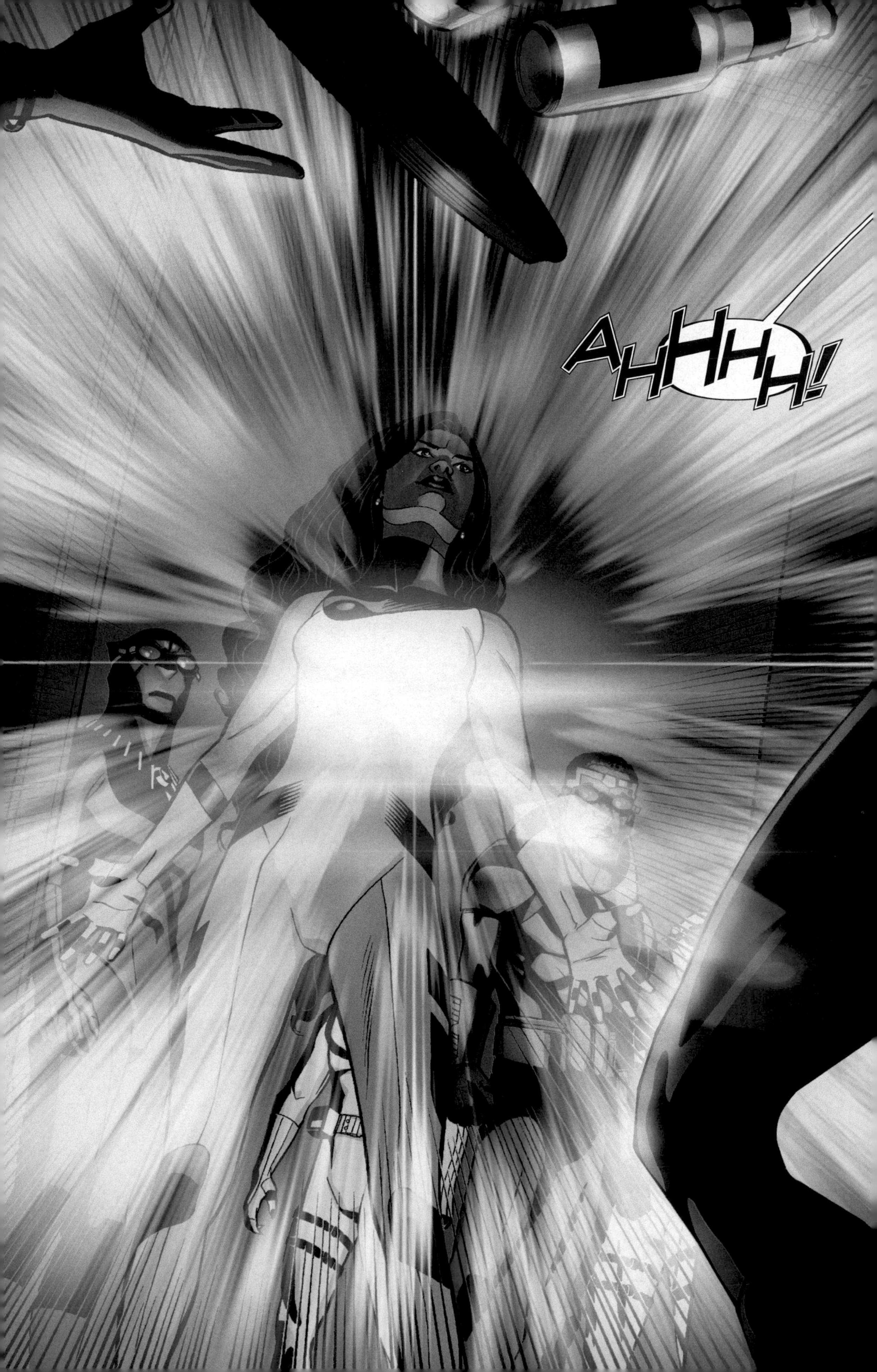
AHHHH!

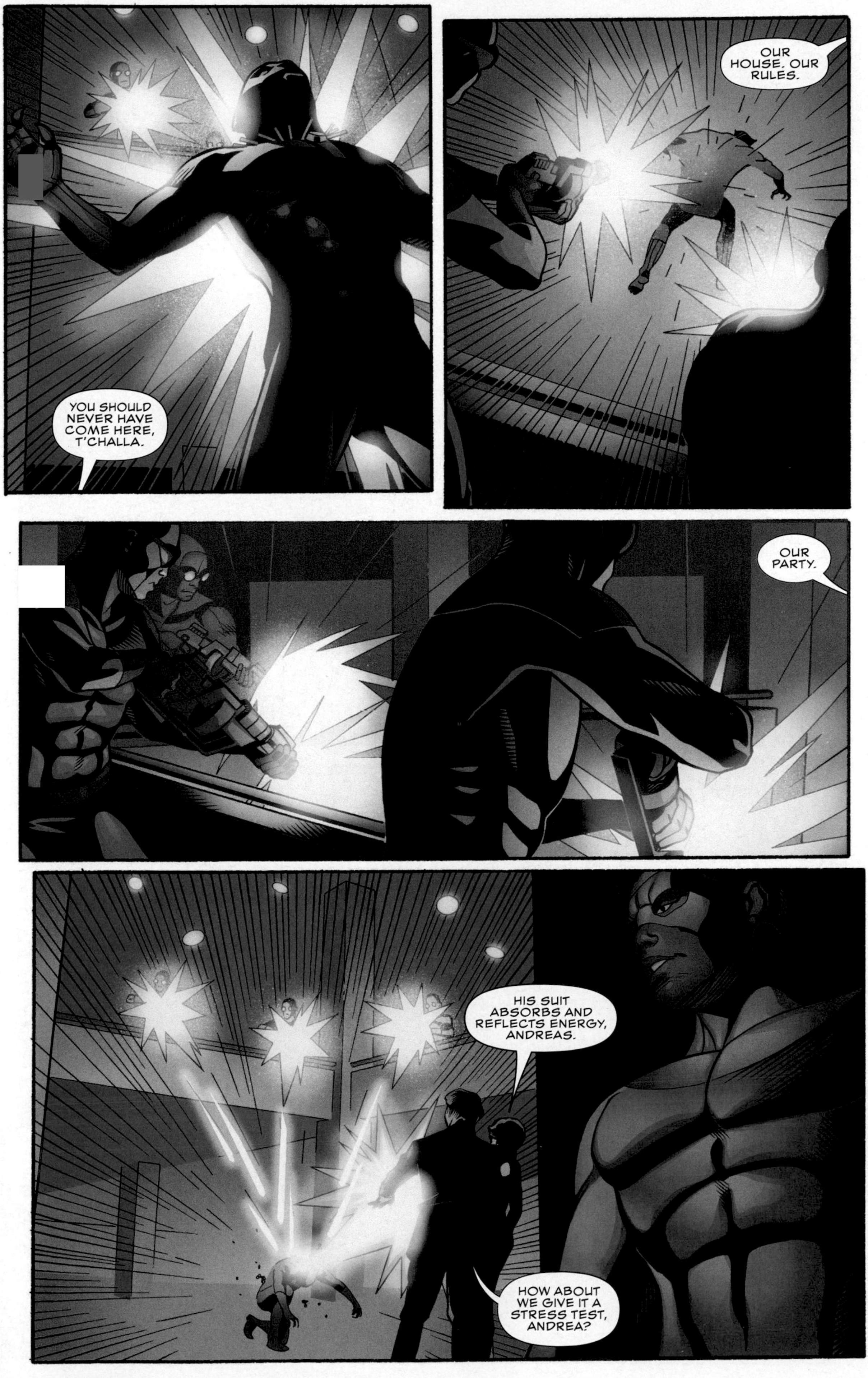
YOU SHOULD NEVER HAVE COME HERE, T'CHALLA.
OUR HOUSE. OUR RULES.
OUR PARTY.
HIS SUIT ABSORBS AND REFLECTS ENERGY, ANDREAS.
HOW ABOUT WE GIVE IT A STRESS TEST, ANDREA?

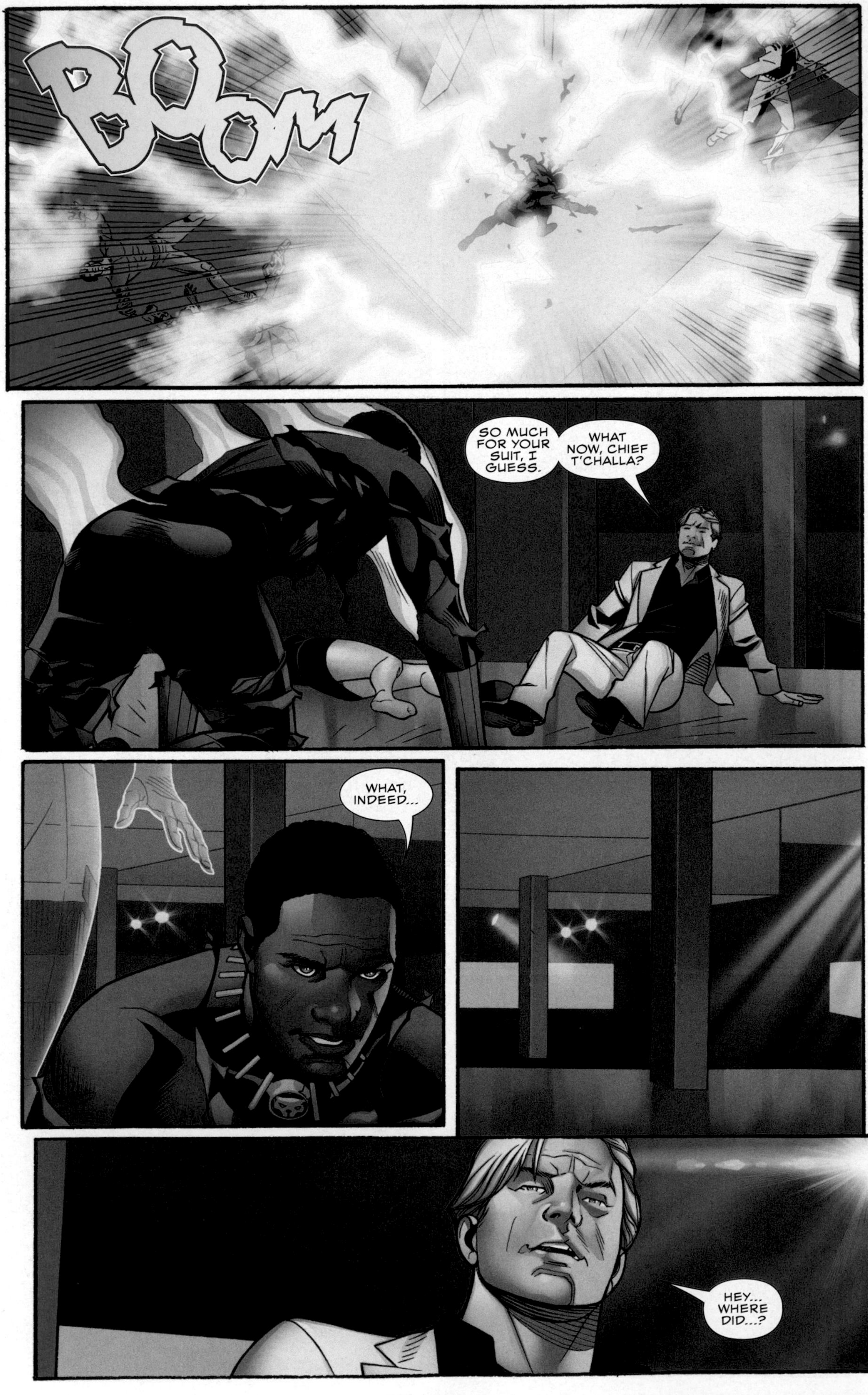
BOOM
SO MUCH FOR YOUR SUIT, I GUESS.
WHAT NOW, CHIEF T'CHALLA?
WHAT, INDEED...
HEY... WHERE DID...?

FIND HIM!

NO NEED.

OPTION ONE: YOU SETTLE YOUR GUARDS DOWN NOW.

OPTION TWO: I DEPLOY THIS ENERGY DAGGER AND WE GET TO SEE EXACTLY WHAT'S ON YOUR MIND.

P-PERHAPS THIS IS A GOOD TIME F-FOR A DETENTE.

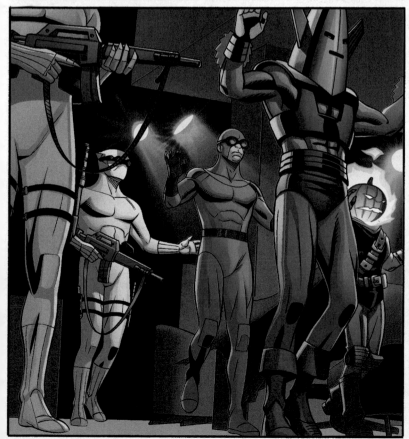

SMART MOVE.

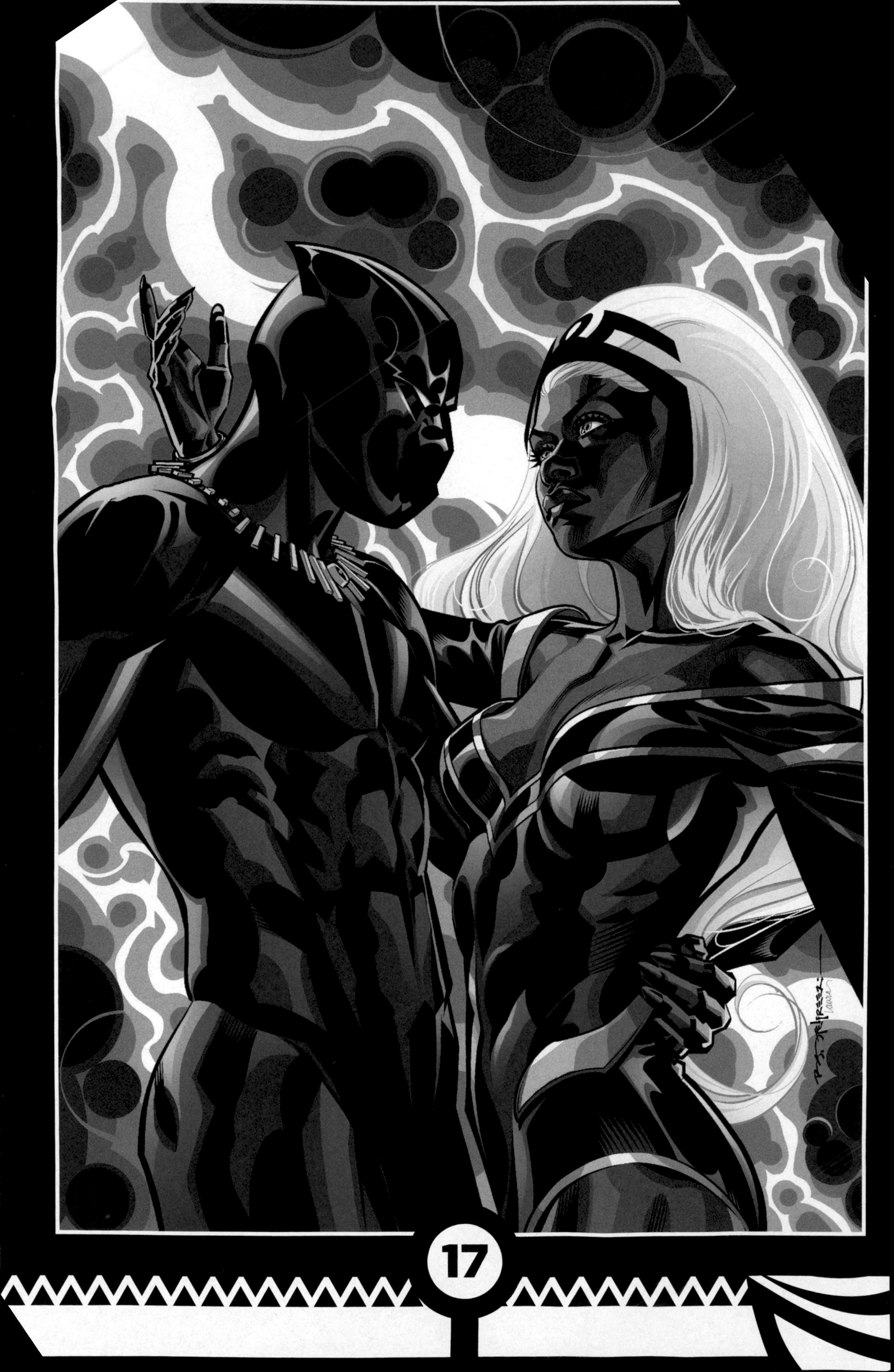
17

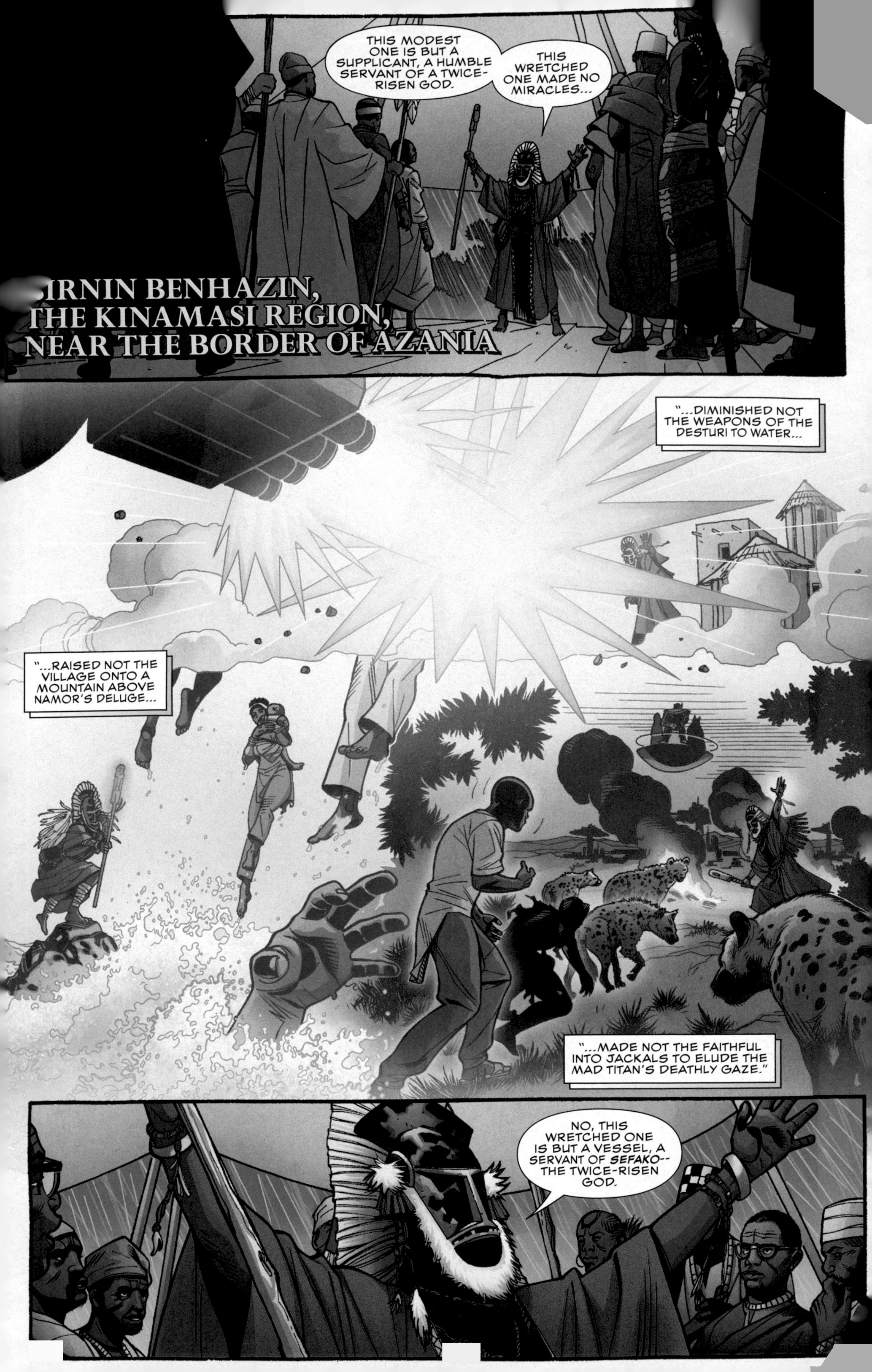
THIS MODEST ONE IS BUT A SUPPLICANT, A HUMBLE SERVANT OF A TWICE-RISEN GOD.
THIS WRETCHED ONE MADE NO MIRACLES...
IRNIN BENHAZIN, THE KINAMASI REGION, NEAR THE BORDER OF AZANIA
"...DIMINISHED NOT THE WEAPONS OF THE DESTURI TO WATER...
"...RAISED NOT THE VILLAGE ONTO A MOUNTAIN ABOVE NAMOR'S DELUGE...
"...MADE NOT THE FAITHFUL INTO JACKALS TO ELUDE THE MAD TITAN'S DEATHLY GAZE."
NO, THIS WRETCHED ONE IS BUT A VESSEL, A SERVANT OF SEFAKO-- THE TWICE-RISEN GOD.

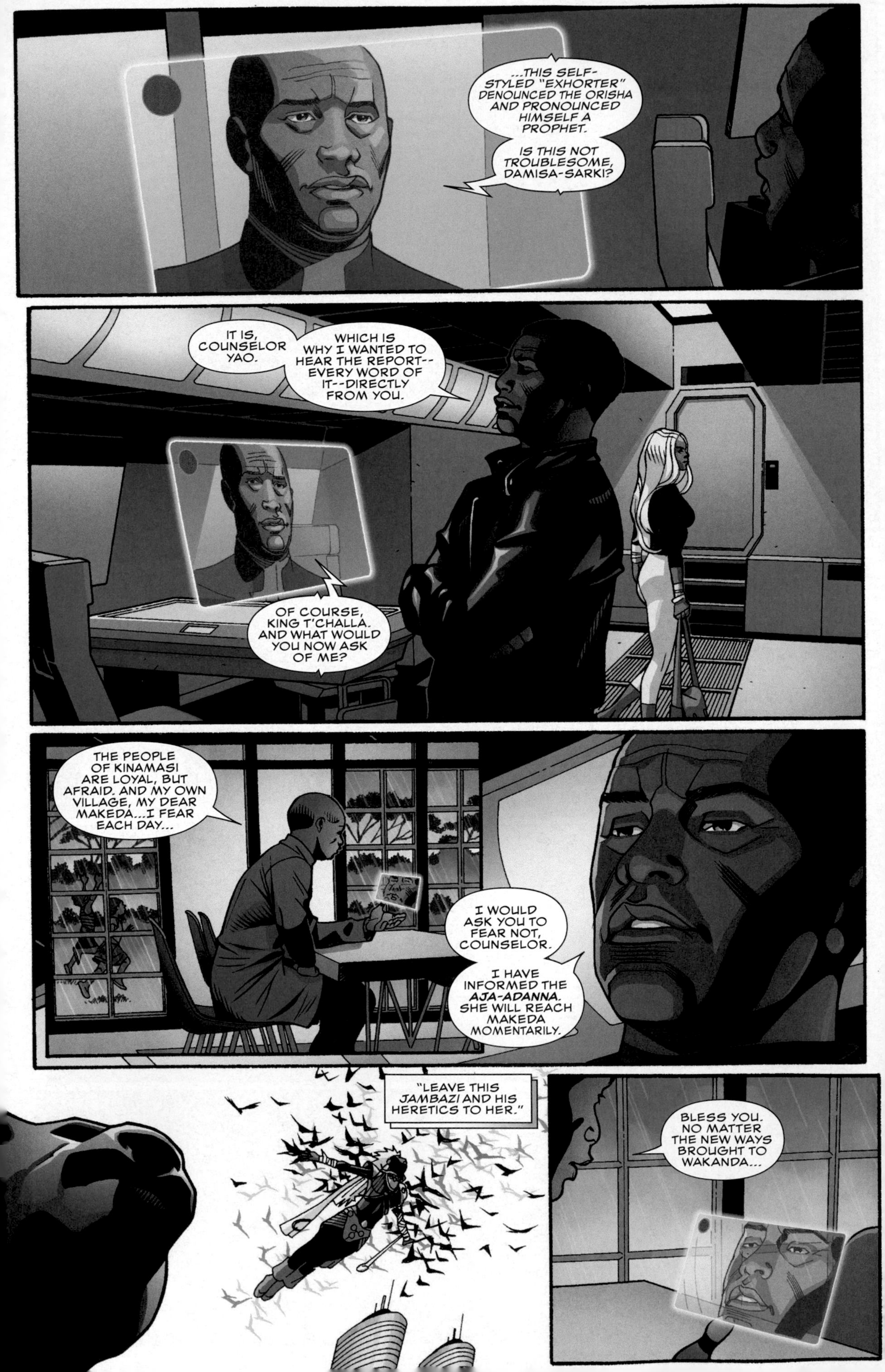
...THIS SELF-STYLED "EXHORTER" DENOUNCED THE ORISHA AND PRONOUNCED HIMSELF A PROPHET.
IS THIS NOT TROUBLESOME, DAMISA-SARKI?
IT IS, COUNSELOR YAO.
WHICH IS WHY I WANTED TO HEAR THE REPORT-- EVERY WORD OF IT--DIRECTLY FROM YOU.
OF COURSE, KING T'CHALLA. AND WHAT WOULD YOU NOW ASK OF ME?
THE PEOPLE OF KINAMASI ARE LOYAL, BUT AFRAID. AND MY OWN VILLAGE, MY DEAR MAKEDA...I FEAR EACH DAY...
I WOULD ASK YOU TO FEAR NOT, COUNSELOR.
I HAVE INFORMED THE AJA-ADANNA. SHE WILL REACH MAKEDA MOMENTARILY.
"LEAVE THIS JAMBAZI AND HIS HERETICS TO HER."
BLESS YOU. NO MATTER THE NEW WAYS BROUGHT TO WAKANDA...

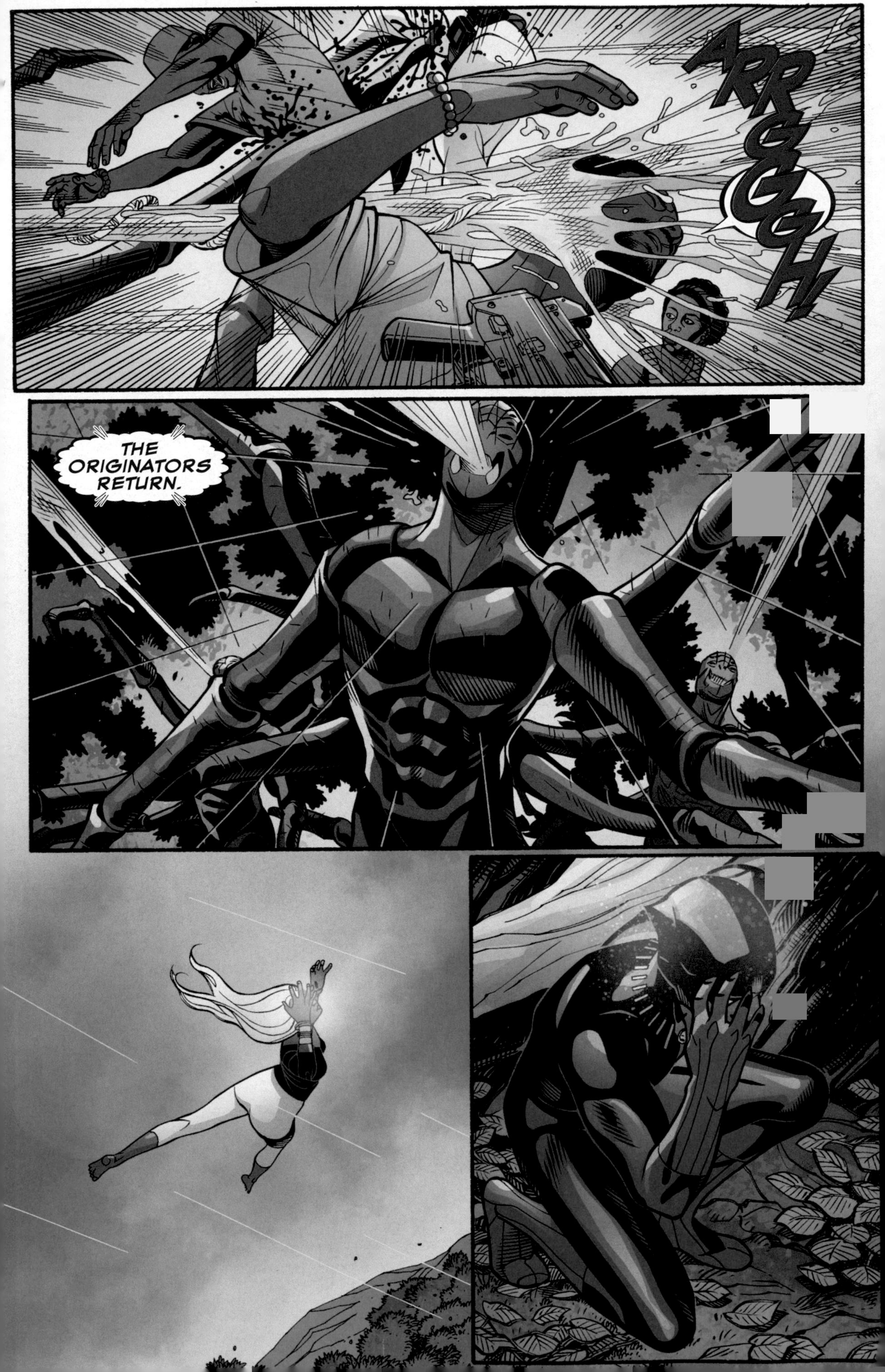
ARRGGGH!
THE ORIGINATORS RETURN.

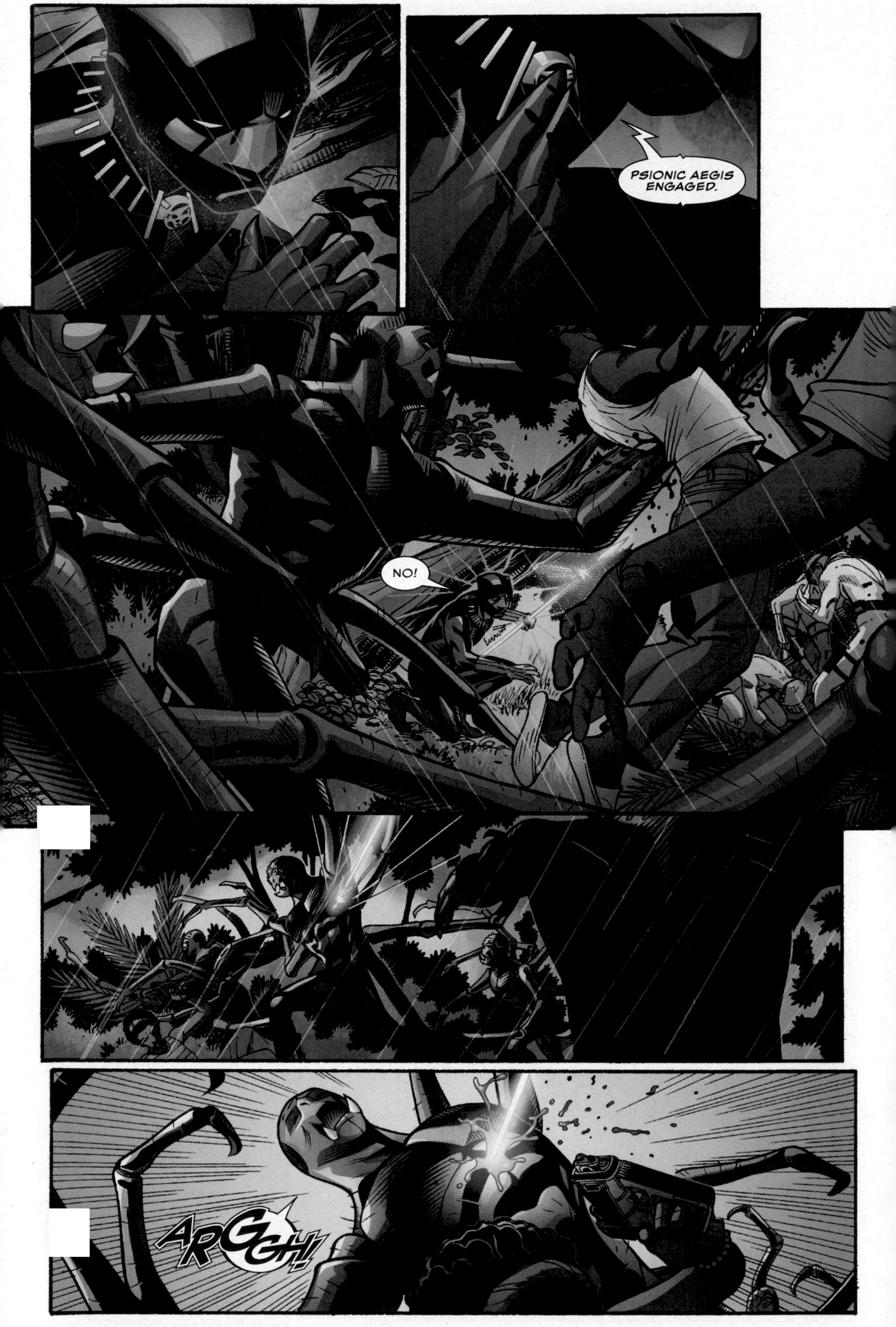
PSIONIC AEGIS ENGAGED.
NO!
ARGGH!

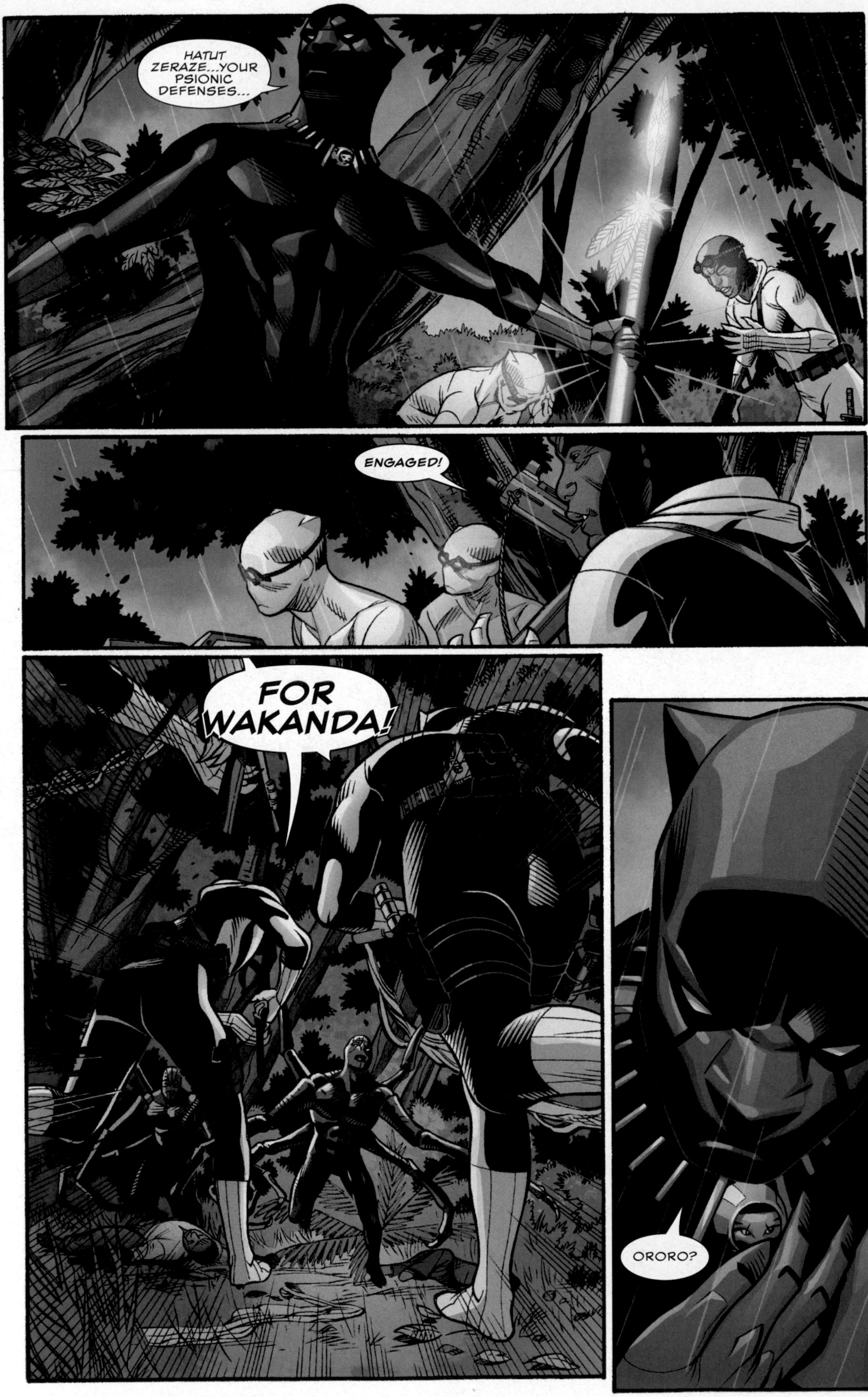
HATUT ZERAZE...YOUR PSIONIC DEFENSES...
ENGAGED!
FOR WAKANDA!
ORORO?

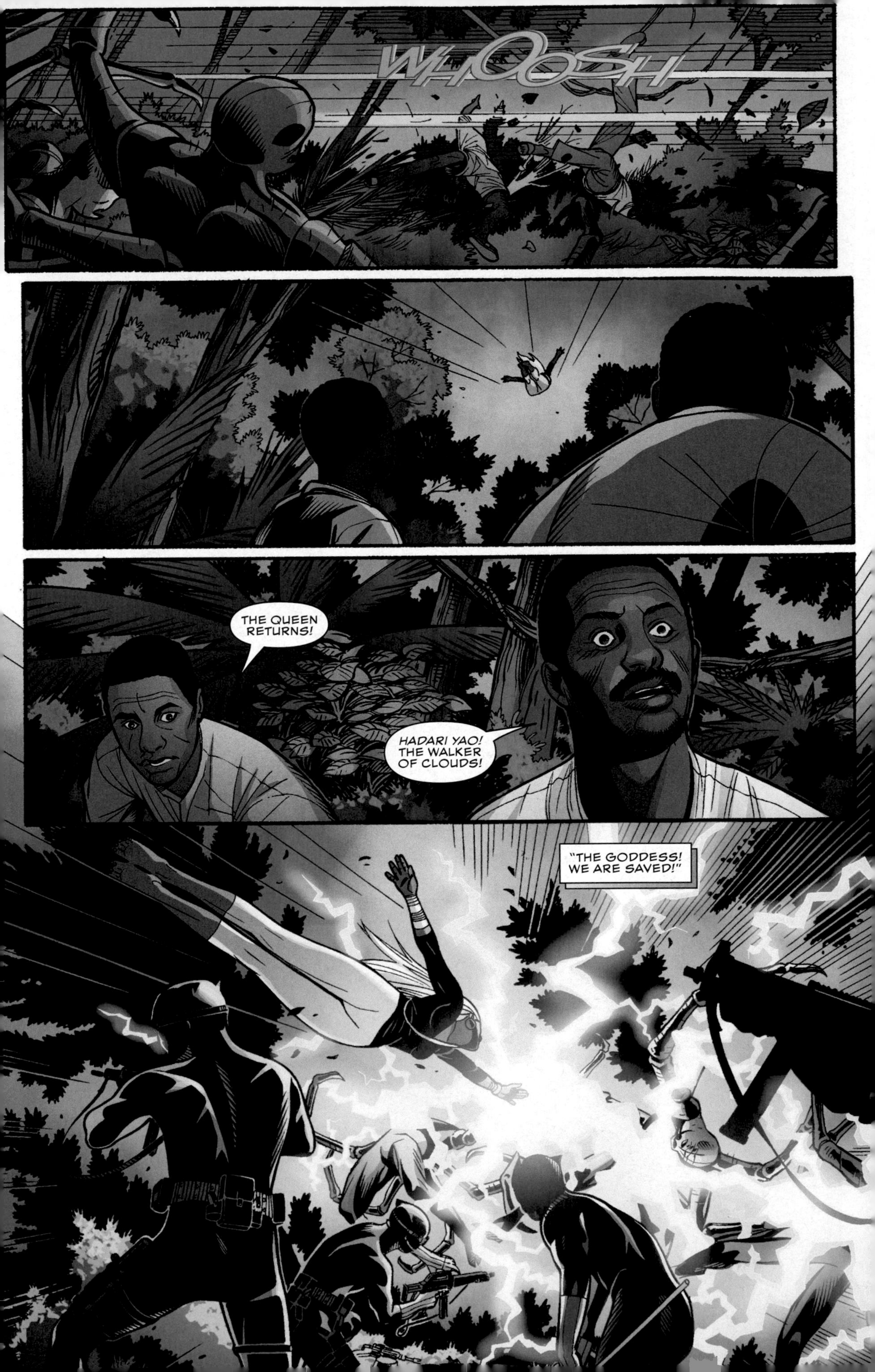
WHOOOSH
THE QUEEN RETURNS!
HADARI YAO! THE WALKER OF CLOUDS!
"THE GODDESS! WE ARE SAVED!"

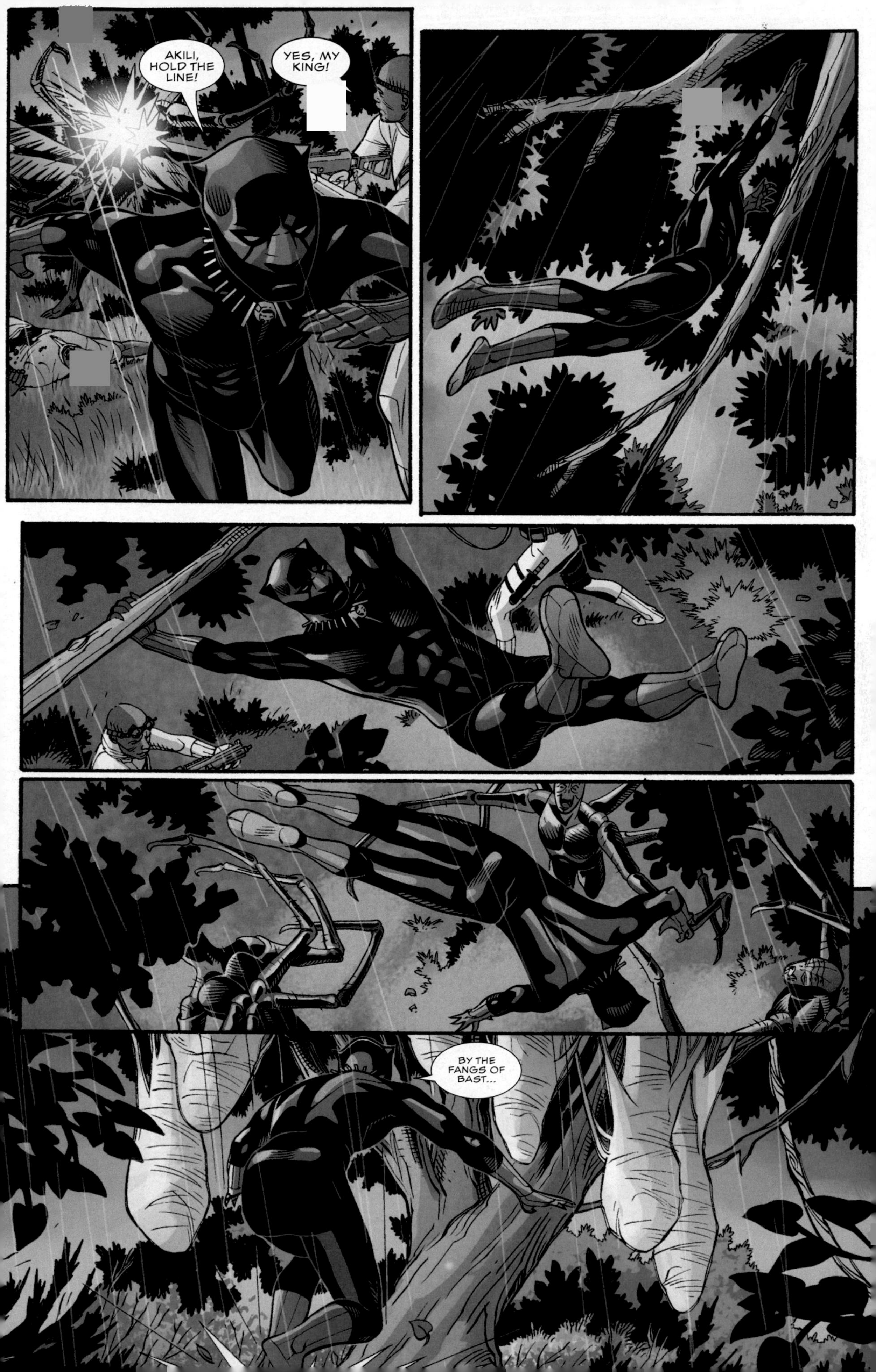
AKILI, HOLD THE LINE!
YES, MY KING!
BY THE FANGS OF BAST...

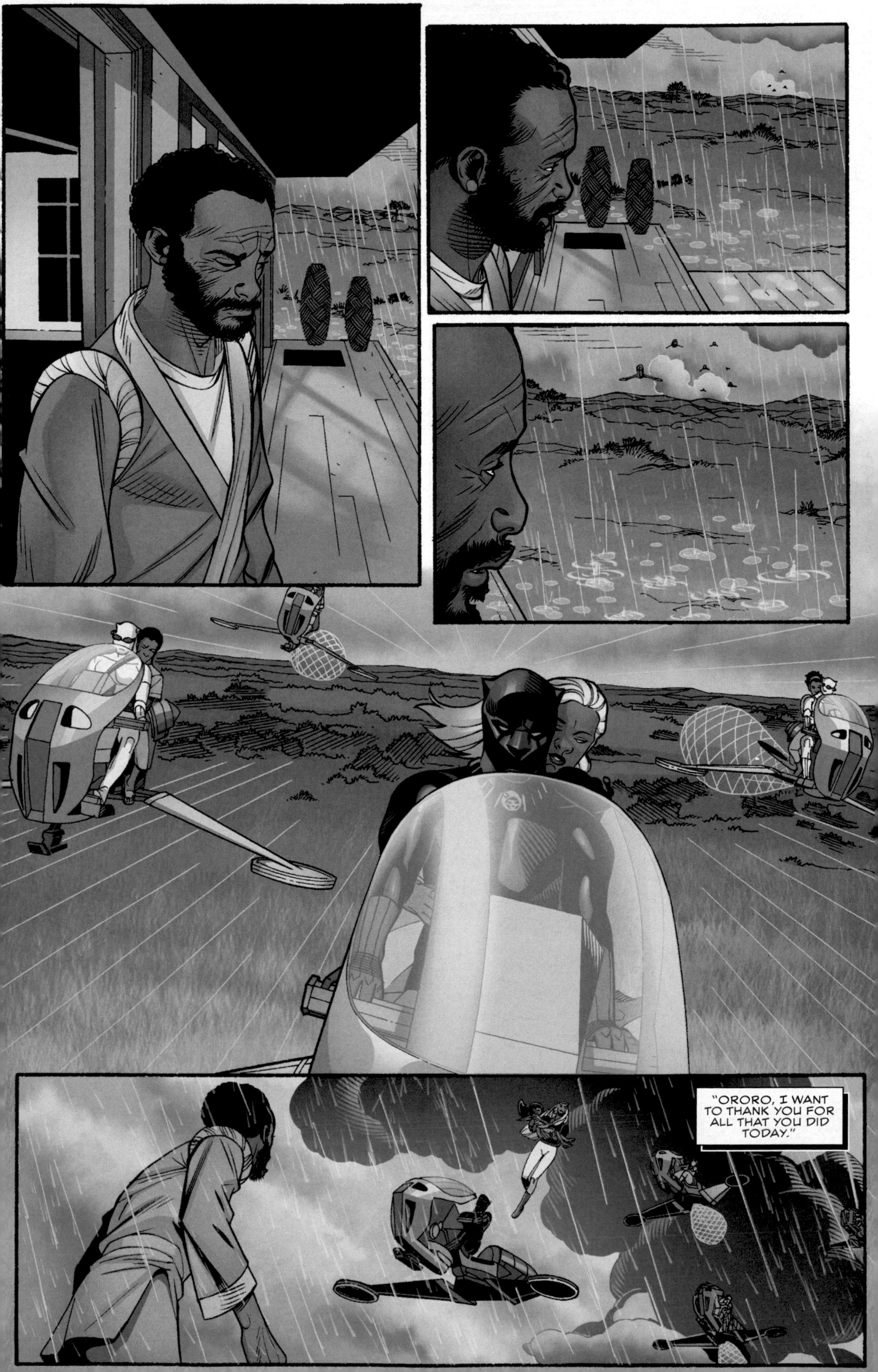
"ORORO, I WANT TO THANK YOU FOR ALL THAT YOU DID TODAY."

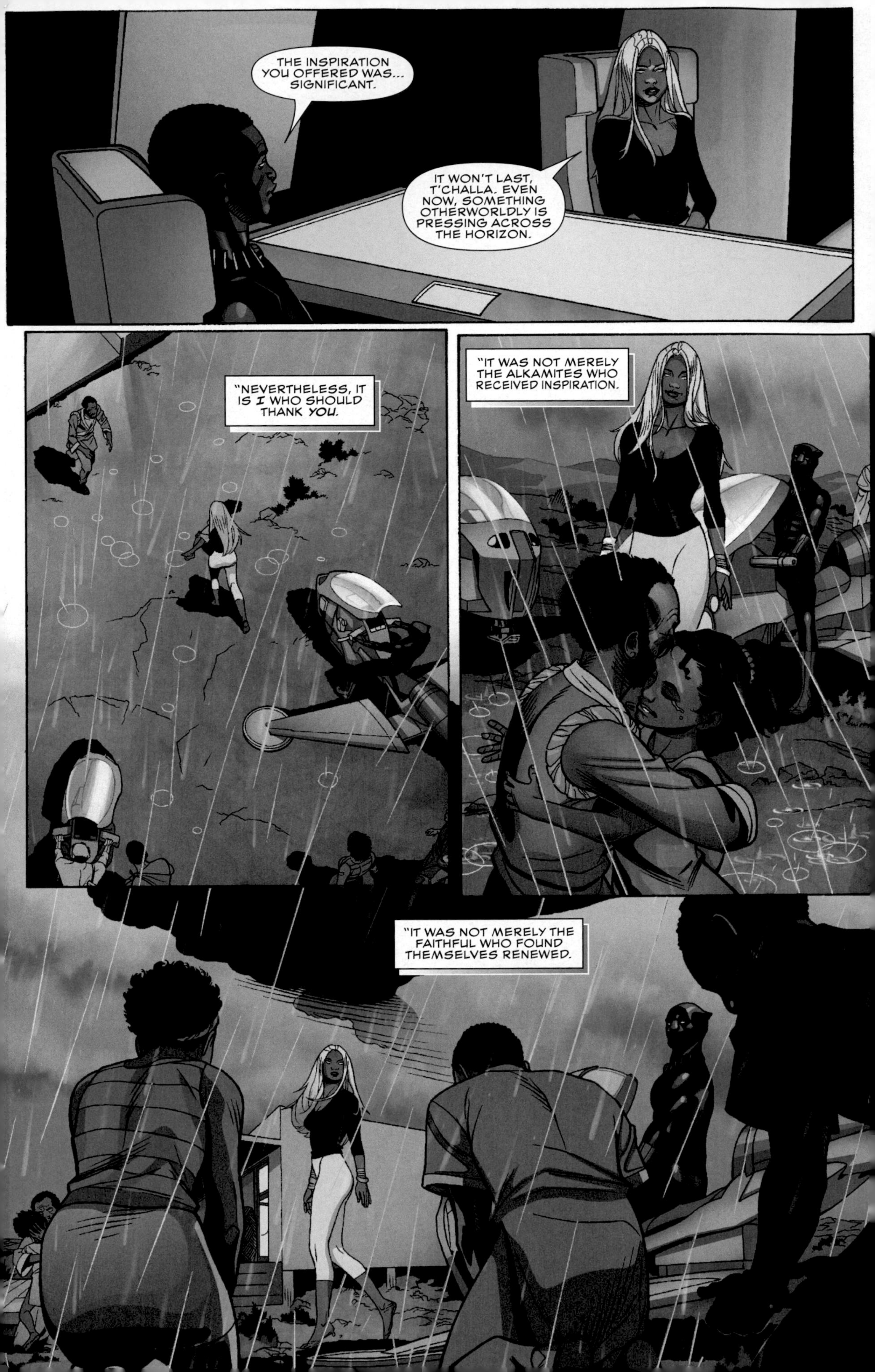
THE INSPIRATION YOU OFFERED WAS... SIGNIFICANT.
IT WON'T LAST, T'CHALLA. EVEN NOW, SOMETHING OTHERWORLDLY IS PRESSING ACROSS THE HORIZON.
"NEVERTHELESS, IT IS I WHO SHOULD THANK YOU.
"IT WAS NOT MERELY THE ALKAMITES WHO RECEIVED INSPIRATION.
"IT WAS NOT MERELY THE FAITHFUL WHO FOUND THEMSELVES RENEWED.

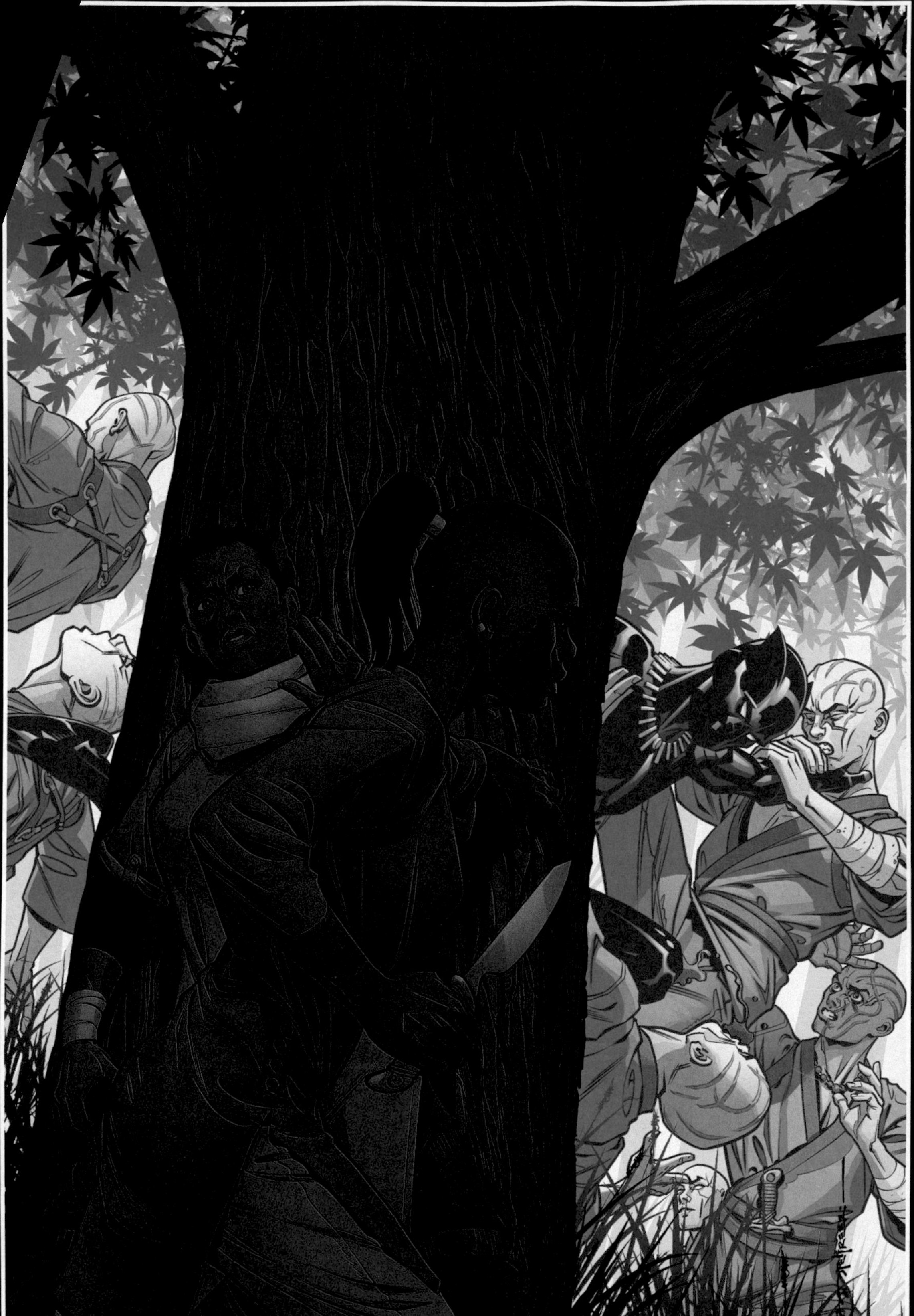

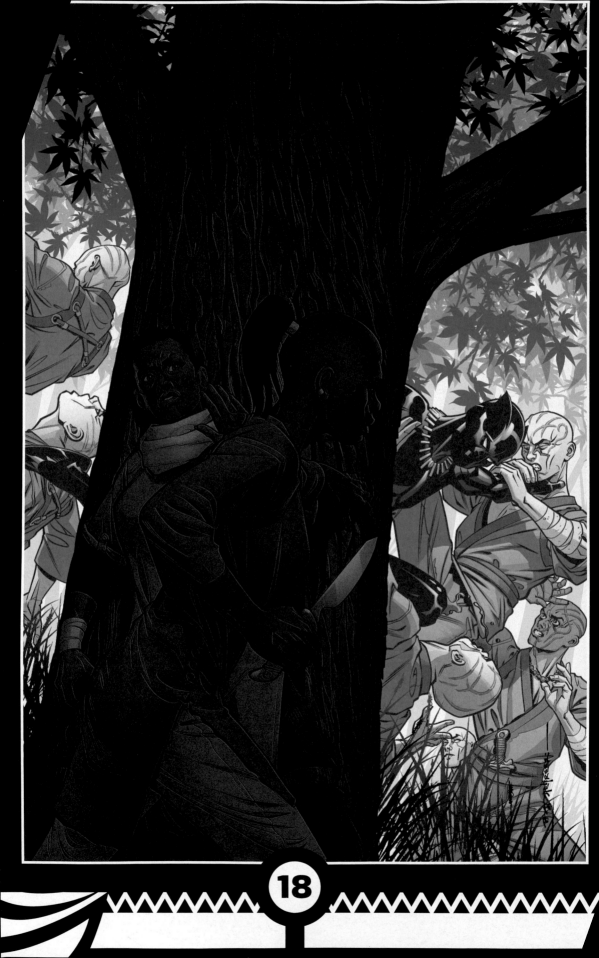

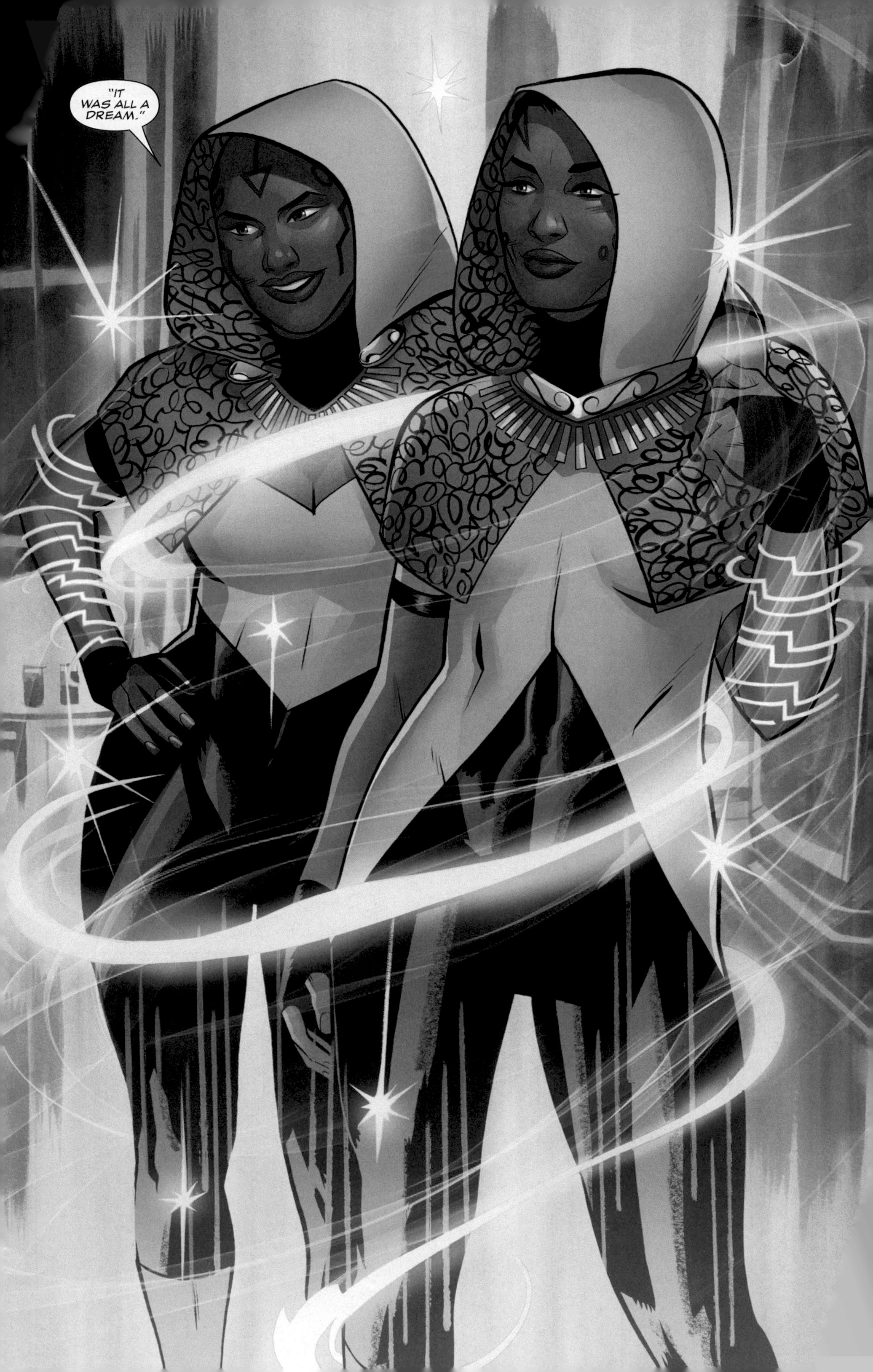
"IT WAS ALL A DREAM."

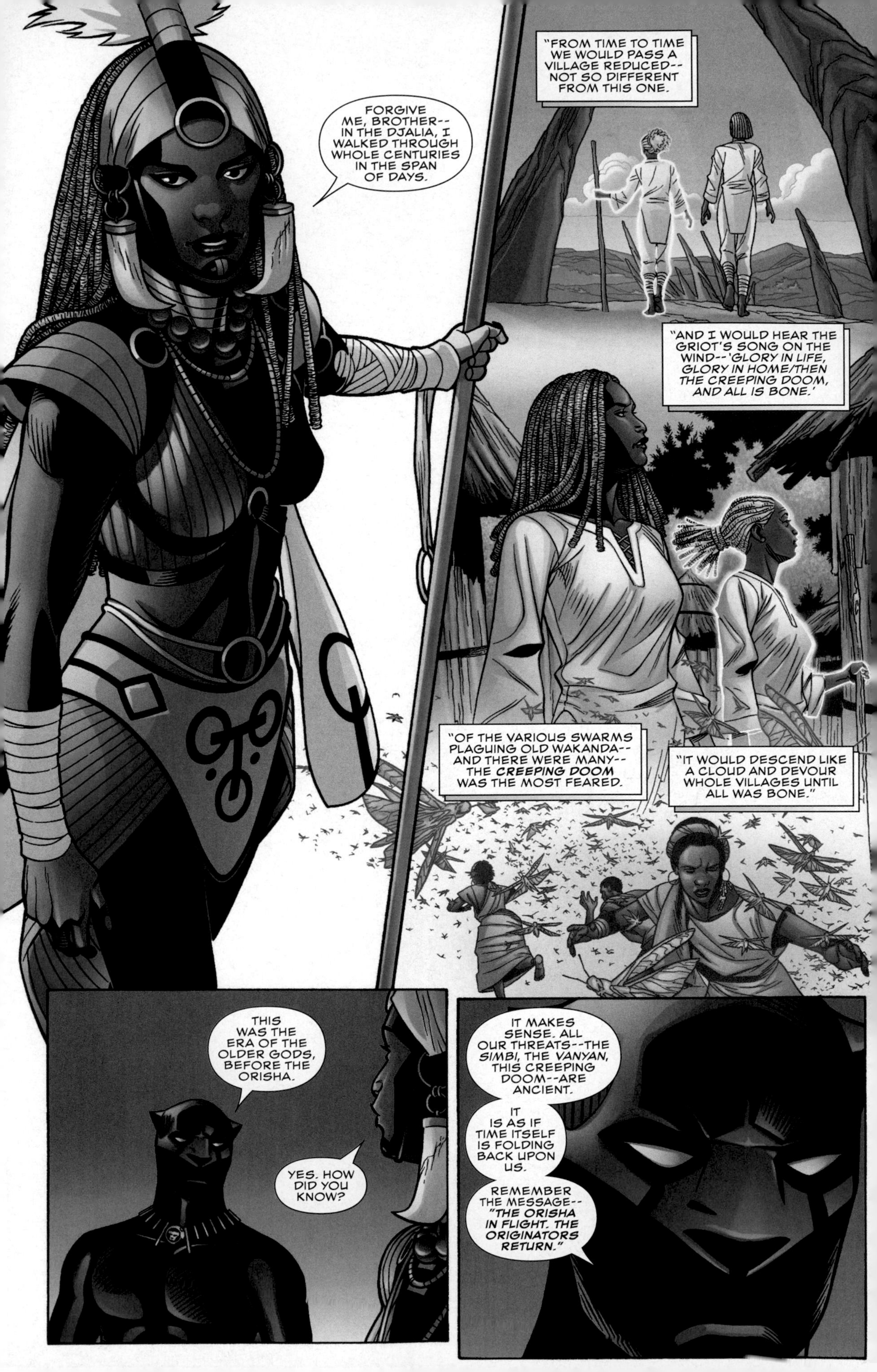
FORGIVE ME, BROTHER-- IN THE DJALIA, I WALKED THROUGH WHOLE CENTURIES IN THE SPAN OF DAYS.
"FROM TIME TO TIME WE WOULD PASS A VILLAGE REDUCED-- NOT SO DIFFERENT FROM THIS ONE.
"AND I WOULD HEAR THE GRIOT'S SONG ON THE WIND--'GLORY IN LIFE, GLORY IN HOME/THEN THE CREEPING DOOM, AND ALL IS BONE.'
"OF THE VARIOUS SWARMS PLAGUING OLD WAKANDA-- AND THERE WERE MANY-- THE *CREEPING DOOM* WAS THE MOST FEARED.
"IT WOULD DESCEND LIKE A CLOUD AND DEVOUR WHOLE VILLAGES UNTIL ALL WAS BONE."
THIS WAS THE ERA OF THE OLDER GODS, BEFORE THE ORISHA.
YES. HOW DID YOU KNOW?
IT MAKES SENSE. ALL OUR THREATS--THE *SIMBI*, THE *VANYAN*, THIS CREEPING DOOM--ARE ANCIENT.
IT IS AS IF TIME ITSELF IS FOLDING BACK UPON US.
REMEMBER THE MESSAGE-- ***"THE ORISHA IN FLIGHT. THE ORIGINATORS RETURN."***

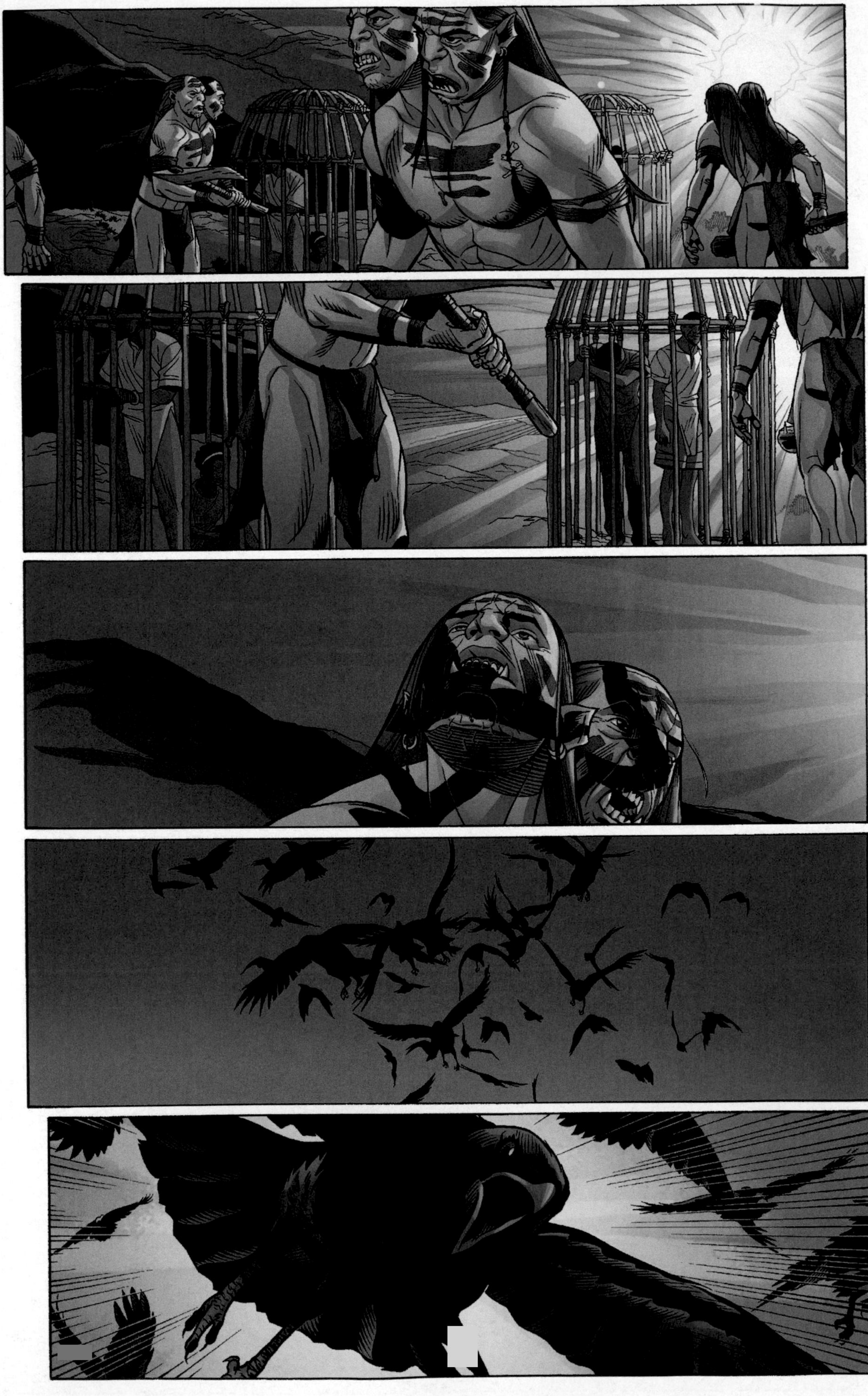

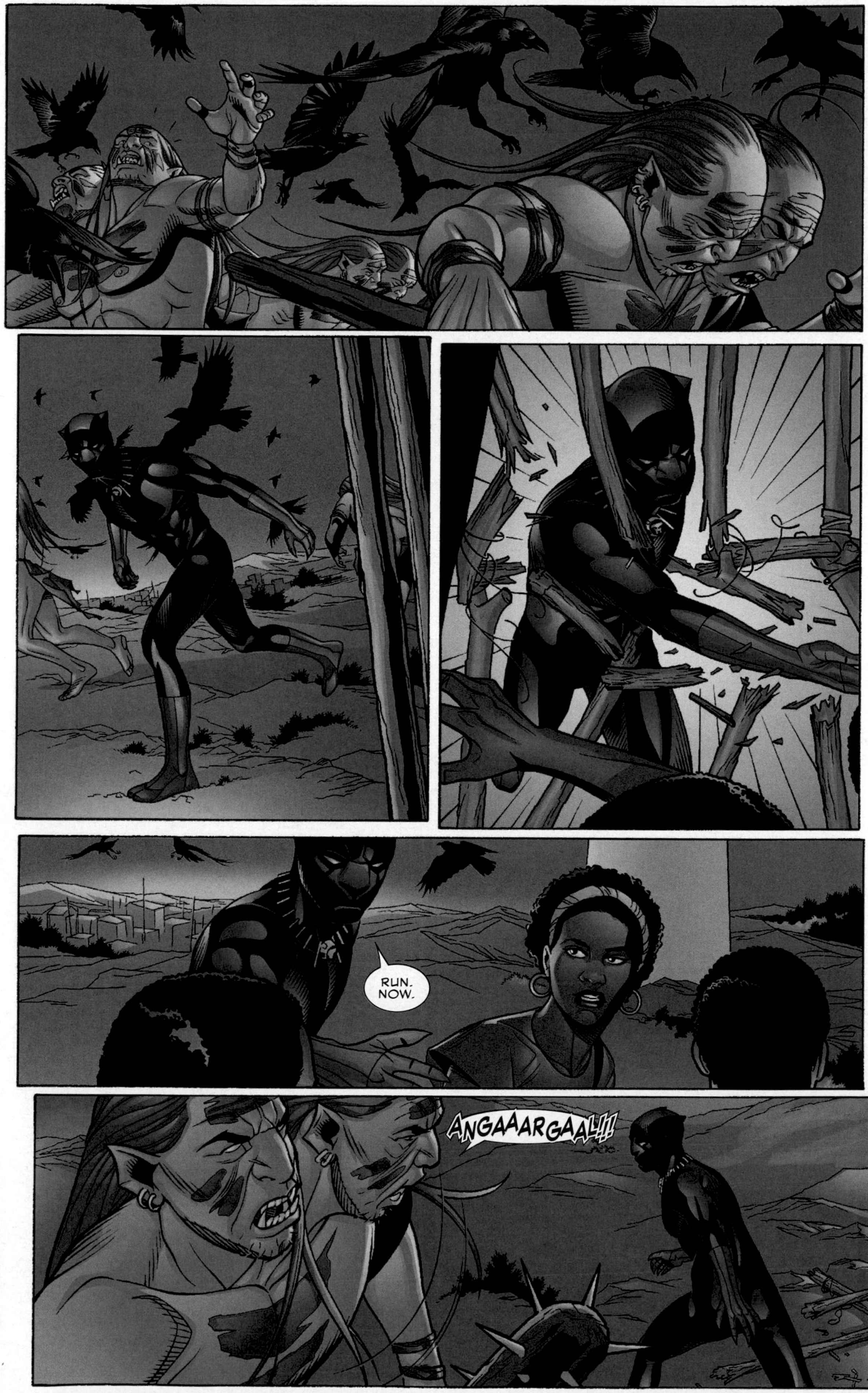
RUN. NOW.
ANGAAARGAAL!!!

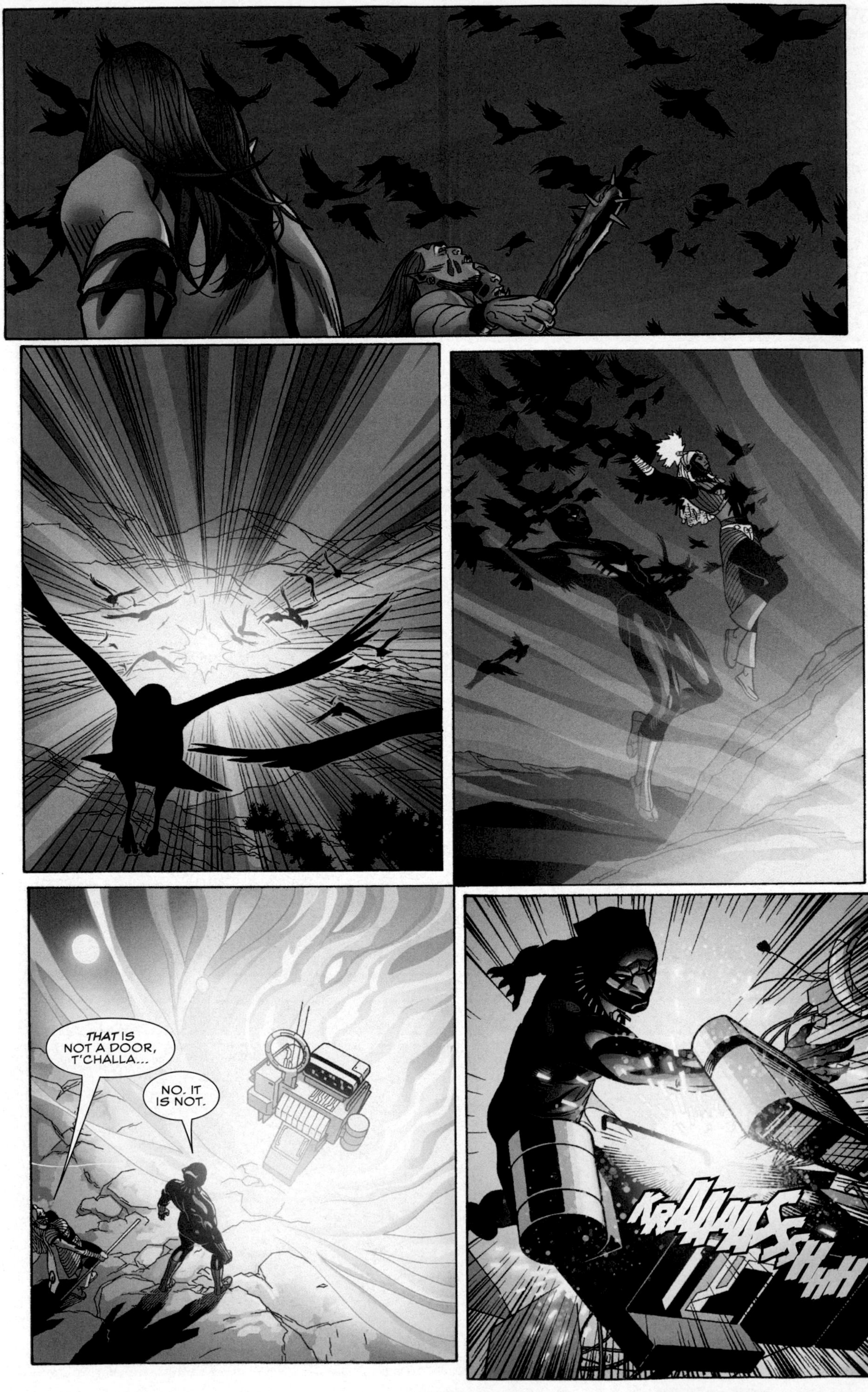
THAT IS NOT A DOOR, T'CHALLA...
NO. IT IS NOT.
KRAAAAASSHHH

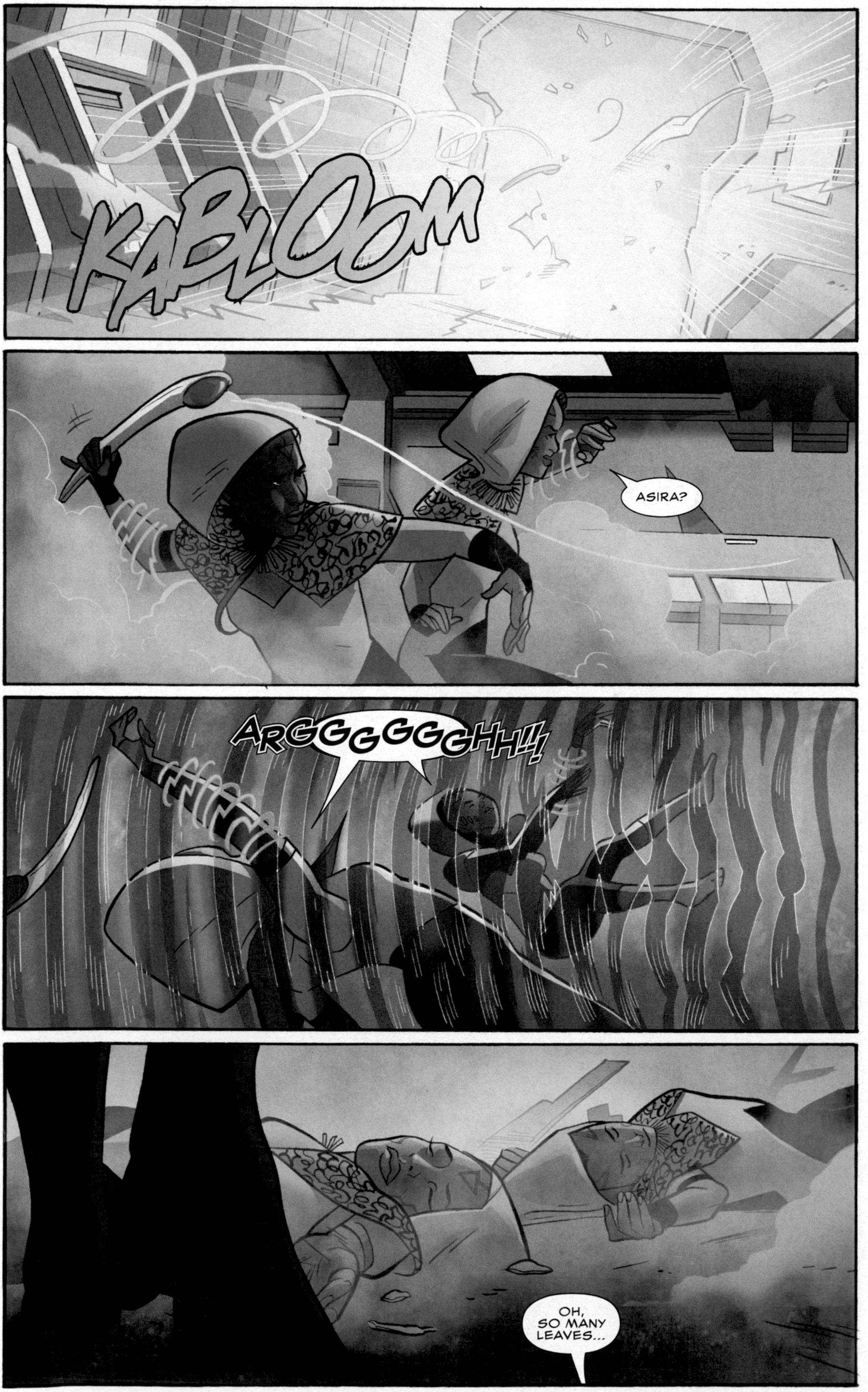
KABLOOM
ASIRA?
ARGGGGGGHH!!
OH, SO MANY LEAVES...

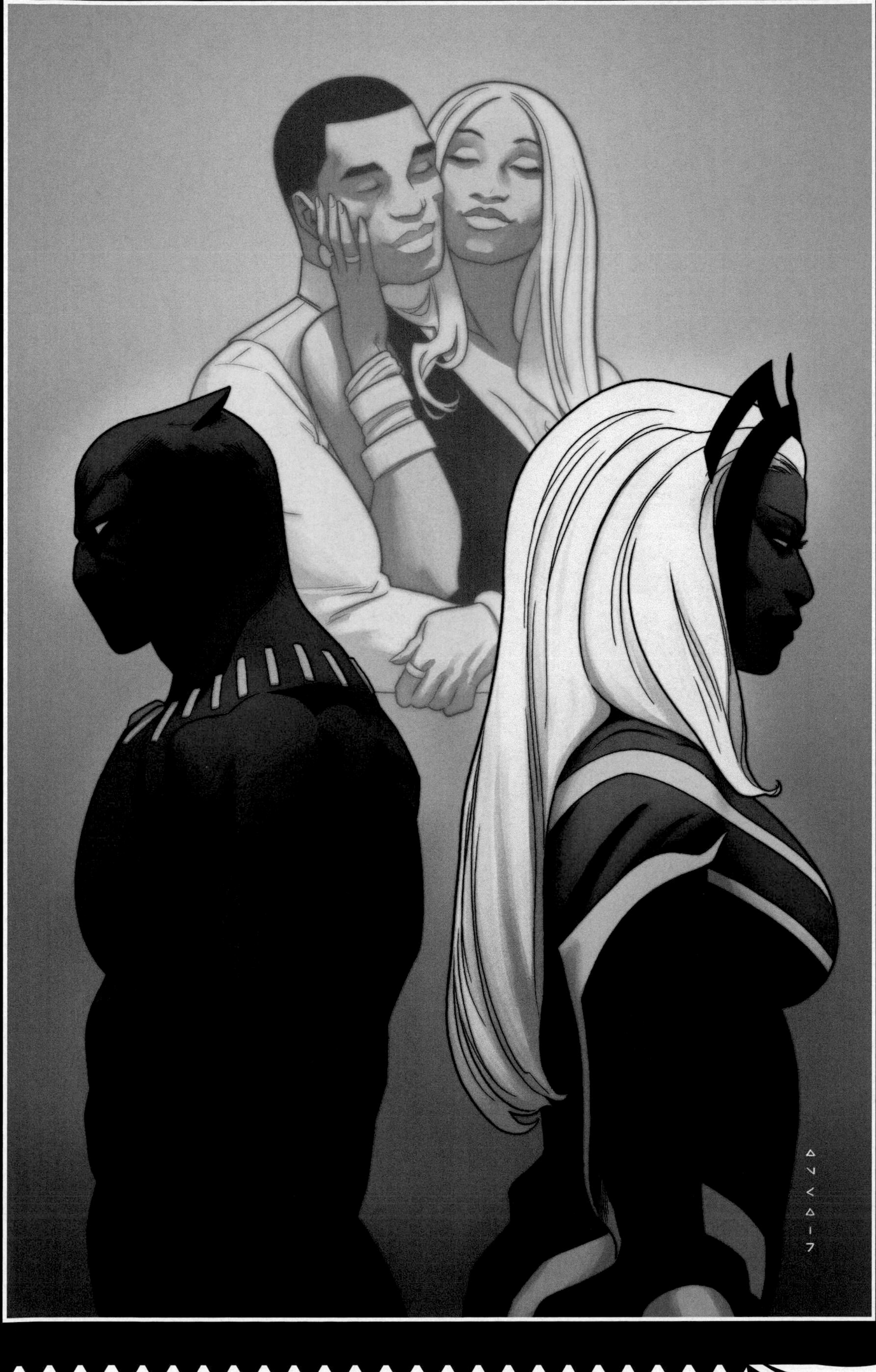

#13 VARIANT BY **KRIS ANKA**

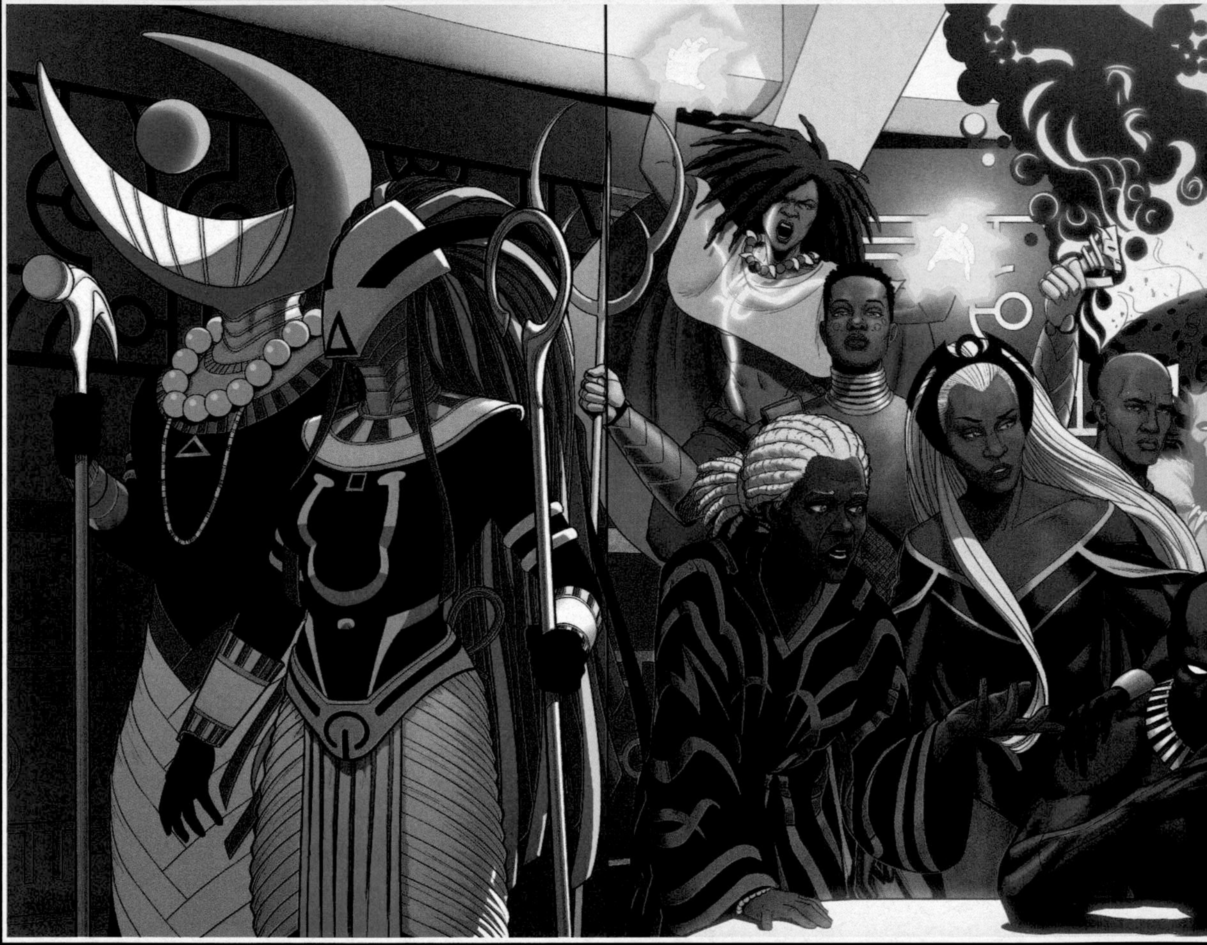

#13-16 COMBINED VARIANTS BY **JAMIE McKELVIE** & **MATTHEW WILSON**

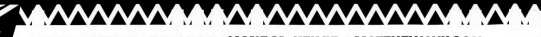

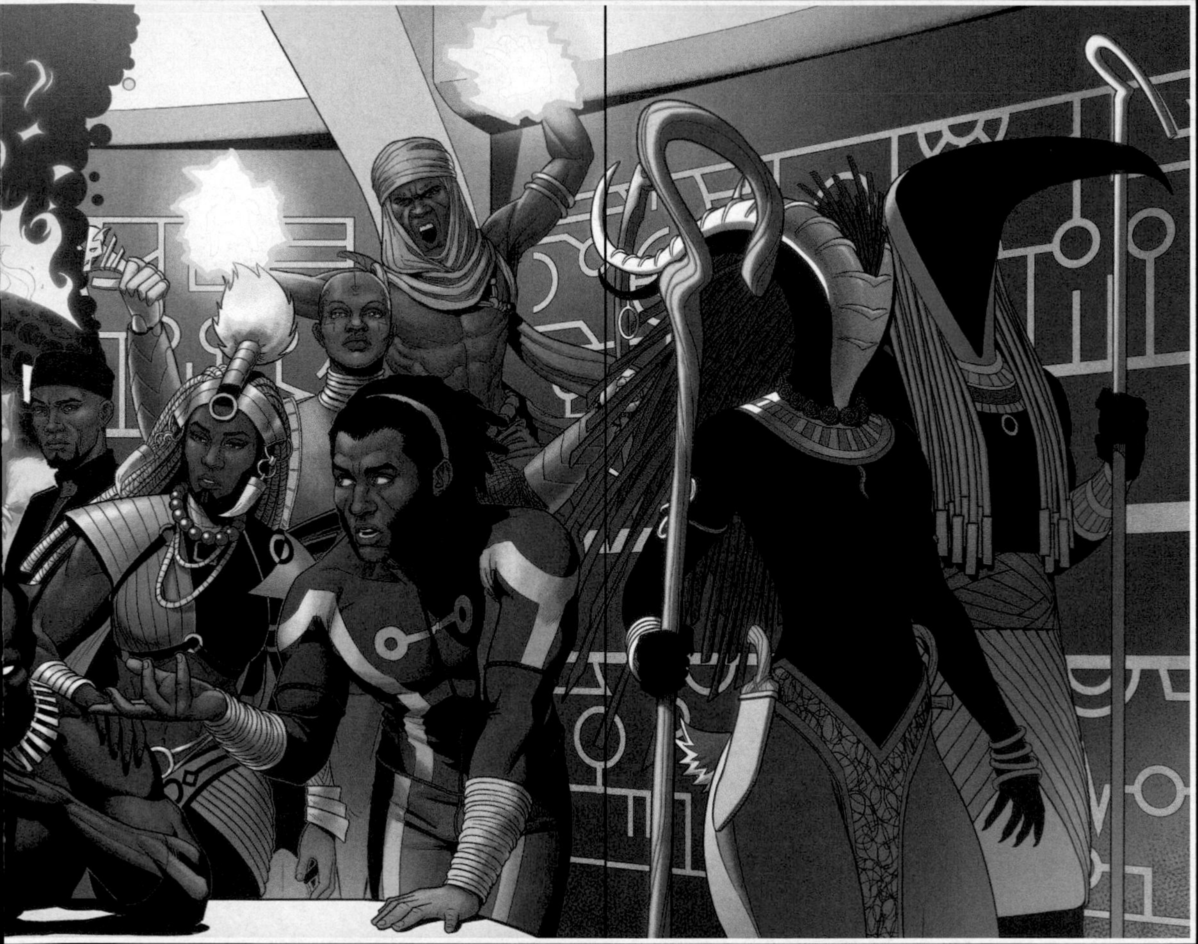

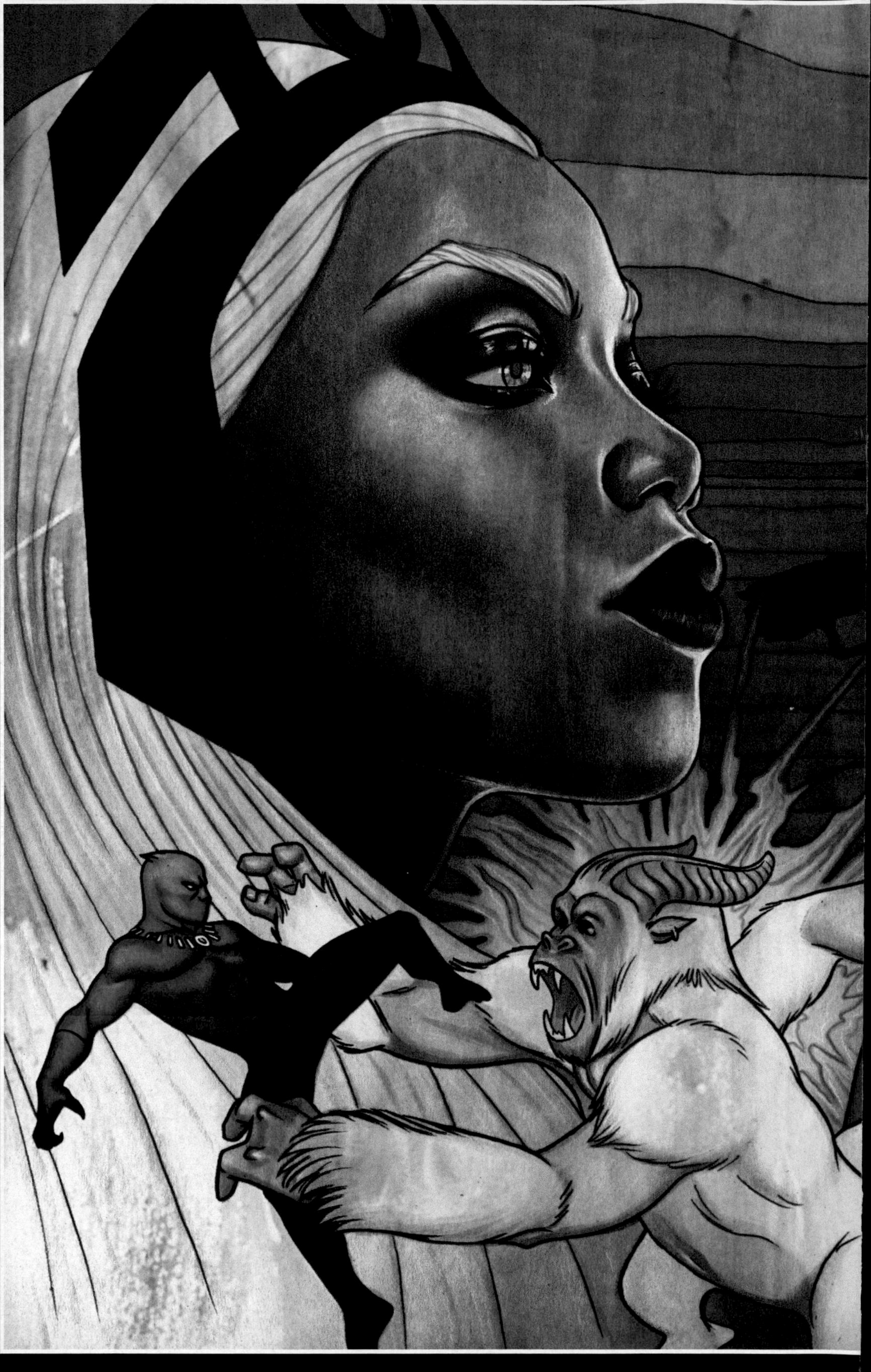

#17-18 COMBINED VARIANTS BY **JENNY FRISON**

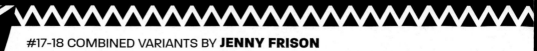

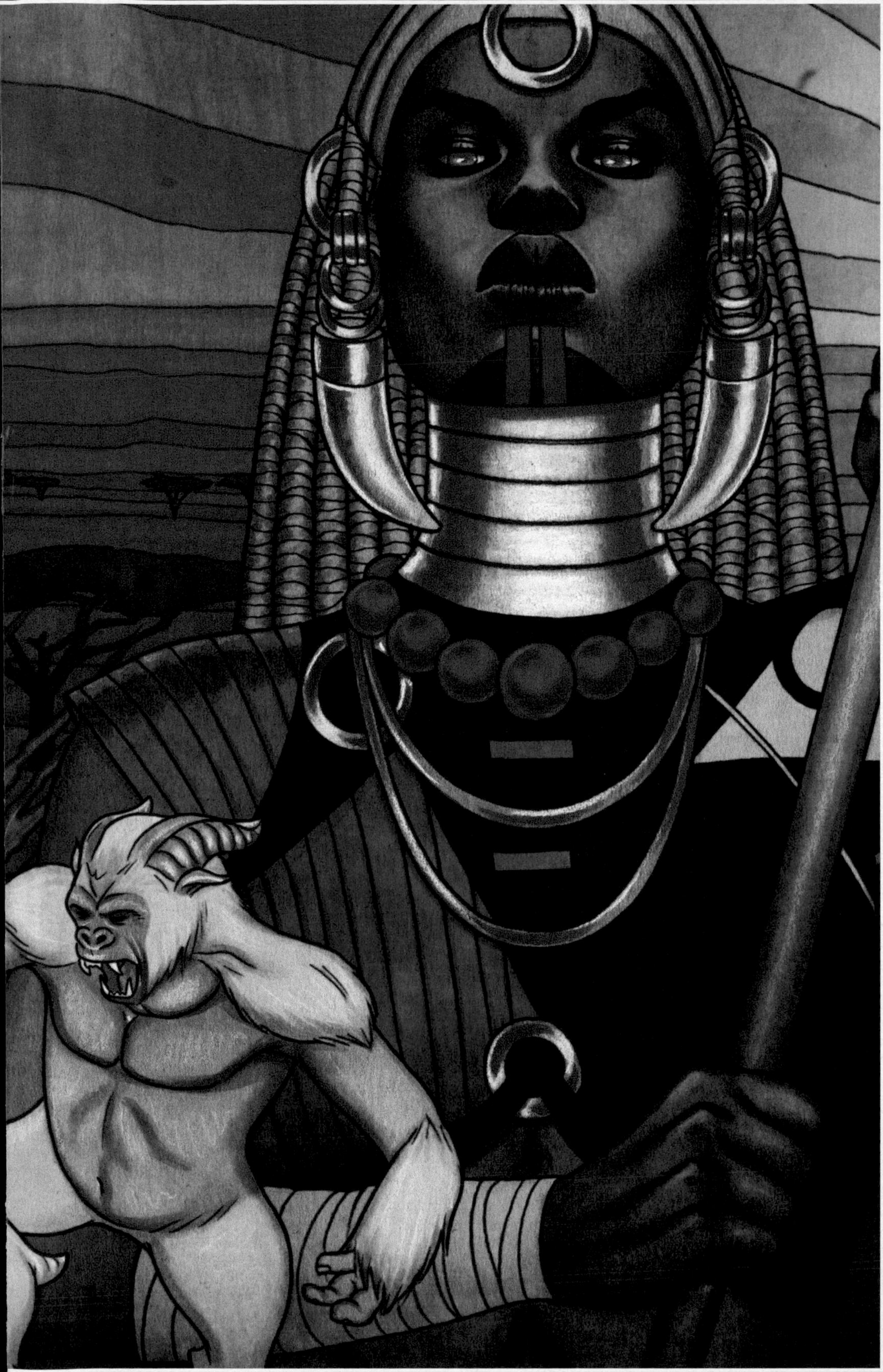

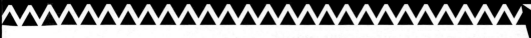

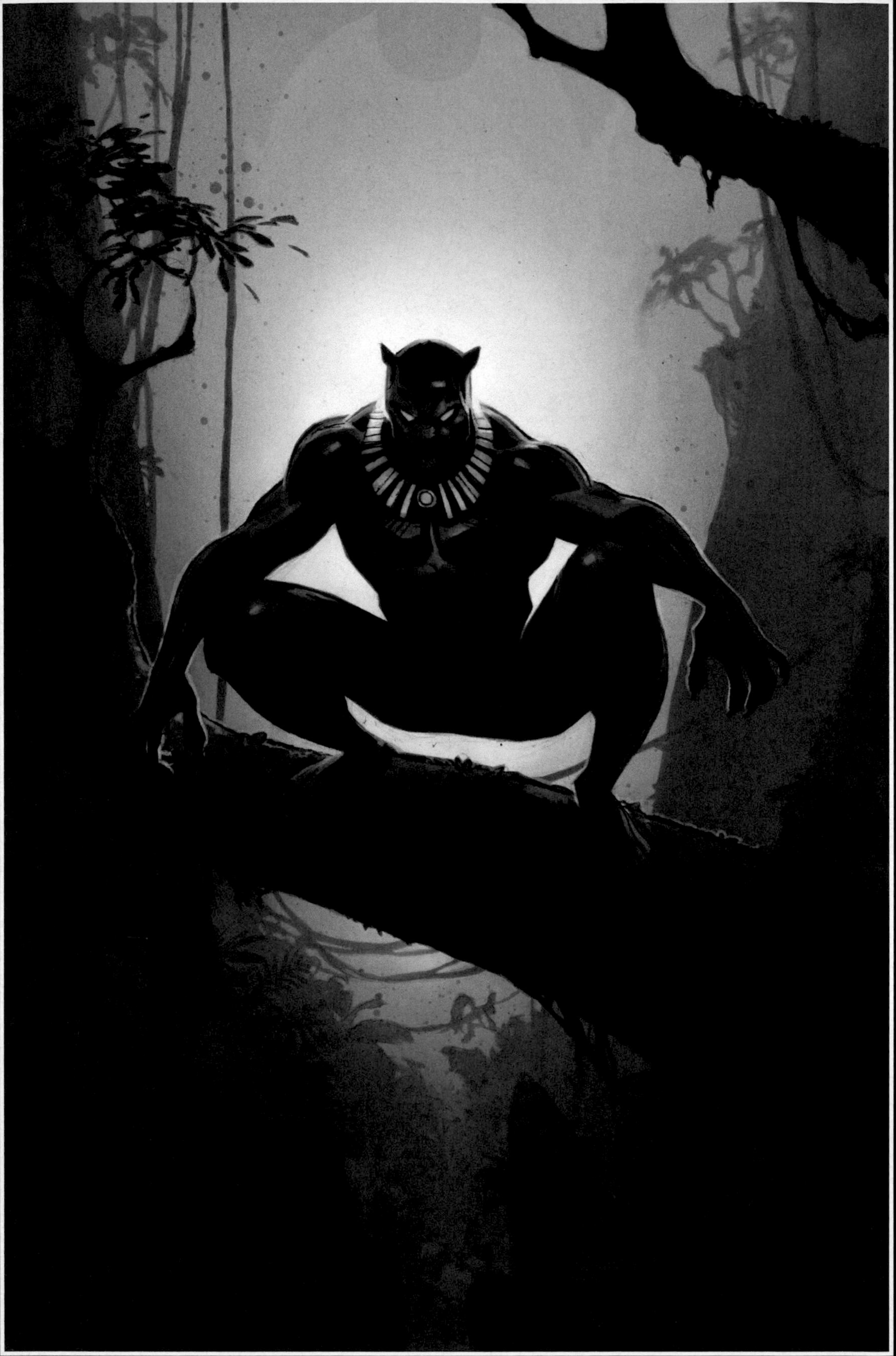

#14 VARIANT BY **ANDREW ROBINSON**

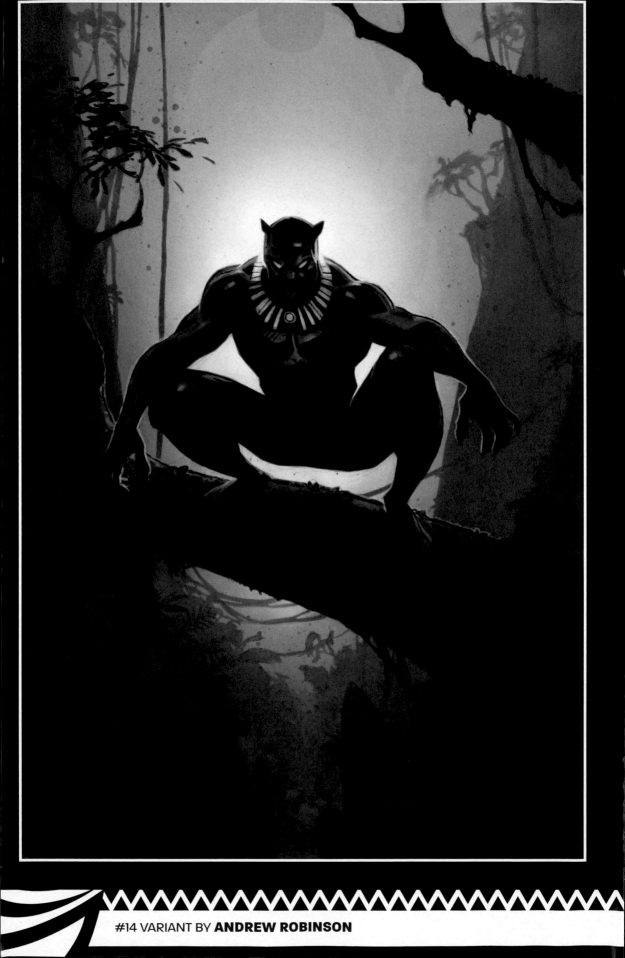

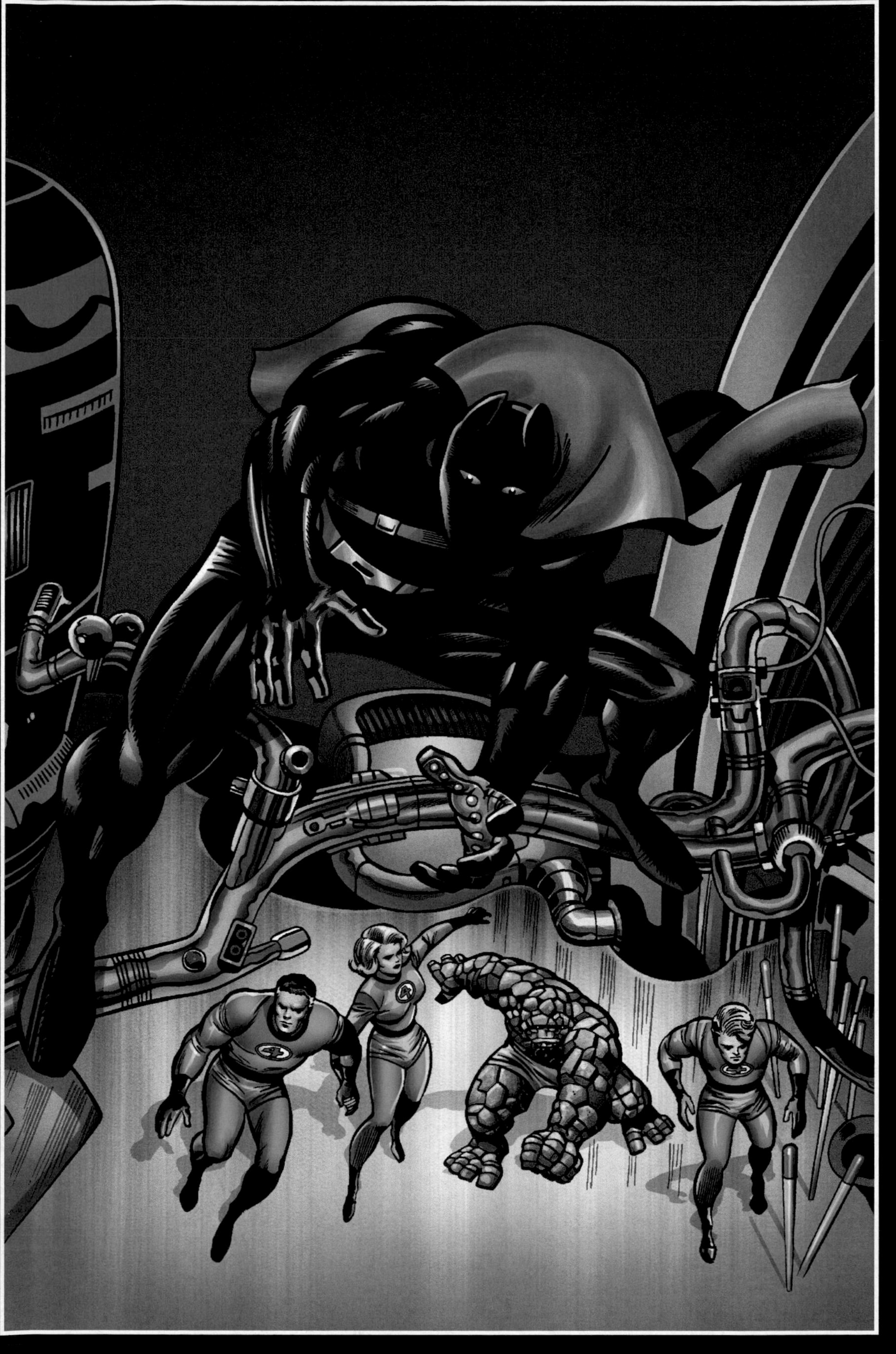

#16 KIRBY 100 VARIANT BY **JACK KIRBY, JOE SINNOTT**
& **PAUL MOUNTS** WITH **JOE FRONTIRRE**

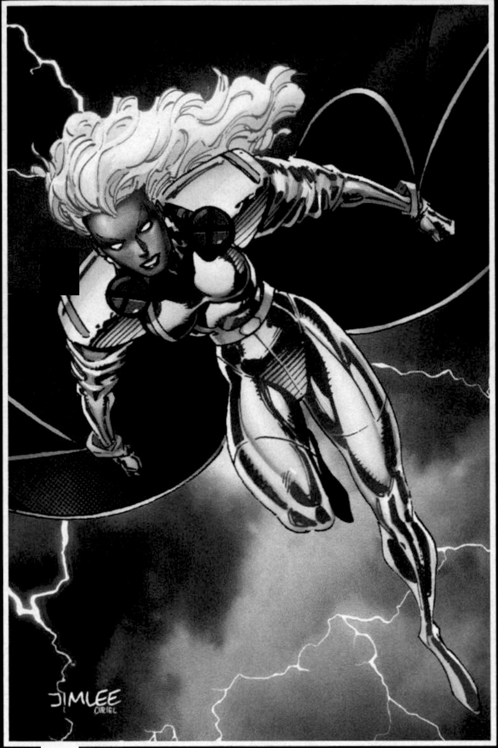
JIMLEE

#16 VARIANT BY **JIM LEE** &
DAVID CURIEL WITH **JOE FRONTIRRE**

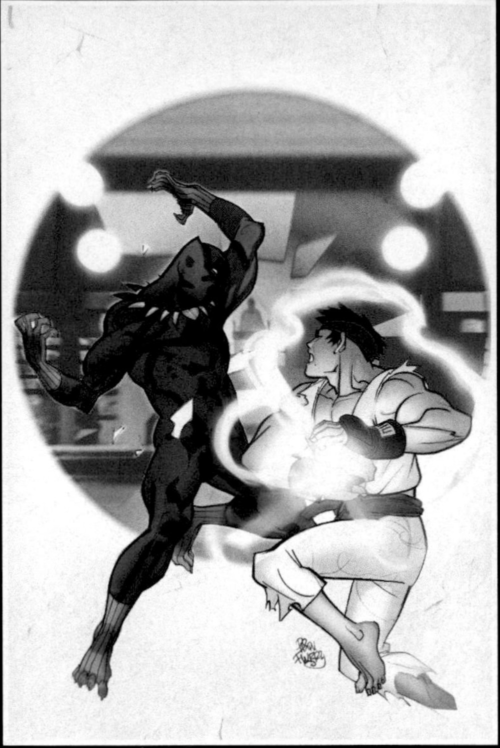

#17 MARVEL VS. CAPCOM VARIANT
BY **PASQUAL FERRY** & **ANDY TROY**

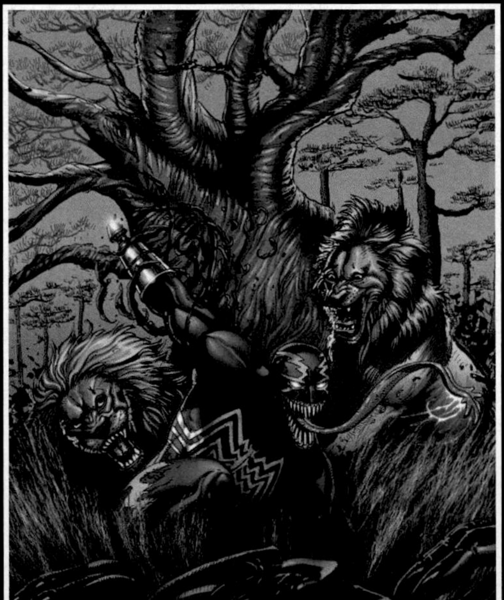

#18 VENOMIZED VILLIANS VARIANT
BY **JOYCE CHIN** & **ANDREW CROSSLEY**

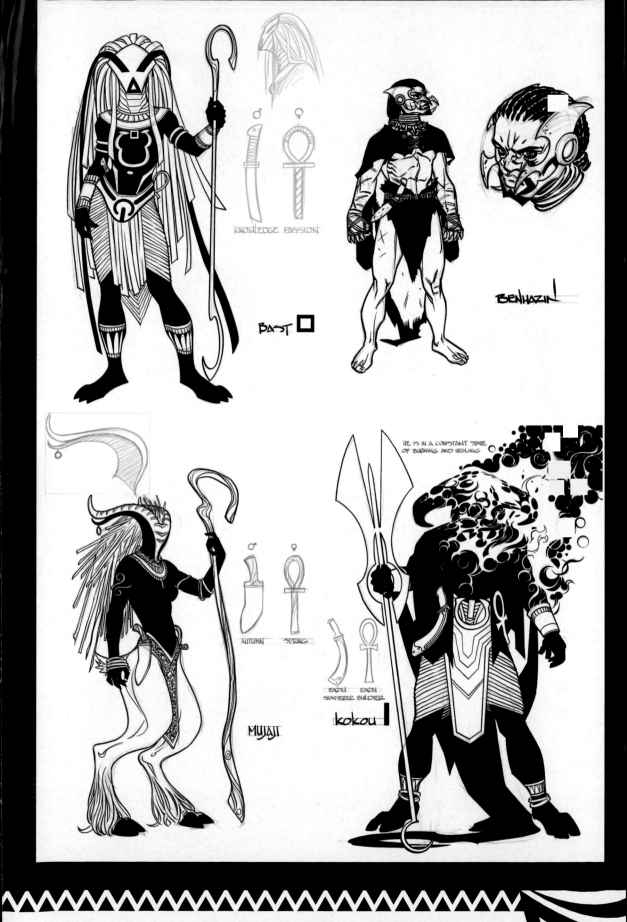

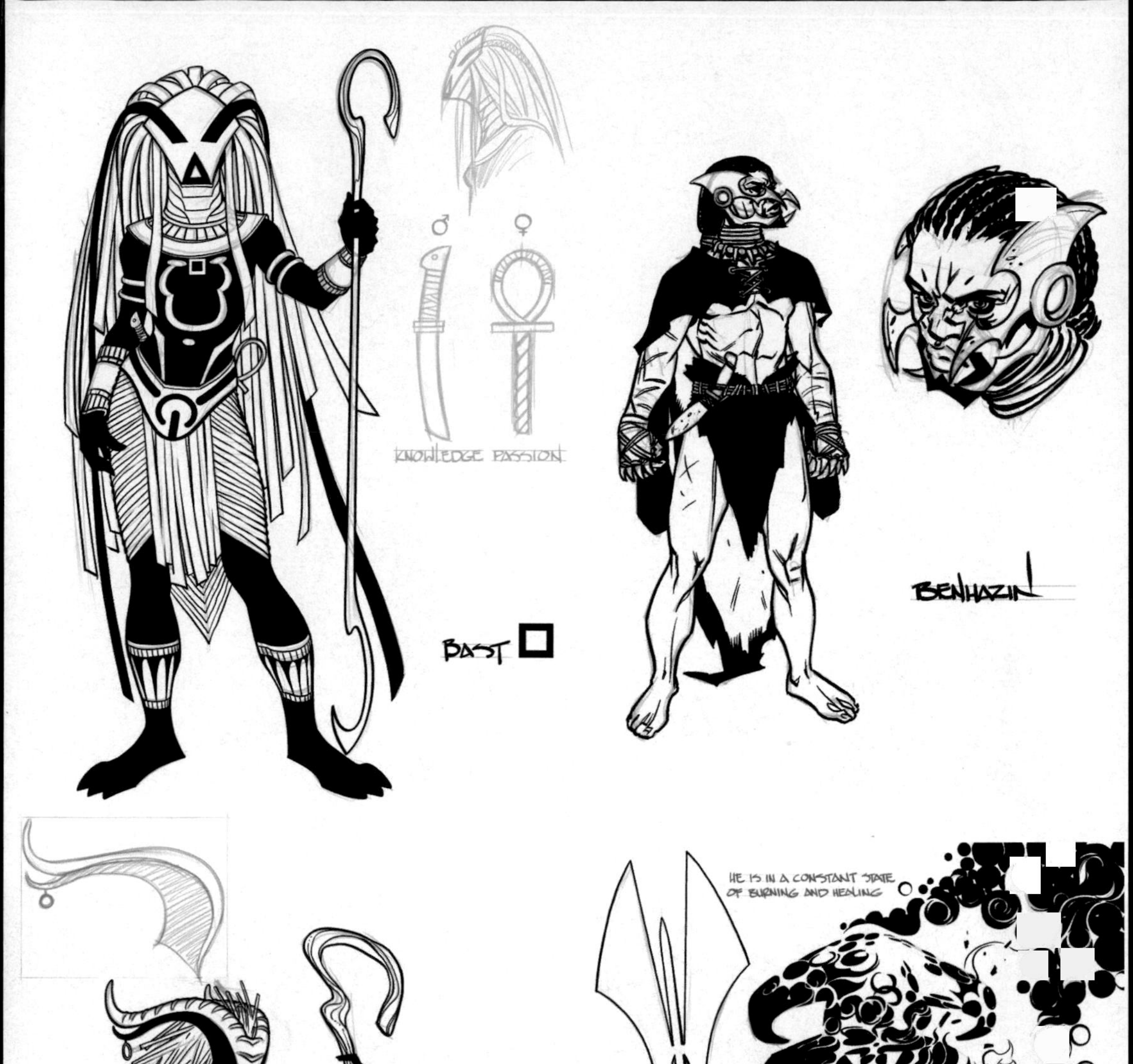
KNOWLEDGE PASSION
BAST
BENHAZIN
HE IS IN A CONSTANT STATE
OF BURNING AND HEALING
AUTUMN
SPRING
MUJAJI
EARTH
SHATTERER
EARTH
BUILDER
KOKOU

CHARACTER DESIGNS BY **BRIAN STELFREEZE**

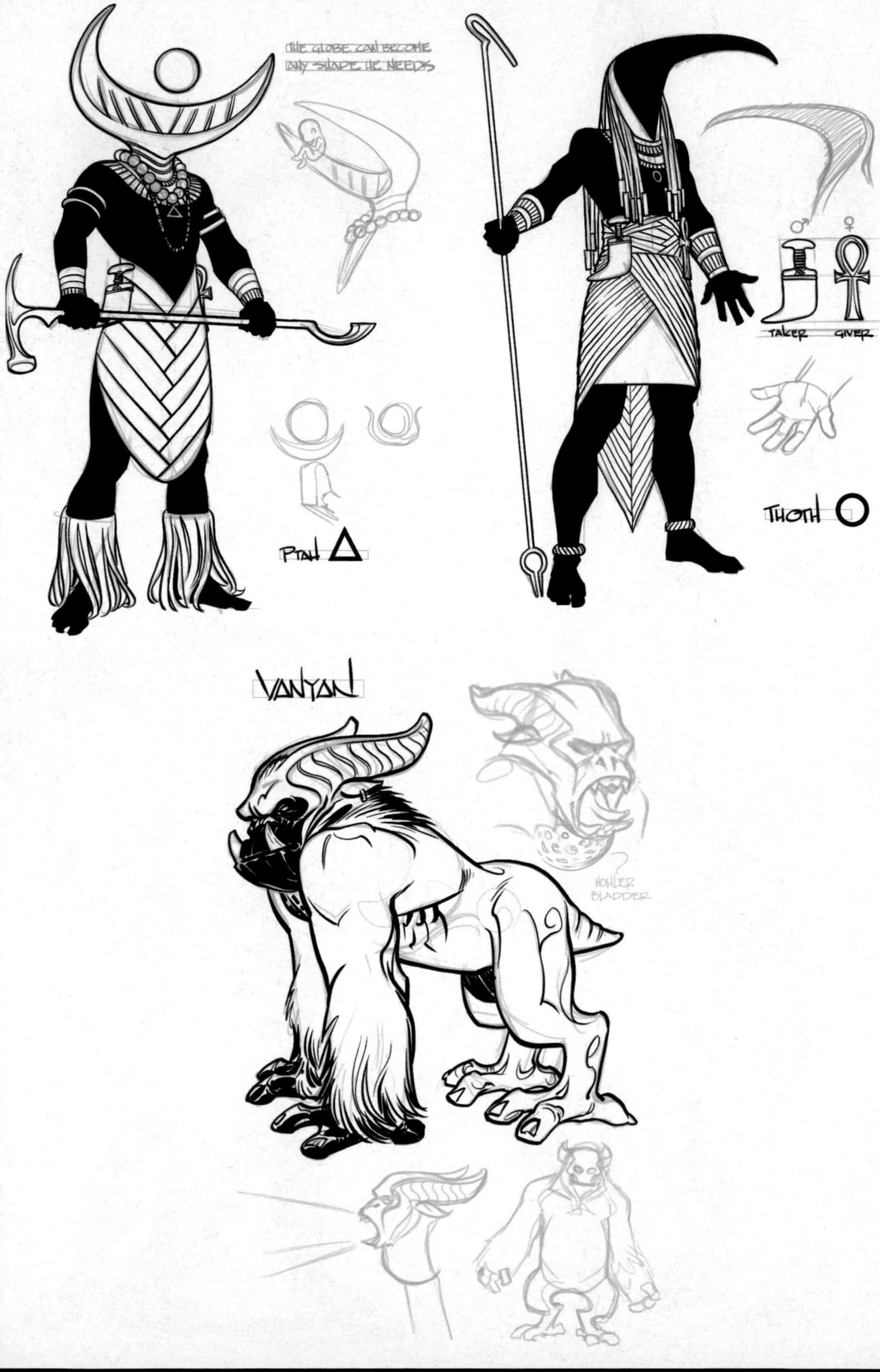
THE GLOBE CAN BECOME
ANY SHAPE HE NEEDS
PTAH
TAKER
GIVER
THOTH
VANYAN
HOWLER
BLADDER

CHARACTER DESIGNS BY **BRIAN STELFREEZE**

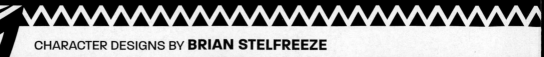